HANS HOTTER
Man and Artist

Hans Hotter in *Die Walküre* (photo Nancy Sorensen, courtesy of Lyric Opera of Chicago)

HANS HOTTER
Man and Artist

PENELOPE TURING

JOHN CALDER · LONDON
RIVERRUN PRESS · NEW YORK

First published in 1983 in Great Britain by
John Calder (Publishers) Ltd,
18 Brewer Street, London W1R 4AS
and in the United States of America by
Riverrun Press Inc.,
175 5th Avenue, New York 10010

British Library Cataloguing in Publication Data
Turing, Penelope
  Hans Hotter.
  1. Hotter, Hans   2. Singers—Germany—Biography
  I. Title
  784'.092'4   ML420.H/

  ISBN 0 7145 3988 0 Casebound
       0 7145 4091 6 Paperbound

Printed in Great Britain by Photobooks (Bristol) Ltd.

To the Memory of

MATTHÄUS ROEMER

A great teacher of singing, uncompromising musician and generous man to whom the public owes much of the artistry of Hans Hotter

This Book is Dedicated

ACKNOWLEDGEMENTS

There are many people to whom my thanks are due for their help and interest while I was working on this book; too many to name them individually. But one has contributed an entire section – Jürgen E. Schmidt of Preiserrecords. He compiled the discography and it was a labour of love by an expert and a friend of the Hotters and of myself, for which I am very grateful.

PENELOPE TURING

CONTENTS

Foreword: Sir Georg Solti, KBE — 13

Introduction: The legend and the man — 15

I   The early years — 29

II   Professional artist — 65

III   International career — 103

IV   Opera producer — 175

V   Lieder singing — 197

VI   Teaching — 263

APPENDICES

Important dates in Hotter's life — 257

Operatic roles — 259

Hotter productions — 262

Discography — 263

Index — 275

Other books by Penelope Turing

YOUR GUIDE TO SICILY (1966)
LANCE FREE (autobiography) (1968)
NEW BAYREUTH (1969)
CONSIDER DEATH (1975)
EGYPT (Thornton Cox Travellers' Guide series) (1982)

ILLUSTRATIONS

Hans Hotter in *Die Walküre*   *frontis*

1   Hans Hotter at Troppau, 1931   *page* *12*

2   Hans Hotter, Prague 1932   23

3   Karl Hotter in the garden of the Spessart   23
    house

4   As Amfortas in *Parsifal,* Breslau 1931   38

5   With Richard Strauss after *Friedenstag,* 1938   38

6   With Julius Patzak in *Palestrina,* Vienna   38
    1949

7   With Viorica Ursuleac in *Arabella,* Munich   48
    1939

8   In *Zaubergeige,* Hamburg 1935   48

9   With Richard Strauss and Rudolf Hart-   48
    mann during a dress rehearsal of
    Arabella, Munich 1939

10   With Anny Konetzni in *Die Walküre,* Vien-   58
    na 1948/49

11   Relaxing with the Begum Aga Khan,   68
    Bayreuth 1950s

12   Making up as Kurwenal in *Tristan,* Flor-   68
    ence 1951

13   As Basilio (a favourite role) in *The Barber of*   83
    Seville, Hamburg 1937

14   As Pizarro in *Fidelio,* Munich 1945   83

15   As Amonasro in *Aida,* Munich 1938   83

16   With Viorica Ursuleac in *Mona Lisa,* Berlin   93
    1938

17   As Jupiter in *Liebe der Danae* at dress re-   93
    hearsal, Salzburg 1944

18   As Don Giovanni with Hilde Güden,   93
    Munich 1941

19	As Mandryka in *Arabella*, Munich 1939	106
20	With Ruth Michaels in *Faust*, Munich 1944	106
21	In the film *Seine Beste Rolle*, 1941	106
22	As Borromeo in *Palastrina*, Vienna 1955	113
23	As Pogner in *Die Meistersinger,* Vienna 1962	113
24	As Gianni Schicchi, Munich 1961	113
25	As Kurwenal in *Tristan*, Bayreuth 1952	123
26	As The Holländer with Leonie Rysanek, Vienna 1955	123
27	With Evelyn Lear and Thomas Stewart after a performance, Bayreuth 1960s	123
28	Hans Hotter in 1959	133
29	With Astrid Varnay and Joseph Keilberth, Bayreuth 1953	143
30	With Gré Brouwenstijn in *Die Meistersinger*, Bayreuth 1956	143
31	With Toni Blankenheim and Wieland Wagner, Bayreuth 1955	143
32	As Gurnemanz in *Parsifal*, Vienna 1960	158
33	As the Grand Inquisitor in *Don Carlos*, Vienna 1962	168
34	As The Holländer, Vienna 1955	178
35	As Scarpia in *Tosca*, Vienna 1968	178
36	As Pogner with Claire Watson in *Die Meistersinger*, Munich 1963	178
37	With Anja Silja in *Die Walküre*, Florence 1963	188
38	As Becket in *Murder in the Cathedral*, Vienna 1960	200
39	As Moses in *Moses und Aron*, Frankfurt 1970	200
40	As The Schoolmaster with Kerstin Meyer in *The Visit of the Old Lady*, Munich 1975	200
41	Hans Hotter, 1976	213
42	With Wieland Wagner and Anja Silja, Naples 1963	228

43 On the twenty-fifth anniversary of the San   228
    Francisco Opera House, November
    1979
44 Hans Hotter, San Francisco, 1979   238

1. Hans Hotter at Troppau, 1931

FOREWORD

In 1943 I was in Zürich and went to a performance of *Die Walküre*, conducted by Clemens Krauss, as part of a Gastspiel by the Munich State Opera. Wotan was sung by a young man, whose name was new to me at that time — Hans Hotter — and I shall never forget his performance. The intensity of his characterisation, stage-presence, musicality and the sheer vocal power was simply wonderful. Little did I imagine that, just four years later, I would have the good fortune to conduct my first *Walküre* in Munich with Hotter as Wotan.

I learned so much from him at that time — what a truly dramatic singer could obtain from a parlando phrase and how Wagner could be sung with a real legato. His 'Abschied' in *Walküre* was so strong and yet so tender and his monologue in the second act was unforgettable. Over twenty minutes would seem to fly by in less than five and included a range from the quietest pianissimo to a violent fortissimo.

We had a number of collaborations in Munich and although we lost touch for a while after these, we resumed work together in the early 1960s when he came to Covent Garden to sing Wotan with me and then to produce the *Ring* Cycle, which he did most excellently, imparting his immense knowledge to a whole new generation of English singers.

I have of Hans the fondest memories, as singer, colleague and musician and perhaps the most typical of these was during out work together on the recording of the *Ring* for Decca. I asked him if he could take a passage in *Walküre* in a particular way. 'Oh', came the reply 'I don't think I have ever tried that before.' 'But Hans,' I replied — 'I learned it from you . . .'

GEORG SOLTI

INTRODUCTION
The Legend and the Man

FOR A QUARTER of a century Hans Hotter strode the international operatic stage as the definitive Wotan in Wagner's mammoth cycle *Der Ring des Nibelungen*. The Wagner public worshipped both the interpretation and the artist, with a devotion tinged with awe.

'He has got everything,' one usually phlegmatic operahouse attendant remarked in the 1950s, and in the eyes of that public he had. Very tall — six foot four — and well built with fine classical features, blue eyes, long-fingered expressive hands, he was visually well equipped to portray a god, either of Nordic saga or Greek mythology. The great rounded bass-baritone voice in the best German vocal tradition, capable of incredible pianissimi, of controlled emotional quality and an amazing range of vocal colour, matched the appearance. There were from time to time problems of unsteadiness inherent in the very size and compass of this voice but with the years his deeply studied musicianship and command of acting controlled these and co-ordinated the natural gifts. It was a whole artist who earned that fame, but the fame was not a whole picture of either the artist or the man.

For one thing, Wotan calling up immortal fire to guard Brünnhilde in a surge of Wagner's most poignant and intoxicating music was only the tip of the iceberg of a much larger and more widely based career, although outside the German speaking countries there were all too few opportunities of seeing and hearing Hotter in his considerable repertory. For another, long and demanding as was his operatic career it was in a way transitional to the full development of his own musical priorities: lieder singing and teaching.

But despite this and the fact that Wagnerian fame

produced in him almost an antipathy to the role, it was as Wotan that Hotter became a legend in his singing lifetime and it is a legend and personification by which other Wotans are still judged. For how long will that image remain?

Art possesses an extra dimension in the finite world, to bring wonder, joy, beauty, even knowledge, to the consciousness of ordinary mortals, not through painstaking study but as a gift which contains a certain divinity. As such it is full of surprises.

For example the performing artist would appear to command an essentially ephemeral glory. The painter, sculptor, composer and poet transmits his inspiration through enduring, tangible media. A lapse of centuries is no bar to the power of such gifts. But with the actor, singer, instrumentalist the situation is very different. Theirs is the heady glory of the live performance, and also the practical endurance and professional technique which must enable them to repeat their creations again and again, always with the flair of spontaneity. They can command an immediate fame and enthusiasm which few other artists enjoy in their lifetime. But how shall that glory endure when they withdraw from the stage or platform which has framed their triumphs?

Yet with the really great, it does. Modern scientific means of recording a performance is not the real reason, although the art of the great performers of this century has been preserved for us with steadily developing accuracy and success, until we now have all the benefits of stereophonic recording and film techniques. But Thomas Betterton and Garrick in the richness of English theatre, and operatic divas like Grisi and Malibran, have remained vividly alive through generations that have not enjoyed these aids thanks to historical mythology.

The reason is the indefinable quality of live performance. It is essentially transient, but for this very reason it is capable of immortality. When tonight's performance is over there will never be another exactly similar because the response of the audience is an integral part of the whole. The cast, the conductor, the world on stage may reassemble many times, but the audience will always be varied, and so the performance brought there to birth will have a particular character, however slight the differences.

Most performing artists acknowledge the effect of different audiences, for better or worse, and it is in the hearts and minds and memories of the audience that a great individual performance lives, perpetuated by their report written or spoken. And this is not a metronomic, or photographic reproduction, it is life on life, human response to art in a living medium. Such reports are handed down, possessing the vividness of an impressionist painter. They are born when the audience stumbles out into the night entranced by a great experience. Centuries later, having acquired a legendary status, they can still illuminate our quest for the nature of that experience.

Only rarely do artists possess the necessary qualities. Most give of their talents, reap their successes and quietly fade from public consciousness. Just a few in each century have both the art and the charisma. Hans Hotter is one of them in our time.

His Wotan is retained for posterity on disc, most magnificently and vividly in the live Bayreuth recording of the complete *Ring* of 1957, conducted by Hans Knappertsbusch, also in the *Walküre* and *Siegfried* of Georg Solti's 'Golden Ring', but his unique personification would survive without records, for it is woven into the living history of opera.

The legendary figure has been long established; the man is less well known. Now a vigorous 74 years old, he divides his time between classes in various cities and his house in Munich, where students from all over the world come to him for private lessons.

He plays golf, swims and enjoys working about the

house doing odd jobs of carpentry, electrical repairs and gardening. After so many years constantly on the move he and his wife Helga revel in home and garden and the companionship of their daughter Gabriele Strauss, married to the grandson of Richard Strauss, who lives not far away with her family. His son Peter and his brother Dr. Karl Hotter both live in Munich. It is a family world but also a very full life with visitors coming from America or Holland, Japan or Australia.

Among his friends now and all through his life his gifts as a raconteur have become famous. Here acting is hilarious mimicry, salted with humour, embracing a wide range of dialects. It is spontaneous, vivid, and very funny, carrying the listeners along in a comradeship of enjoyment.

Behind this Hotter of today lies a lifetime of service to music; indeed several lifetimes lived concurrently, and round that career is the aura of greatness which established him as a unique figure quite early. Only those who know him really well can escape from a certain inhibition of awe in approaching him. 'I saw the god today,' Viennese concertgoers still say quite naturally.

It is a far cry from the little boy playing with his brother in the woods of the Spessart hills, from the student in Munich dreaming of becoming a conductor, doubtful of turning to singing as his teacher urged. But his mother was a widow with slender resources, and if he could succeed as a singer he would be able to earn his living fairly soon. . .

And so the decision was taken, and the career built, through small provincial operahouses, great and famous ones, in war and its aftermath, and out into the demanding world of the international star.

At the end of the 1940s he suffered a vocal crisis which provoked some commentators to declare he had passed his prime. But by determined effort, and by mobilising all he had learned and experienced, he not only survived it but moved on to the greatest phase of his career. It was a valley of shadows while it lasted, but now in his teaching it enables him to help others with such problems.

All the time the image of a handsome, rather unapproachable celebrity was growing.

London saw him and worshipped; very properly, since at Covent Garden he has appeared as Wagner's chief god far more often than in any other role. On stage he sang and acted with a command which made the godhead credible and the agony of Wotan's erring and perplexed character amazingly poignant.

At the end of a performance, particularly after *Die Walküre*, there was usually a breathless silence before the applause. Then the leading singers would appear before the curtain.

Some stars clasp their hands on their breasts, smile, nod, bob or even blow kisses to their audience. Hotter did none of these things. His expression was still in Wotan's character: austere, even frosty. 'Hotter looks as though the audience was a nasty smell,' was said about him.

It was little wonder that he often wanted to escape the crowds of waiting fans for he has never really liked basking in adulation. Hotter was adept as discovering alternative exits, and would often be far away, eating supper after the performance, while his fans still waited patiently at the stage door. All artists who achieve international fame have to develop techniques to prevent admirers from invading the small amount of privacy which their careers permit. Hotter became experienced at this through the years, aided perhaps by the sense of awe his fans felt towards his personality, and his physical and musical stature. But he has always had a real gratitude and affection for his public. 'They carry us in their arms, but they are very critical!' he said once of his devoted Viennese audience.

Within the profession the picture was rather different. Among his fellow leading singers there have been long standing friendships, the camaraderie of colleagues who meet and work together all over the world. With younger artists who have come to know Hotter by working with him there has usually been profound admiration and often a deep affection.

This is something inspired by the individual and his approach to his profession. The most caustic assessment of a performer often comes from those with him on stage in supporting roles. For various reasons the assessment may not be wholly balanced but it is realistic. Colleagues will often have a genuine admiration (sometimes tinged with envy) for the rare, superb natural voice, but they have no patience with the possessor of that voice if he or she has not the intelligence or dedication to train it for its proper use, musically and dramatically. In Hotter they have seen a master craftsman who knows precisely what he is seeking to present and why and how to achieve it.

That is what his colleagues acknowledged. They are a highly critical body, quick to recognise an 'off night' or to scorn undue public adulation, but generous in their respect and admiration for the true professional and the physical and psychological control of a master.

Hotter sang the role of Gurnemanz many times in the Bayreuth Festivals. Gurnemanz is on stage throughout the first and third acts of *Parsifal* but does not appear in the second. With Bayreuth's long intervals this means that the singer has a break of some three hours between the two parts of his performance. Two young members of the Covent Garden company visiting Bayreuth asked Hotter how he spent the long hot summer's evening in the Festspielhaus and he admitted that he slipped away in his car and had a swim. They were amused, but also deeply impressed by the professional sureness which could use that kind of relaxation within a single major musical performance.

If the balance between the gift of a rare voice, musicianship and intellect is what has made Hotter the

2. Hans Hotter, Prague 1932

3. Karl Hotter in the garden of Spessart house

artist that he is, discipline is the cement which binds those qualities together. Self-discipline and the acceptance of the professional disciplines of conductor, producer and ensemble.

Meeting Hotter in relaxed mood, telling stories at an informal supper party, the disciplinarian is not apparent. But his whole career has been built and maintained by this quality, often considered far removed from the artistic temperament.

Without an acceptance of the need for discipline he would probably say that he can do relatively little with the students who come to him now for study. Much of the teaching and coaching will be wasted if the student will not or cannot accept that when music becomes a profession it carries responsibilities like any other job. But with a pupil who is willing to work, and to sacrifice much social enjoyment or the indulgence of moods and feelings, Hotter has found a kindred spirit. The talent may be small, but he will take infinite pains to help and develop it to its fullest extent.

The voluntary disciplines form a vital part in creating a whole and a great artist, and in maintaining a stable and enduring career. Probably it is to this as much as to his possession of a strong physical constitution that Hotter owed his phenomenally long singing career of well over forty years. But there are other disciplines to which international celebrities are subjected. Since the second world war all such personalities are to a greater or lesser extent members of the jet set.

This is a much publicised stress and hazard, but only those whose work involves constant travel really know what intercontinental commuting means. The greater the traveller's fame, or the fees he can command, the more comfort he will obtain, but there are certain problems such as long hours of flying, change of climate, change of time, in which there is a harsh equality. These things are equally trying to all.

The ordinary traveller on professional work copes

with such difficulties according to his own resilience. If the work is done and well done, personal wear and tear is an acceptable price to pay. The singer, even more than other performing artists, is in a different category. His instrument is a physical one, sensitive to climatic changes, to infections, to sheer weariness in a way that no amount of heroic endurance and willpower can overcome. A singer with laryngitis is temporarily a broken man.

Hotter has done his share of this kind of artistic shuttle. In the '50s and the '60s he appeared from one day to the next in Vienna and Munich, Rome, London, New York. Because of his personal standards of discipline he made few mistakes, though he has not escaped criticism for attempting too much and in consequence sounding vocally tired. In counselling other artists he would certainly admit the danger of this.

Some artists are foolhardy in the extent of the pressures they accept, but this general way of life is today inseparable from an international career. There is no time to travel long distances except by air with the inevitable airport delays, constant changes of hotel, new people to meet, old friends to be recognised, rehearsals on different stages, unfamiliar acoustics, dressing rooms and dressers, varying local backstage customs and audience reaction. A famous star will be welcomed, shepherded and watched over, and subsequent visits may mean a very pleasant and enjoyable return, but there are problems of another kind inherent in this: the international artist is a figure of absorbing interest to most people backstage as well as across the footlights, a subject for anecdotes, gossip and reflected glory. It is natural that the object of so much attention will often choose the strain of another double flight between performances in order to spend a night or two in the normal atmosphere of home and family.

It was not Hans Hotter's first choice to be a singer, though he is far too honest to pretend that he has not enjoyed his long singing career. He is and always has been a true musician, dedicated to, and finding his reward in making music for its own sake. He had early dreams of conducting, and many years later became a producer of operas. The concept is similar: the creation of an artistic whole from many parts.

Producing and teaching has developed another side of Hotter's character, the ability to make easy, unforced human contact. Earlier in his career he had many personal friends and innumerable admirers, but there was an element of reserve in his response to strangers. Once he began to co-ordinate the work of others, to help, advise and inspire, he found a new flexibility and human understanding and his gifts as a teacher and communicator became apparent.

Hotter the producer, Hotter the teacher, the counsellor, the enthusiast, is a fulfilment of the singer and the actor. The fruits of decades of glory and success, sometimes of frustration and disappointment, are now as the service of the professor and those who study with him.

The public personality of stage and concert platform, like Wagner'a Wotan, seemed to possess an almost inhuman artistic magnificence. The Hotter of the last decade is no less respected, but is also loved and trusted by his students in a quite different way. He sang Hans Sachs less than any of his other great Wagnerian roles, but it is the maturity and wisdom, the humour and warmth, as well as the command of Sachs, that is now revealed.

One of the art forms which Hans Hotter has never seriously attempted is writing. His are the gifts of song and speech, and of such acting that he might have made a notable stage career apart from music. Parallel with much of Hotter's career I have followed the writer's path. I have attended many of his performances through the last thirty years, and have been a personal friend of Hans Hotter and his wife for more than twenty. This book is therefore a collaboration, a new experiment for both of us. In much of this book he speaks directly. For the rest the words and comments are mine and the life is his. The subject is human: Hans Hotter, man and artist. All famous artists are sometimes idolised. The purpose of this particular portrait is to bring the reader through the likeness into direct contact with Hans Hotter's whole personality.

PART ONE
The Early Years

ALTHOUGH HANS HOTTER was born in Offenbach that busy city of the Main can claim no influence on his life and there are few memories of the brief early years spent there. He is essentially a Bavarian, with the practical commonsense, the humour and the deep love of art and nature which southern Germany often bestows upon its sons. Both his parents came from Munich, and the Bavarian capital has been his home for most of his life.

The first records of his father's family come from Badan-Württemberg, at Esslingen on the Neckar east of Stuttgart and date from the 17th century. When Esslingen's gothic church of St. Dionys was restored the factor for the building work was named Hotter, and several of his sons assisted him, a clothmaker, a goldsmith and a cooper. Late in the following century a Sippe Hotter lived in neighbouring Kennenburg and in 1832 one Eberhard Hotter was a servant at the royal chateau of Weil. A branch of the Hotters had moved to Bavaria and one of them, after spending his early years in the service of the Habsburgs at the Hofburg Palace in Vienna, returned to settle in Haidhausen just outside the gates of Munich. There he became a master smith with royal appointment to the Wittelsbachs.

Karl Hotter, father of Hans, was born in Munich in 1877 and trained as an architect. Here again royal patronage played a part in the pattern of the family's life. Grand Duke Ernst Ludwig of the adjacent state of Hessen-Darmstadt was a cultured man drawn to the vitality and artistic richness of the Wittelsbachs' Bavarian capital Munich, not only for its material treasures but also for the people who worked and congregated there. From Munich the Grand Duke drew a number of

31

his artistic advisers and experts and something of a small Munich colony settled in Offenbach, among them Karl Hotter who was appointed teacher of architectural drawing at the Baugewerkschule, a technical school for art and industry.

He came to Offenbach in 1904 or 1905, bringing with him his young wife Crescentia, née Winklmayr, (always known to the family as Centa) and here their two sons were born, Karl in 1906 and Hans on January 19, 1909.

For the next seven years home was divided between the Offenbach flat, (first at 20 Speier Strasse, then in Ludwig Strasse), a simple country home in the neighbouring Spessart hills and a sojourn in Switzerland. During that time certain very deep impressions were made on the two boys, especially in the Spessart, though it is difficult to say just how much is actual memory and how much has been recreated through their mother's recollections.

The span of Crescentia Hotter's marriage was brief and overshadowed by anxiety. Her husband developed a lung complaint. The only practical treatment known at the time was to send the patient to a high altitude and Swiss sanatoria were filled with consumptives.

Karl Hotter did not want to leave his work and absolutely refused to part from his family. But he agreed to take sick leave and go to the mountains and it was arranged that his wife and the two little boys, Hans scarcely more than a baby, would accompany him.

They settled in Arosa, spending about a year and a half there. The therapy of the clear, dry, alpine air suited Karl Hotter, his health improved and the Swiss doctors urged him to stay and to make Arosa a permanent home. Swiss resorts were developing for both patients and holidaymakers; there would be plenty of work for an architect.

But he was homesick for Germany, for his teaching work, his friends and music and what he must have felt would be a more normal background for his children.

The invalid atmosphere of Arosa oppressed him. They returned to Offenbach and the disease advanced again. He was able to continue work for a time, but the last year of his life was spent in the Spessart house. He died there on Christmas Day 1916 at the age of thirty-nine.

It would be interesting to know how his sons' lives would have developed if Karl Hotter had lived and the family had remained in Arosa. For the elder, Dr. Karl Hotter, who entered the Roman Catholic priesthood and became a schoolmaster the pattern would probably not have been very different. But for Hans? Without the rich artistic and musical life of Munich to which Crescentia Hotter returned with her children it is unlikely that he would have taken up music professionally, and almost certainly would not have become a singer. We may have cause to be grateful for Karl Hotter's instinct, even at the cost of his early death. Length of life is a matter of relative value. He was blessed with a happy marriage, a richly rewarding home life and a circle of like-minded friends. It is hardly surprising that he preferred not to to risk those gifts in the clinically-minded exile of Arosa.

But it must have been an agonising decision for his wife if she realised that he was probably rejecting his only real chance of health and that their close-knit and devoted family life would not be of very long duration.

Back in Offenbach they took up that life again. They were surrounded by friends, many of them with a Munich background, and always there was music: the ardent love of it and the gift for it which both sons developed came from their father. Crescentia Hotter, even though her own mother had a deep understanding of music and her sister taught piano in Munich, was not herself a practising musician. She listened and provided the appreciative background, and she remembered. One of her great gifts was an amazing memory.

Her husband played the piano, lute and guitar, and had a good if not outstanding baritone voice. He had sung in a church choir as a boy soprano and then joined a well-known choral society in Munich. Apparently he said afterwards that he had damaged his voice for later life by continuing to sing with the society while his voice was breaking. His father had a fine singing voice and Karl was a natural musician who recognised his own shortcomings, but sang for pleasure with his friends. There had been a time when he had thought seriously of taking up music as a career, and it always remained for him much more than a hobby.

He was a devoted father and spent a great deal of time with his children, playing and singing with them the folk songs of his country. There were no dull evenings. He also made toys for them. His particular knowledge and feeling for design in architecture had its domesticated form in the hobby of cabinet making. The long, sensitive fingers took delight in the functional beauty which could be created from wood and he made not only toys for his sons, but all the furniture for the country home in the hills.

When the river Main leaves the vineyard-covered hills round Würzburg it winds past forests to Aschaffenburg and so eventually to Offenbach, Frankfurt and to the last sophisticated reach leading to the Rhine at Mainz. Those wooded hills just north and east of Aschaffenburg are part of the Spessart range and even today they possess a remote and unspoilt beauty. In 1912 they were totally undeveloped, an area of scattered hamlets, small farms and foresters' cottages through which the railway ran as it does now, leaving the river and climbing up over the shoulder of the hills, past a small halt where a neat little garden grows a crop of sunflowers. The station for Steiger.

There, near the point where the railway and autobahn now cross, is the small village and the house to which the Hotter family came at weekends and whenever Karl Hotter could get away from his work. This main line from Frankfurt to Würzburg made access from Offenbach simple, for trains stopped at the halt, although in those days a second engine was added at the back of the train to help it up the steep incline and incidentally to provide some extra excitement for young travellers.

This area of the Spessart was and is still part of Bavaria although being Lower Franconia, a region in the north-west which was a later addition to the old Wittelsbach kingdom, it does not wholly qualify as true Bavaria. Still the journey from town to country meant crossing into another state, and there is no doubt that whether or not Steiger was typical Bavaria it was much more deeply loved by the Bavarian Hotters than was Offenbach.

Here was country life of the simplest kind, woods, birds, flowers, small practical gardens. A love of nature which Hans Hotter has had all his life probably springs from this part of his childhood. After the circumscribed city flat, this freedom to run in and out and to play with the raw elements of life, was a priceless discovery.

Again it is the father's personality which emerges from that time with extraordinary clarity and conviction. A tall, quiet, bearded man, never wholly well in the small boy's memory, for Hans was only seven when his father died, yet a warm and powerful influence, he introduced all the unknown wonders of bird, beast and flower to his sons.

Hans spent 1915 at an elementary school in Offenbach, but by the end of that year Karl Hotter's health had deteriorated so much that he had to resign from his work. The family did not give up their town flat at the time, but moved to the Spessart house although in fact they never returned to Offenbach.

Eight months of happy country life followed for Hans, who most clearly remembers the summer, though the snows and darkness of winter impressed him too. His brother, having reached the age of ten, was living with friends in Aschaffenburg where he went to school, coming home for weekends. Hans attended the small country school for local children. In the background was the mother, gently reminding her children that their father had to rest and must not be worried, but somehow contriving not to cloud their lives with her own anxiety.

She also had the difficulties of living and running a home in wartime. The family suffered no serious privations, but food was short even in the country, and Crescentia Hotter went out to the farms for supplies, especially for extra nourishment needed for her husband. Despite her efforts his death was probably hastened by the limited wartime diet, but his final illness was mercifully not a very long one. Hans remembers that his father was confined to bed for only about three weeks at the end.

So ended the exile from Munich for Crescentia Hotter. Little more than a dozen years, but they contained virtually the whole of her married life, the birth of her children, and the loss of her husband to whose memory she remained devoted until her own death fifty years later.

Perhaps she idealised those years in retrospect, but the fact remains that Hans Hotter's own impressions are happy ones. There was a loving stability; home as the basis of an enduring, developing life of boundless interest, of things to learn and do and make, music being always an essential element. But also there was a child's dawning awareness of the meaning of responsibility.

Much of the harmony of that simple and, for the parents, often painful life almost certainly sprang from their religious faith. Both were born and brought up in the Roman Catholic Church and as such were not so extrovert about the practice of their faith as the convert who is busy making up for lost time. To the Catholic born, church and faith are simply the framework of life, and this is how it seems to have been with the Hotters. There is nothing to show that Karl Hotter was an excessively devout man, his wife was almost certainly always the more religious of the two, but there was faith in the home, and the boys were brought up in the practices of the Church. In her widowhood Crescentia Hotter turned more and more to the strength of her faith, and it must have been a great joy to her that the elder son, christened Karl after his father, became both a priest and a schoolmaster. She was greatly in favour of teaching as a profession.

Let Hans Hotter himself sum up the Spessart days.

'I remember one occasion before I went to school — so I could not have been even six years of age at the time — when my father took Saturday off from his school work to take us to the Spessart where we already had the house. It was a special event because it was not normal for him to be free then. Saturday was an ordinary working day for everyone, in school too, but my father made up some hours on other days to get those two days' holiday. I can remember the train ride of about an hour and then we had to walk and climb up for another thirty minutes to reach the house, with rucksacks on our backs . . .

'There was always a lot of walking there. Later when we lived in Steiger there was the long walk to the country school for there was no school in our village. It seemed to me an hour at least. Probably it did take us an hour though it was only three or four kilometres and for grownups it would have been not more than thirty minutes. In winter we had to get up at 5 or 6 o'clock to reach school by 7.30, and of course in darkness. Sometimes we went in two groups, boys in one and girls in the other.

'It was quite a small school. I think there were three classes in one room, boys and girls, and not more than six or eight children in each class. We were given lunch at school and walked home in the afternoon.

'The village was up in the mountains — about 1800 feet — and our house was some three hundred yards

4. As Amfortas in *Parsifal*, Breslau 1931

5. *(Below, left)* With Richard Strauss after Friedenstag, 1938 (photo Hanns Holdt)

6. With Julius Patzak in *Palestrina*, Vienna 1949 (photo Rudolf Pittner)

from the village. Of course it was very simple. Not even piped water. There was a well about fifty yards from the house and we had to carry the water in pails. And no electric light. We had oil lamps, and of course we went to bed when it was dark . . . The fires were of wood. There was a big stove and every drop of water had to be heated in kettles or pans. But we were not so spoiled at that time and we washed in cold water!

'You can imagine the problems to get food during the war. We were rationed and of course it was easier in the country. We had friends among the farmers, but I remember my mother going on forays to find food. There was a doctor who came every week or ten days, but he had to walk or come by horse carriage. There were no telephones. It was in a way a very independent life.

'At that time in the war there were Russian prisoners on some of the farms. Not interned, but working with the farmers and they had meetings in one of the farmhouses. I remember that Karl and I went there sometimes and heard them singing in Russian. Years afterwards my mother told me that we were already learning some Russian from them — especially the rude words!

'In later years I have gone back to Steiger several times, but it has changed a lot. The house is still there, but it has changed too, and my father's workshop where he made the furniture and toys is now a garage. It overlooks the valley where the railway line lies, and from the train you can see the village and the church perhaps half a mile from where the autobahn now runs. Our old walk to school would now mean crossing the autobahn.

'I remember all the holiday times. Tobogganning in winter — that was long before ski-ing developed in Germany. And so much of nature. The forest started right behind the house and went on for miles and miles.

'We had no piano up there in the Spessart, but my

father played the lute in the evenings There was always music. Always music.'

If his father's artistic nature shaped Hans Hotter's earliest years, guiding the child's first perceptions and inherent love of beauty, it was the mother who taught him the practicalities of life. Crescentia Hotter was a remarkable woman, a woman of courage, unselfishness and what Rudyard Kipling called 'truth and God's own common sense'.

The early years of the twentieth century, those years which ended with the first world war, formed a period so different from the modern world that few people today can enter into its thinking and approach to life. Those who, like Crescentia Hotter, grew up at the end of the 1800s were trained in the old acceptance of existing orders, and their view of the intellectual adventures of the new century was coloured by that philosophy, especially when they had great personal responsibilities. In her case these came to her in the midst of a war, then unparalleled in its magnitude, which was to end with her country's defeat. It was a dark world as well as a time of deep personal grief in which, with her small sons, she had to plan their practical living.

Today most widowed mothers would first seek for well paid work to support the family, and reckon that some loss of home life and personal care for the children is an inevitable if regrettable necessity. So much is talked about the problems of one parent homes in today's environment that it is sometimes overlooked that this situation has been a reality through the death of father or mother since the adventure of parenthood began.

Civilisations, centuries and individuals meet the problem in different ways, but there is nothing new about it. Crescentia Hotter met it in the spirit of her upbringing and of her own character. For her provision of the home background for her sons was a paramount consideration. She was deeply conscious of the need to stand for them in the place of father as well as mother, and that they should not lack the stability and wisdom of home, even though economic factors would make that home a simple one.

It was natural that she should return to Munich. Her husband's work was the only reason they had gone away. For most of the last year of his life they had not been living in Offenbach, and the friends there were probably basically his. The Spessart house provided a country idyll but was remote, out of touch with their professional world and there was no education beyond the elementary school. Munich was home. Her mother Frau Rüttenauer (she had made a second marriage) was living in the south of Munich and close to the grandmother's home a flat was found for Crescentia.

Until he was ten years old Hans attended an elementary school in the district, his brother had already reached the high school stage, and here they found their first real identification with a home environment wider than the family dwelling. They made friends among the other children and there was the background of grandparents and relatives, for Karl Hotter's family also still lived in Munich.

Here Crescentia Hotter coped, and coped successfully, with the economic problems of running her home and bringing up her children, but it meant a simple standard of life — very far from luxurious, in Hans' memory. She had of course already learned many things about living within a budget during her husband's illness, among them to be an excellent cook. Years later she used to say that you must be poor before you really learn to be a good cook.

Due to Karl Hotter's early death his widow received only a very small pension. But even that pension was a blessing, and long afterwards Crescentia Hotter used to say that without it she would not have been able to give her sons a full academic education.

41

That was her goal for them: a good education leading to eventual economic security. Her own struggle against poverty made her realistic, entertaining no glamorous ambitions for them but a determination that they should be equipped to earn a solid living in a safe profession. For this she wanted them to have a good education, and in this there was also a dedication to her husband's wishes. Karl Hotter himself did not complete a full academic course. His architect's training had ended with an engineer's diploma, and he always regretted that he was not able to continue studies for a doctorate. It was his ambition that he would at least enable his sons to achieve that, and so for his wife this aim was also a memorial to him.

During the difficult years some friends advised her not to attempt so much, but to have the boys trained in some craft which would also provide a sound living and support for her at an earlier stage, but she was not to be changed. Crescentia Hotter was a woman not easily turned from her beliefs and aims. The first were tested in the fire of experience and endurance, and to achieve the second she was ready to give of herself and all that she had.

The impression of this indomitable lady may sound somewhat daunting, and yet this was not the whole Crescentia. She had a tremendous sense of humour which coloured her approach to life and gave a vitality and sanity to her loving and her wisdom. All through her life her sons turned to her as a sound counsellor as well as a proud and devoted sharer in their achievements or their problems. They both loved and respected her, and perhaps while remaining extremely feminine she did in fact represent for them also something of a father's strength.

At ten years Hans was sent to a high school, the Theresien Gymnasium which is also on the south side of Munich. At that time he had no thoughts for the future, no real ambitions and most certainly not artistic ones.

Football was the thing. To football he devoted all his available time and enthusiasm. The mother smiled and waited. It was a healthy passion, a very natural sport for a schoolboy.

Music, however, was still in the background. Both boys were taught the piano by Crescentia Hotter's sister who was assistant to a piano teacher at the musical high school — Hermann Zilcher, a fine musician who founded the Würzburg Mozart festivals — and both had good soprano voices. When Hans went to the gymnasium he was immediately put into the choir without waiting for the usual period of training. Later he became one of the boy soloists. But this was very much incidental at that stage, it did not enter into his personal enthusiasms. Music had always been an integral part of life and at all times he enjoyed making music, but his mother was anxious that it should remain firmly in the realm of hobbies. As a career it was far too uncertain.

Rather to her horror her own mother had other ideas. Frau Rüttenauer was more musical than her daughter, more perceptive of gifts and less restrained in imagination. Listening to the boy Hans singing she said 'This is a voice — he should be a singer!' Crescentia protested; she had to steer her little family's economic ship to ports of security and there was no room on board for artistic also-rans. Frau Rüttenauer did not press the matter. She too waited, for after all in singing the child is by no means always the father to the man. Few famous boy sopranos become great singers in later life.

When he was about fourteen a new and wholly absorbing interest came into Hans' life: the Jugendbewegung or youth movement which was sweeping through Germany.

The Jugendbewegung became an important part of the country's living and thinking at that time. Germany was defeated, disillusioned, financially broken and the young who had followed the militarist period and seen its disintegration turned away from all that imperial

43

Germany had been, and sought a new meaning in life and a new pacific if not pacifist expression and ideal. They were the parellel of much later anti-establishment groups in many countries, but less aggressive and vocal than many youth movements which followed the second world war.

In the 1920s the young had less money, less assurance of their rights, less mission to take up militant causes and to demonstrate. These young Germans were more concerned to get away from the old patterns of life which their elders had followed. Away from social etiquette and class distinction and militarism and out into a natural, idyllic, simple world. Boys and men alike they all wore blouses and shorts, and idealised the simple life.

The origins of the Jugendbewegung went back to the *wandervogel* started in Germany before the first world war, which in its turn had been inspired by the boy scout movement in England, but its real development came after 1919.

Within the one broad youth movement there were many different groups and organisations spread all over the country. Several were organised by the Roman Catholic Church. Some were definitely political, socialist and tending even to communism. Most were of socialist ideals even if not politically attached.

Much later, leaders of the Hitler Youth movements adapted some of the ideas of the Jugendbewegung to their own militaristic theme, but by then the original groups had been banned or driven underground where only some of the Church ones survived, and were re-established after the second world war. There is quite a strong Jugendbewegung today, Church inspired by both catholics and protestants, and found mainly in the high schools and universities.

Open air life, athletics, restoration of the old traditional music, these were the main preoccupations. They condemned as decadent the modern dance music of their time. Girls and young women could join some of the groups, but in the main they were for boys and young men, and definitely anti-militarist.

In the '20s the groups were known in general as the Wandervogel and they walked and sang their way through the mountains and villages of Germany, and from time to time held big gatherings in one of the old castles. National Socialism destroyed that kind of spirit, but in their day they were one of the happier manifestations of the young people of a country seeking new birth in the aftermath of destruction.

Hans spent seven years at the Theresien Gymnasium and then transferred for his last two years at high school to the Max Gymnasium, a famous school in the north of Munich where a number of the city's well known personalities have studied. One was the nuclear scientist Werner Karl Heisenberg, eight years older than Hotter, and later Franz Josef Strauss was a pupil there.

A principal cause for the change was Hans' own enthusiasm to belong to a youth group called Neudeutschland which had a particularly live branch in the Max Gymnasium. Founded in Cologne in 1919 by a Jesuit priest, Father Ludwig Esch, Neudeutschland was one of the Roman Catholic groups which spread throughout Germany. It was also one of those which, renamed 'Singing Circle' managed to exist during the Nazi period, holding its religious meetings in secret, and as Neudeutschland again it is very much alive today.

By fourteen Hans' singleminded devotion to football had waned somewhat, and changed to other sports, and the diverse interests and companionship of the group provided a new world outside the limitations of school. His mother was wholly in favour of it as a safe outlet with plenty of activities which did in fact occupy the whole of his interest and spare time for about four years. His brother was also a keen youth movement member, but of a different group.

'The Jugendbewegung played a very important part

in my development, indeed the most important part during my years between fifteen and eighteen when it took all my time and I was completely devoted to it. Neudeutschland was — and is, for it exists again now — one of the Church groups. It was quite organised but not regimented. There was always a priest or seminarian as companion of each group, they influenced us but did not lead; that was a part of the whole conception.

'We were principally devoted to nature, old music, simple things. Sports too. When the Nazis began to use some of the Jugendbewegung concept they developed it with sport as a goal. We also wanted to be good in sports but as a general interest, not to produce super sportsmen.

'There were circles within the group which met every week and we were very dedicated — no smoking, no drinking! We rejected modern dance tunes and devoted ourselves to the old traditional folk music. No classical playing of course, but we had little orchestras of fiddles, flutes and guitars, and we sang old folk songs. And we went on tours — that was the real *wandervogel*. We would walk for weeks and weeks, sleeping in tents or at the monasteries. They were very good to us, we could always stay overnight at a monastery and eat there and sing. Sometimes we were away four or five weeks together, and managed on almost no money... We sang in the local churches and the monasteries. Sometimes we went to smaller places, villages or hamlets and acted plays at night by torchlight. Real, simple amateur acting with no special costumes, and the plays were those of Hans Sachs' time. Boys played the women's roles as they did in those days, for there were no girls in Neudeutschland — we were very strict about that!

'We had no interest in girl friends at that age, and the youth activities left us no time, and perhaps kept us away from contacts too early... When I was seventeen girls of my own age seemed too old for me, too far above me, and the fourteen and fifteen-year-olds were too young, but of course we studied with some girls, there were always a few in each class at the gymnasium.

'There were other groups which did have girl members. One was Quickborn, a rather similar group to ourselves, also Church based, but it was more sophisticated, and especially interested in music. In Neudeutschland we were keener on sport, and the *wandervogel* walking and nature side. But music was important too, and we had joint meetings with Quickborn and competitions in summer.

'As I got older music was becoming more important in my own life, and I ran a musical circle in Neudeutschland, a group of boys of my own age and a little younger. Josef Greindl was in that group of mine; he was two or three years younger than I, though he actually left Neudeutschland a little earlier than I did.

'There were many people who took an active part in this particular Neudeutschland branch of the Jugendbewegung in their formative years. One was Karl Holzamer who became very well known in the postwar world of public affairs and for years was the head of the German second television programme. He was a few years older than I was, and I remember him very well as a leading figure in the all-Germany meetings when he was in his early twenties.

'Looking back on that time I know the youth movement broadened my outlook and experience, and helped me a great deal. It kept me out of trouble which I might have drifted into without a father . . . All the *wandervogel* groups were socialistic and certainly anti-establishment, though in a very mild way compared with youth today. Still we stirred things up quite a bit!'

In the first sixteen or seventeen years of Hans Hotter's life there was nothing to indicate his future fame or even his artistic career. A sheltered early life in a happy home of the professional class, though one in which he soon came to know the realities of sorrow and a struggle for existence. Normal school years with a boy's love of

47

7. With Viorica Ursuleac in *Arabella*, Munich 1939 (photo Hanns Holdt)

8. In *Zaubergeige*, Hamburg 1935

9. With Richard Strauss and Rudolf Hartmann during a dress rehearsal of *Arabella*, Munich 1939 (photo Hanns Holdt)

sport. Then the development and give and take of companionship with his own generation and its ideals and pleasures. Countless other boys have shared such a youth.

He was in no way an infant prodigy and his mother, unlike many fond parents, was determined that he should not be made one. She carried her realism to the point of scepticism, even though it was lightened by a sense of humour. She herself would have liked to be a teacher, being well-read, a thinker with a fine brain and wide-ranging interests. But in her youth an attractive girl was destined for marriage and not a career, and so she rejoiced in her family life. But she was much too wise ever to project her own unfulfilled ambitions onto her sons.

After those years when the Jugendbewegung and its way of life was all important to the adolescent Hans Hotter he grew up quite suddenly, and grew out of the youth movement. Others might continue teenage interests well into their twenties, but for him there was a sharp change. He was a man and ready, or almost ready, to face a man's responsibilities towards his mother and his own life. In the facing of them he made his first big decision and chose music.

Gradually in the high school years music began to play a more important part in Hans' life, fostered probably by the musical side of the youth movement, although at school the music was classical.

Dr. Josef Saam was then a musical professor at the Max Gymnasium, young, still in his twenties, keen, and one of those who recognised the musician in the young Hotter. Outside his school activities Dr. Saam was organist and choirmaster at the small church of St. George in Milbertshofen, a district in the north of Munich. Then he was offered an appointment as professor of music at Passau, and when he left he suggested

Hans Hotter as his successor at St. George's church. It was a landmark, even if a small one, for here Hans got his first practical experience as an organist and in directing a choir. And Josef Saam always remained a friend, admirer, and one who encouraged him in the early days.

In 1929 he invited the young Hotter to sing in the *Messiah* in Passau cathedral which seats more than 4,000 people. 'You will never sing before a larger audience!' said Saam, and two years later in 1931 it was thanks to him that Hotter gave his first recital, also in Passau and with Saam accompanying him.

When at last the time came to study for a future career Hans finally faced the fact that music had become the paramount interest of his life and the field where his gifts lay. This was something of a shock to many who were interested in him. His mother even when she accepted that his heart was in it, insisted that his career must be a steady one, that he should be a teacher of music and not an itinerant artist. Professors of other subjects at the gymnasium felt that he was betraying the true academic field in which he might have had a fine career. To the middle class academics of that time, and perhaps to some extent even today, a practising musician does not appear the intellectual equal of a university professor.

So he went to Munich University at the age of nineteen to study philosophy — which included musical science — and with no very great outside enthusiasm to support him, except from his music teacher at school and his grandmother. At the same time he joined the Hochschule für Musik to study organ and piano. Singing he did not enter for, and kept secret.

The first real contact with singing in its own right and the larger world of music as a practical profession came almost by accident. He had begun to feel that as he had dreams of becoming a conductor it would be useful to learn something from professional singers, and just at that point Josef Saam introduced him to a private teacher of singing in Munich. So entered Hotter's life one of its most important personalities and certainly the greatest single influence on his musical development — Matthäus Roemer.

At that time Roemer was a man in his early fifties. He had started his professional life as a schoolmaster teaching modern languages at a gymnasium or high school, and was also a tutor in languages to the Wittelsbach royal family. Later he became a singer, making his main career in concert and oratorio work, though he also had a rather limited fame as an operatic Heldentenor. This came after he went to Paris to study under Jean de Reszke at the suggestion and with the help of his wife, who was also a singer. Later he became a friend of Siegfried Wagner who invited him to sing at Bayreuth where he appeared as Parsifal in 1909.

Years afterwards he was to tell Hotter that he learned the real essence of singing from de Reszke, but it was then perhaps too late to equip him for a great operatic career. Instead what he learned he was able to pass on to others. In teaching, Roemer found his real musical fulfilment.

That seems to have been typical of the man. He was a great artist and musician, and also a warm, wise, understanding mentor, generous to a fault. Indeed he probably lacked those practical worldly qualities which Hotter himself was later to describe as so important to a singer: the power to know and reckon with balancing a financial budget through having to manage on very little. But Roemer was essentially practical and down to earth in his teaching, and he possessed an uncanny instinct for assessing the potential of a young singer.

He heard Hans sing at a concert in the gymnasium, sought him out through Josef Saam and offered him lessons. To him, then, came Hans in 1927, eager to learn from a master all that Matthäus Roemer could teach him, but by no means intending that it should shape his

51

career. Roemer took him on, saw and heard what he was at that stage and worked with him.

It is sometimes said that there are no great teachers, only good pupils, meaning that however good the teacher may be he or she cannot create an outstanding artist out of mediocre material. Where the student has the necessary gifts then the wise teacher will become famous through his or her success. This is of course an oversimplification. No one can make the proverbial silk purse out of a sow's ear, but lack of a really fine teacher may prevent a gifted artist from reaching the Olympian heights, as was probably the case with Matthäus Roemer. Instead he found his star pupil in Hans Hotter.

Roemer had an extraordinary dual approach to Hotter's singing at that time which to this day Hans still finds hard to explain, or indeed understand. He recognised in the young untrained and still hardly formed voice an instrument of such rare beauty and power, coupled with a personality of depth and intelligence that he predicted a great future with certainty. It was to him a matter not of hope or luck but something which time would witness — *provided* Hotter worked and gave total singleness of mind to a singing career. Roemer never showered praise on him in the present. He was in this as deflating and realistic as Crescentia Hotter was in other issues.

And Hans continued to doubt, both his own capabilities for this kind of life and also his wish to attempt it. He was conditioned to the aim of a steady professional career probably within the government educational system, and even though he had discovered that for him life must be devoted to music he still saw music within that framework. Or possibly in the great world on the conductor's rostrum... So he continued his studies at the Hochschule für Musik and privately with Roemer.

Finally after more than a year Roemer brought the matter firmly to a head. By then he probably knew that the young man not only had it in him to win through to the real goal, but also that the home background was a strong restraining influence. Matthäus Roemer went to see Crescentia Hotter and took with him all his powers of confident prediction and his own personal generosity.

He had never taken fees for Hans' lessons, and now he offered to give him his full training and only to claim payment later if Hans fulfilled Roemer's own prophecy of success.

He won over the doubtful mother. It would have been ungrateful not to accept such an offer, and scarcely human not to have been somewhat infected by confidence backed by such a practical manifestation of faith. Hans Hotter became a singer.

'Roemer was a very unique person in many ways. Without him not only as a teacher but as a personality and with his persuasiveness, his urgency, I should probably never have taken the decision to be a singer. There was the point when he said - "Now is the time when you must choose: *either to be a singer or to give it up.*" He did not actually put the knife in, but he said "Now you must stop discussing it. Stop the Hochschule. Stop the organist's training. Stop your idea of being a conductor. There are many good conductors and school teachers, but not so many great singers." And that really forced me to decide.

'About that time I was introduced to a retired producer who had been in Munich for many years — Willi Wirk. It is a kind of fate that you meet certain people at the right time. And then you have to have the instinct, intuition to know whom to believe, to whom to listen. At many times in my life there have been colleagues or one of the conductors or a director who would say one thing, advise in one way, and others would say just the contrary. How does one know which to follow? You need a kind of sixth sense to know which is the way for you.

'Willi Wirk at that time was already over seventy —

seventy-one or two I think — and I cannot remember now how I went to him; probably it was arranged by my grandmother. Through him I had my first experiences in acting. We had meetings twice a week. He had a large apartment with an anteroom big enough to play scenes out of opera, and we could bring along our friends on Saturday afternoons. This was exactly at the time when Roemer wanted me to make the decision for singing, and then came this first training in acting. Wirk gave me hours of discussion. He went through the score with me and explained the story and the character I was going to play. What the character is, in which way it is drawn, and the personalities of the other characters. So there was a lesson in practical opera acting and producing.

'Wirk had been the teacher of Rudolf Hartmann about six years earlier. He taught him in the same way, going through the score with him and explaining. In my own scores of that time I still have the old man's notes. He too had been an operatic tenor who appeared in small parts at Bayreuth and also sang in Munich where he played David and Mime for a number of years, way back before the first world war. He had great experience and had worked with Toscanini and also with Bruno Walter. He taught us the basic things too: how to walk on the stage, how to sit down, move, and so on.

'It was at his apartment that I met the famous baritone Anton Van Rooy. He was a well known Wotan who first sang the role at Bayreuth about thirty years before I met him. I think he was the first who afterwards committed the crime of singing Wagner in the States and was thereby expelled from Bayreuth! I remember he was there at Willi Wirk's apartment when I was doing the Dutchman's aria in late 1929. Eight or ten months later I signed my first contract.'

Hotter's unique place on the operatic stage in later years came from his near perfect balance of musical and dramatic gifts. Each great singer has his or her particular qualities of voice and musicianship. Very few can match these with an equal art in acting. Conversely there are good average singers who are outstanding actors and who achieve very considerable fame from this, combined with intelligent use of their vocal resources. Only once or twice in a generation is the ideal marriage of these arts found in a single artist.

Wirk's training was for Hans Hotter the first step towards the meaning of operatic acting, the deeper study both of the particular drama of a given work and the place in it of the character to be assumed. As such it was of great importance by showing him the meaning and possibilities of using his own intellectual powers to see and convey the intention of the composer and librettist's joint creations. At that early stage of course he would have seen it as no more than wise training in undertaking each individual role and the mechanics of being at ease on the stage, but it was the beginning of a lifetime study of dramatic possibilities and expression.

But if Wirk played a vital part in helping Hotter to become the great singing actor who later emerged, it was Roemer who was godfather to the whole artist. Without the strength of Roemer's conviction, the urgency, even fierceness of his challenge, Hotter would almost certainly have remained in quieter backwaters of music. Without his wisdom, knowledge and flair for teaching Hotter's gifts as a singer might never have been fully developed. And without experience of this remarkably selfless musician he might not have become the teacher that he himself is now.

Roemer with his enthusiasm, his patience, his realism at times caustically expressed, was more than a teacher. A man of strong religious faith, his influence was something like that of a prophet promising glory but commanding obedience, resilience, self sacrifice before the end could be achieved.

All through his musical life Hans Hotter has reaped the harvest of Roemer's teaching. Much of it, heard and acted on in the early years, he only fully understood much later in the light of experience.

'I learned from Roemer the qualified approach to music with taste and knowledge. Never to teach a cold technique, never to work without music. It was so enlightening to me that I have tried to adopt this always in my own teaching.' There is no stronger basis for trust than this personal proof of it in one's own life, and evidence of that is in the number of times that Roemer's name and Roemer's maxims are on Hotter's lips today when speaking to his own students,

Yet the actual period of his full time study with Roemer was very short. He started lessons with him in late 1927 but the first year was divided between the high school and these private lessons. Nonetheless Hans worked hard with him, impressed and attracted by the teacher's musical personality. After Roemer brought him to the crucial decision to leave the Hochschule there was just one year of intensive study — and this was the time when he was working with Wirk also — before the chance came to join the opera company at Troppau and launch into working life. It was a very vital year.

But of course Hans' departure from Munich did not break the association. Whenever he returned there he went back to Roemer for more study and to tell the master about his progress, the successes and the problems. Roemer was Hans Hotter's only singing teacher — with one specialised exception.

While Hotter was with the Prague Opera in 1932 the director sent him to Berlin to study with Rudolf Bockelmann. He worked with him for three weeks, not for general vocal studies but for coaching and practical advice on the singing of particular roles from another baritone. 'If you get through this phrase well you will be safe at the end,' Bockelmann would say, 'If this doesn't work, be careful — it may be disastrous!'

The actual study time with Bockelmann was short, but because of the pressures of his Prague day-to-day musical life Hans did not see Roemer for about two years, and then returned with something of the anxious feelings of a prodigal.

Arriving back in Munich he telephoned and Roemer said nothing about his long silence; Simply told him to come at 10 o'clock the next morning in the old way. When they met still nothing was said. The old relationship was re-established, the lessons proceeded as though there had been no break.

Some time later Roemer asked 'With whom did you study during the time I did not see you?' Hans told him. 'Well, I always thought I might send you to a baritone sometime, but I would not have chosen Bockelmann.' The incident was closed.

But to return to the student years. Roemer was probably impressed by one who was so remarkably free of vanity that he did not at once build dream castles of fame on the teacher's prophecies. He must also have been surprised, perhaps even piqued, to find the young Hotter was not deeply interested in the career he advocated. For Hans really did not want to be a singer.

Although music has been the expression of life for him from very early childhood its form changed and developed through the years. In those years of his middle and late teens he passed through a whole gamut of awakening musical perceptions and unsuspected responsibilities and decisions quite as deep rooted, and in his case perhaps as inevitable, as the changes of adolescence itself.

As a small child music had been part of the warm loving safety of home. The father singing with and for his children the simple immemorial folk music of Germany; music linked with fairy tales which is probably the best of all introductions when it comes with the naturalness of human beings to whom it is a way of life. At that stage the small Karl and Hans sang instinctively as many children do, for it was their first way of making music. And making music was to remain the real joy

10. With Anny Konetzni in *Die Walküre*, Vienna 1948/49 (photo Bruno Völkel)

and aim for Hans throughout his life.

In his youth movement phase simple traditional music was still the form, but with growing interest and practice, with the amateur's dedication and enthusiasm. In his case it was more than a hobby because of the depth of the early background, but it was something to be followed purely for enjoyment.

At the same time there was the more practical and obligatory discipline of piano lessons. Exercises and simple classical pieces to be learned, with enjoyment but also with the aim of making music in a more adult way; a way which made demands of training. Parallel with the piano was singing in a choir and the opening up of the world of church music, the meaning and art of highly trained choral singing and the place of the organ, and through these the knowledge of another vast part of Europe's musical heritage in the form of sacred music. It was here that he first found the composer to whom he has always given his greatest devotion — Johann Sebastian Bach.

Music once it is approached as a participant can also be a chore. No one can perform well, as amateur or professional, without hard and often wearisome practice and study, and so by his high school time when Hans decided to follow music as a profession it was already work, even though work that he enjoyed. The form and approach had changed. Once you have decided to make any art your living the perspective is never quite the same again. some of the unquestioning enjoyment (and the sweeping criticism) will inevitably give place to another kind of appreciation.

Hans Hotter planned to teach, therefore he would need to know musical theory, musical history, all the nuts and bolts of musical life, background, training. So this formed the ground of much of his study. He also chose the organ as his instrument, and if he was to train choirs and soloists he needed to know about singing... Behind it all was his growing love for and appreciation of music as a whole — the endless fount of beauty and experience, of laughter and anguish which music bestows like an extra dimension of life. Therefore his dream of conducting, of making music totally.

Singing, he privately considered, was a rather inferior form of making music. Today with a mischievous smile he recalls that. It was only the possession of an exceptional voice and Matthäus Roemer's recognition of it that forced him, at that stage really against his inclination, to be a singer. Very few of us avoid prejudices when young, and Hans Hotter's prejudice seems to have been against singing, at least from the point of view of his own career.

For lieder singing he had an early admiration. The mother of a school friend first introduced him to lieder, and though he himself did not really develop this kind of singing for ten years or more he studied lieder with Roemer who considerd it vital to the technique of an opera singer quite as much as a concert artist. He urged his pupils to test their voices by singing a lied after a heavy operatic role. If the result was not good they were oversinging. The precision, colour and delicacy of the classical lied can be regarded as a thermometer to indicate vocal health.

Roemer was of course a singer, and a singer who had perhaps missed achieving his full potential. When he saw that potential in the young Hotter he was determined that this voice should not be lost. Probably his hardest task was not teaching him how to use that voice — for Hans was always a 'quick study' and a naturally disciplined person — but in making him realise the splendour of singing as an art and his own vocation for it. Roemer succeeded, but in the field of opera Hans had reservations for a long time. Indeed his attitude was that having decided to adopt singing as his musical expression he had to sing opera, and he settled to it with more sense of duty than of joy.

Those who still regard opera as something of a

bastard form of music may be surprised that one of the great stars of the operatic firmament for more than thirty years started with much the same outlook. This was largely due to the rudimentary conventional acting which held the operatic stage in the '20s and early '30s and to some extent until after the second world war.

Hans, growing up in Munich where there was a virile artistic life, developed an early love for the straight theatre. At that time the German theatre was full of new experimental ideas. Fresh impetus in acting at least in modern plays had expelled the old classical 'ham' style, and there was inventive, artistic decor. But the winds of change had not reached opera.

In Bayreuth, where Cosima Wagner lived on until 1930, she influenced her son Siegfried to honour to the letter his father's stage instructions, so that the composer's ideas, which were new and revolutionary fifty years before, became rather mummified with repetition. Bayreuth had held its place in the world through great singing and conducting. The same was true of other houses where grand opera was performed as a sacrosanct art form, with the result that when the standard of singing and conducting fell below the highest level, as they must do everywhere for a good deal of the time, the results from the dramatic point of view were meat for parody. Today we often see the faults of the other side of that coin: ill judged innovations also floundering when musical excellence is absent, but at that time those wheels had not even begun to turn.

For pleasure Hans did not go to operas. Plays, concerts, recitals, but scarcely ever opera. Here again Roemer forced him. And so he did his first serious opera going in Munich in those years from 1927 to 1930. Production and acting apart, they were great days, with Knappertsbusch in the pit and many famous singers, names like Elisabeth Feuge, Hildegarde Ranczak, Felicie Huni-Mihacsek, Paul Bender, Hans Hermann Nissen, Wilhelm Rode (Hans' first Wotan) and Luise Willer who was a fine lieder singer as well as an operatic mezzo.

That experience came only a very short time before he was to stand on an operatic stage himself. Unlike playgoing, he saw opera from the first with the eye of a future performer, and at the same time he was working with Willi Wirk, a producer with a real understanding of what operatic acting and stagecraft could be. But if his approach to the performances was an informed one his reaction to the music was that of normal youthful enthusiasm.

He describes his developing musical tastes as a natural scale of idols. With operagoing he found Puccini who for a time became a firm favourite, as Edvard Grieg was in the non-operatic field, both probably something of a reaction to the classical composers who formed the basis of his piano and organ studies. For a time he turned delightedly to the romantics, though Bach towered above them all, and his love for Bach's music has never wavered. Mozart and Schubert, two of Hotter's great loves, took their places much later, and he only really discovered Verdi when he began to sing in Verdi's operas.

And Wagner? Not unnaturally he was caught by the Wagnerian magic when he first encountered it, and with Roemer's certainty that he was destined for Bayreuth and a Wagner career it must be counted among his very important musical phases. But his enthusiasm lessened with the years. Partly because of the political overtones caused by Hitler's fondness for Wagner's music, but probably more because the golden yoke of fame as a Wagner singer is heavy and sometimes oppressive. Over the years Hans Hotter was to have too much of Wagner

But that was all far ahead. When the twenty-one-year old young man set out for his first regular engagement as a member of the Troppau opera company he had simpler and more basic aims: to earn his living and so lift a financial burden from his mother, to prove that his own choice of profession had been right, and to justify the faith, inspiration and generosity of Matthäus Roemer. That was enough, coupled with living and working away from his home city for the first time.

PART TWO
Professional Artist

WHEN MATTHAUS ROEMER asserted with such conviction that the young Hotter would one day sing at Bayreuth he did not leave the matter on the lap of the gods, Wagnerian or otherwise. Knowing Siegfried Wagner as a friend he was able to recommend his student to Richard Wagner's son, sole director of the Bayreuth festivals, even before that student was installed as a member of the Troppau opera, and Hans had an audition with him in 1930. Siegfried Wagner was impressed by his voice and stage potential and said there should be an opportunity for him to sing one of the esquires in *Parsifal*. He even mentioned the role of the Herald in *Lohengrin*.

It was a thrilling, though probably rather terrifying prospect for a young man of twenty-one still very unsure of his vocation as a singer, but it was one of the visions which did not materialise. Three weeks later Siegfried Wagner died. His mother Cosima had died earlier the same year. The Bayreuth festivals passed into a new phase under the direction of Winifred Wagner, Siegfried's widow. Any notes that he may have made about Hans Hotter were not followed up, and the Bayreuth prospect faded. Much later Winifred was to invite him to sing the Dutchman in 1939, but he did not wish to join the company then because of its political affiliations. It was more than twenty years after that first audition that Hotter came to Bayreuth in 1952, and by then he was a world star. It has always been a sorrow to him that Roemer, then in failing health, was never able to see and hear him on the stage of the Festspielhaus.

Apart from Siegfried Wagner he had a number of auditions, but none of them successful in producing the offer of a contract. Roemer was anxious to get him out

11. Relaxing with the Begum Aga Khan, Bayreuth 1950s

12. Making up as Kurwenal in *Tristan*, Florence 1951

of Munich and into a regular company because he felt that his pupil was still drawn to other forms of music; being a member of an operahouse ensemble would settle him into the profession.

In fact the Troppau offer came quite unexpectedly. Hans sang the baritone solo part in Hindemith's *Lehrstück*, an oratorio with words by Bert Brecht, at a Munich concert conducted by Hermann Scherchen. A critic gave him high praise in his notice which appeared in a Vienna paper. Arthur Löwenstein, the director of the Troppau opera heard of this, and when he came to Munich looking for new singers for his company he sought him out. Hans went to Troppau with a contract for the 1930-31 season, providing a very small salary, but the opportunity to perform a number of leading roles including some of the great Wagnerian parts: Wolfram in *Tannhäuser*, the Wanderer in *Siegfried*, even Hans Sachs. An amazing chance for an unfledged singer.

Perhaps fortunately, that *Meistersinger* came to nothing. 'Thanks to God!' says Hans Hotter today, considering how at the age of twenty-two he would have coped with Sachs, one of the longest, greatest, and most psychologically mature roles in all opera. Rehearsals for it started the following spring, but the municipal authorities cut down on finances and the production was cancelled.

However he sang other roles. As well as the Wanderer and Wolfram there was a very successful Tonio in *Pagliacci* and the Speaker in *Die Zauberflöte*, and he also gave a lieder concert in April 1931.

Although he does not look back on Troppau in the rosy light with which some singers regard their first company engagement, it was an interesting, fruitful, hard-working eight months. The artistic standard was not very high. Troppau was then a town of some 40,000 people in the German-speaking part of Czechoslovakia known as the Sudetenland. Before the first world war it had belonged to Austria and retained, as well as the language, much of the social and artistic atmosphere of the old Austro-Hungarian empire.

The company was composed mostly of young singers with a few others who had passed their prime. In general it was like a continuation of university life, all young and keen, all with very little money. Löwenstein and his wife were kind and invited the young baritone to their home for lunch soon after he arrived. He was lucky in finding good 'digs'. In a letter to his mother he describes the place, in the centre of the town and only five minutes from the theatre. Everything was large — bed, wardrobe, cupboards, a six-foot mirror — and it contained a piano! All this for the equivalent of about 40 marks a month.

The piano must have been a godsend. Much of Hans' study with Roemer had been devoted to lieder and oratorio parts and he only had a repertoire of four or five operatic roles when he came to Troppau. In those days a promising young singer was not limited to a few roles. Within his '*fach*' or range of parts, for which he was vocally and dramatically suited he might be called upon to sing a great many important parts and often at short notice. Coaching was given by the musical staff but much of the work of preparation and learning roles was done by the young artist alone. Having inherited his mother's remarkable memory this presented no particular problems and he was of course a trained pianist. No wonder he was delighted with the piano in his room.

During that season he realised that he should soon go to another company where there would be wider experience of working with more mature singers. And he wanted to be in Germany. Georg Hartmann who was intendant at Munich in the late forties and early fifties was then director of the Breslau opera, and from time to time he came to Troppau to look for new young talent for his company. In this way he heard Hotter and several others, and as a result Hans went to Breslau for

70

the 1931-32 season. Once again the salary was a very low one, but there would be the opportunity to tackle new roles in a more testing environment.

At Breslau he sang his first Jochanaan, his first Amonasro and even Amfortas, as well as lesser parts such as Schlemihl in *The Tales of Hoffmann*. The general standard of performance was provincial, the artistic level not very high, although higher than Troppau. Still the challenge was exciting for a young singer and, despite two spells when he had relatively little to do, the sheer amount and variety of work — which included operetta — proved a valuable part of his training. By the end of 1931 he had given his first hundred operatic performances.

On the whole the Breslau time was not, however, a very happy one. Years later his mother used to remember how often he felt discouraged and doubtful in the early years of his singing career. There was also a rupture with Hartmann. Colleagues advised that he should sing Hans Sachs which angered Hartmann who demoted him to a super's part as the king in *Macbeth*, gave him virtually no work in the last two months of the season and no farewell performance.

There were other problems too. Political changes were making themselves felt in Germany. There was a sense of anxiety and uncertainty. But the town had a lively musical life and he went to many concerts. For the first time he heard Furtwängler conduct and Walter Gieseking play, and admired a number of other artists.

Breslau also proved to be a single-season stage in his career. Two provincial houses and only two years of professional work lay behind him, but they included probably four times as much varied experience as most beginners of his age can obtain in comparable companies today. If the opportunity offered he now wanted to try his luck in a bigger city.

Richard Lert (husband of Vicki Baum) whom he got to know during the Breslau season urged him to try for

71

Berlin. This proved to be the first of several occasions when he almost committed himself to what was then Germany's capital city, and then for one reason or another drew back. About a dozen years later he held a contract with Berlin concurrently with Munich, Hamburg and Vienna and he has made many guest appearances there, but fate — and his own preference for southern Germany — have always prevented a very close relationship with the town.

The reason he drew back at his first encounter in 1932 was Dr. Paul Eger. Hans himself was probably then very much attracted by the thought of Berlin.

Eger, already an experienced theatre director, was at that time head of an association of theatres in Berlin called the *Bühnenverein*, but had just been appointed intendant of the German Theatre in Prague. In this capacity he offered Hans Hotter a contract. He knew that the Berlin Staatsoper was in the air, and made his own suggestion first, backed by considerable wisdom and fatherly counsel.

When Hans was in Berlin for the opera audition, Eger's secretary telephoned to say that Eger would like to talk to him first. On arrival Paul Eger said that he believed Hans would be offered a contract by the opera, but that he was convinced that he was still too young and inexperienced for what it was likely to entail. Either he would be taken up with enthusiasm and induced to oversing, possibly damaging his voice and certainly his artistic development, or in a large company he would not be given enough to do which would be just as bad. Berlin, he said, was a dangerous place for a young man with time on his hands.

Instead he offered him a chance to work in Prague with a good company where there would be a number of fine singers in his own range; men from whom he could learn much. He would not be the glittering young star of a mediocre company but a young gifted member of a high quality ensemble.

With considerable prescience he said that the political upheavals in Germany would probably send many more experienced singers to Prague; Hans, already conscious of these nationalist undercurrents in Breslau and unhappy about them, saw this was likely to be true.

Two generous gestures by Eger won him over. First Eger promised that he would not try to hold him in Prague when he felt ready to move on, to Berlin or another major company. Secondly he asked Hans if he had any debts, and offered to pay them. For a young man on the very limited salary then being paid by Breslau, Eger said, debts were to be expected. Hans explained that his main liability was to Matthäus Roemer who had refused to accept any payment until his career was launched. So Eger advanced him the necessary money, saying it would be deducted in instalments from his second year's salary. When the contract for that second year at Prague came to be signed Eger wrote off the debt.

Hotter went to Prague and never regretted it. Eger proved to be the wise and understanding counsellor he had appeared, and though he certainly wanted this brilliant young singer for his company and did his utmost to get him, he was genuinely and unselfishly interested in helping him to build his career. 'Use the Prague time as your apprenticeship,' said Eger, 'I will see that you have enough to do, but not too much, so that you have time to learn.'

Events followed the pattern Eger had predicted. With the rising tide of Nazi power many musicians, Jews and others, left Germany. A number, especially those from Berlin, went to Prague because of good contacts with Eger. Some stayed for quite a long time.

To Hans Prague was wholly delightful, a beautiful, lively city with a vital cultural and particularly musical life. Like Troppau it still had the charm and cachet of the days when it had been part of imperial Austria, but while Troppau was distinctly provincial, perhaps almost parochial, Prague was a capital city.

A great many of its inhabitants, perhaps ten per cent, were of German origin and German speaking. Much of the culture came from or was fostered by Germans. But there was also Czech art and culture. There was a lively social life and a lot of sport, football, ice hockey, tennis. Hans enjoyed it all, and found life inspiring in this 'little Paris'. He and his young fellow artists were hard up, but money was not essential. They could have a good time on very little.

Here he heard Bruno Walter again, whom he remembered from his youth in Munich and was to know personally and work with in later years. Great names in the theatre appeared on the Prague stage — Paula Wessaly, Ernst Deutsch, August Bassermann, Paul Demel, Frederick Valk who later came to England and whom I remember as a fine Othello with the Old Vic Company in 1942. All came and gave of their art to Prague at that time.

George Szell was then leading conductor at the Prague opera and to him Hans owed a great deal for encouragement and trust when he was given leading parts at that early stage. This was a friendship that developed later when they met again through concerts in Chicago in the 1950s and when Szell conducted *Die Zauberflöte* at the Salzburg Festival in 1959.

It was during the Prague time that he finally decided to remain a singer, and the crucial influence was an artist whom in fact he never met personally — Feodor Chaliapin. The great Russian bass revealed to him that it was possible to resolve the artist's problem of true music drama: to reconcile what he calls the discrepancies of singing and acting.

He was impressed by others such as Wilhelm Rode, his first interpreter of great Wagnerian parts, but Chaliapin was different from all the others. Today we should probably regard Chaliapin's acting style as very old fashioned, but the power was there, the mastery which transcends all passing styles, the great artist who compels belief. It was a tremendous revelation, an opening up of the possibilities of an operatic career, a challenge and an ideal.

Chaliapin's voice was not always beautiful; it was distinctive, it was a means of conveying character, a dimension of drama or feeling or tragedy. By the time Hans heard him he was no longer in his prime, but the vocal timbre and acting fascinated him. When listening to Chaliapin's records in later years he describes it as stage presence in the voice, the acting power of a great personality conveyed in the actual singing.

Here then was the answer to the young man who had still felt out of sympathy with the career into which he had launched. Chaliapin was the living example of what a singer might be, and it was something which called for every quality of brain and musicianship and personality to be united.

When Virgil Thomson wrote in the *New York Herald Tribune* about Hotter's first Dutchman in New York in 1950, he remarked that there was an aura of Chaliapin about him even before he began to sing. By then he had truly inherited the mantle of his ideal model.

If Chaliapin was an unconscious power in Hotter's life, the Prague years also brought his first contact with a musician who was to play an enormous part in his later career and fame: the conductor Clemens Krauss. At that time Krauss was musical director of the Vienna Opera. He came to Prague for some concerts, and happened to audition a young tenor in the company, who was a friend of Hans'.

'I was not asked for an audition. It was a colleague of mine, and when he told me I said "My God, I wish I could do that too!" He said, "Yes, but I cannot fix that". Then I had the glorious idea to say "Let me accompany you!" I accompanied him. I still remember that it was in a big concert hall, and Clemens Krauss sat in the front row. My colleague sang, and after that Krauss made some polite remarks. I had of course brought my music with me, and at the end this colleague — who was a real friend! — said "May I say something? My accompanist sings also". Krauss looked up in his ironic way "Ah — a singing coach! Then I shall have to accompany you." It was really very kind of him, and he went over to the piano and sat down. I sang "Abendlich strahl" from the end of *Rheingold*. I always sang that for auditions. It is short, and for auditions it is always better to sing something short and impressive. I think I also sang Wolfram's "Evening Star" from *Tannhäuser*.

'Then came Krauss' remark which I should always remember "This impresses me. Are you singing here?" I said "Yes, I am singing dramatic roles, and smaller parts too" and he said "Yes, you'd better! How old are you?" I told him I was twenty-four. He said "I would like to take you to Vienna, but for the smaller parts you are too tall. I cannot put you beside a leading man who is a head shorter . . . and for the leading parts you are too young. But I shall know what you do."

'It was almost another five years before he got into contact with me again, but I came to know later that after that first audition he wrote to his wife Viorica Ursuleac, the leading soprano in so many of his opera performances, "I do not think I am mistaken that today I have heard the Wotan of the future."'

Hans Hotter's public of course already adored him. Firstly the admirers of the shy young man in Troppau, then the Breslau audience and afterwards the habitués of the German musical theatre in Prague. The critics gave him quite a lot of attention. In those early notices there was almost universal praise for the beauty and quality of the young Hotter's voice. Some were less enthusiastic about his histrionic understanding and ability to tackle major roles. Not unnaturally. When he had completed his second season at Prague and moved to the more testing world of Hamburg, he was still no more than twenty-five.

He himself was worried about his acting. The revelation of a great operatic actor and stage presence such as Chaliapin made him all the more conscious of what he knew were his own shortcomings. Later he used to recall that he was shy and stiff, and very conscious of his long arms and legs. Like many others before and since he felt awkward on stage. Those who saw him in later years and counted his poise, economy of gesture and grace of movement among his most striking accomplishments find it hard to believe that he ever felt himself gauche and wooden. But actors are not always 'born', indeed many of the greatest only achieve their personal expression on stage by long and arduous study and practice.

Intelligence is not always a popular word in relation to singers; it is often used as qualified praise for one whose vocal endowments are mediocre. No amount of intelligence by itself will create a great singer or actor. Greatness in these arts comes from the gift which enables a person to grasp, to feel, to *be* the music or the character. But without intelligence and self sacrificing hard work in acquiring technique this cannot be conveyed to an audience. By his own intelligence and self discipline Hotter overcame the early inhibitions, and by the second year at Prague the critics were beginning to credit him with growing insight and interpretive powers.

It was during 1932 that Dr. Eger, casting him for some of the great taxing roles, Wagnerian and others, sent him to Berlin to study with Rudolf Bockelmann. Although that series of lessons lasted only three weeks Bockelmann continued to take an interest in Hotter, and it was he who obtained for him an introduction to Hamburg.

Eger heard of it. He had promised that he would not stand in Hotter's way when the time came for a move from Prague, but he made one stipulation. He would not release him unless the next operahouse who offered him a contract was prepared to pay more than he, Eger, could offer him. It was a farseeing and generous condition.

Bockelmann was one of the great artists then appearing at the Hamburg Staatsoper, but he was ending his regular contract and he suggested that Hotter should be auditioned for a place in the bass-baritone range. The director H.K. Strohm had already found a successor to Bockelmann in Karl Kronenberg who was due to come the following year. He explained that he really had no vacancy for a young baritone, but on Bockelmann's word agreed to give him an audition as he had been so warmly recommended.

That Hamburg audition took place at 1 p.m. on the rehearsal stage; afterwards the director said, 'I would be interested to hear you on stage, but there is no time. However we have a performance of *Cavalleria rusticana* and *Pagliacci* tonight. Would you be prepared to sing in it?' Hans, on the spur of the moment, said yes. And he sang both Alfio and Tonio. But Strohm did not wait for that. He came to his dressing room before the performance and offered him a contract. Next morning there was another brief meeting before Hotter had to rush back to Prague for a performance, and it was then that Eger's condition regarding salary came out. Strohm was not a little surprised. He expected Hotter to jump at the chance to join the Hamburg Staatsoper on any terms, but he was impressed by Eger's opinion of the worth of a still relatively little known singer. Eger's stipulation won the day. Hotter had his contract at a higher salary than Prague could offer him.

He was not at that time very much drawn to Hamburg. His heart was in southern Germany, his ultimate ambition to join the Munich opera. He had tried Breslau and not liked it very greatly. Both the Czech cities of Troppau and Prague had more of the character of Austria and Bavaria. He had consulted with Paul Eger before the Hamburg audition and told him privately that he would much rather go to Vienna. Hamburg seemed far away, remote not only geographically but in mood and people from the world he knew.

Here again Eger stepped in with wise advice. He could foresee the political avalanche which would overtake all these lands. No peaceful cultural havens would remain, and as he had counselled Hotter two years earlier to come to Prague to serve his apprenticeship to a singing career, now he advised him, as a German, to return to Germany and take his place for better or worse in one of his country's major opera companies.

In 1934 Hamburg was indeed a very different city from any in which Hans Hotter had lived, and the opera company and his place in it were on a new level. Young as he was he joined the company as a leading singer. In Prague under Eger's guidance he appeared in many small parts as well as certain important ones. In Hamburg the small part phase was over. Here he sang the star roles not, it may be said, at first in new productions, but he took over the roles from other singers in the regular repertory. Karl Kronenberg who had been engaged to follow Bockelmann came in 1935. But Hotter was given and held his own place in the company and soon became increasingly well known as a handsome and gifted young leading baritone among a constellation of well known names.

During the years that were to follow, Hamburg became home in a real sense. Here he met his wife, and here they lived until 1940. Here he became a star of the operatic world, famous throughout German speaking countries and to a limited extent internationally too. Here the second world war overtook them.

As the Nazi regime tightened its grip on the country, Hamburg remained for a long time one of the more free-thinking centres. A port, a commercial centre with businessmen coming from all parts of the globe, the city was in contact with the thinking of the outside world. In cultural life there were fewer political pressures, and Hotter coming to the opera company as an already established singer was never put under any party pressures in regard to his artistic life and work.

There was a good deal of smart social life going on in Hamburg, more public and sophisticated in this cool, handsome city of the north than in the southern towns with their nostalgic Habsburg heritage. One of the major events of 1935 was a film ball at the Atlantic Hotel. Hans Hotter was invited among other leading artists of the entertainment world.

He did not particularly want to attend. Large public events of this kind were not his favourite relaxation and he hated the formality of full evening dress; white tie and tails were to him the uniform of the concert platform. Still, he had only been in Hamburg about six months and friends persuaded him that it was important for his career that he should be seen at the film ball. On arrival he was taken to an artists' table where there was a number of theatrical celebrities and some of the young members of the Thalia Theatre company.

Hans was introduced to one of these, Helga Fischer, a tall slender blue-eyed daughter of northern Germany. They danced together and after a while Hans suggested that they should go to a bar where there was a more personal and *gemütlich* atmosphere. Helga had come to the ball as the guest of her drama teacher, the well-known actor Ernst Leudesdorff, and she said she must ask his permission. 'With Hotter you may go!' was the verdict. So began the romance which led to their engagement some months later and their marriage the following summer.

In many ways they are opposites, though not in appearance. Both are very tall, both have blue eyes and fine drawn, classical features. When they were young this 'family' likeness led to their sometimes being taken for brother and sister. But under the surface Helga is essentially a northerner with love of the high, rain-washed skies and salt winds of the North Sea and the Baltic in her nature, while Hans belongs to Bavaria's mountains and forests, music and laughter. It was an attraction of contrast, not least because paradoxically he is the more practical and industrious of the two.

Their backgrounds were also different. Helga's father was a prosperous businessman who had several factories at Chemnitz in Saxony, one for hosiery, another for motor-cycles, as well as a wide-ranging export business in Hamburg. His wife to his great delight presented him with five children, four daughters and a son, and he would have welcomed more having himself been one of a family of sixteen. His wife had expensive tastes in clothes and houses and he, although his own tastes were simple, always revelled in providing handsomely for his family.

Through business contacts he had developed a great interest in and affection for England and in the mid-1930s he owned a hosiery factory in Nottingham and moved his family home there. This was not wholly popular. His wife's health was never good in England and well before the outbreak of war, she had returned to Germany. Helga, the eldest child, had been sent to a family in Leicester to learn English in 1932 after she left high school, had been very bored and unhappy there, and on that account did not go to Nottingham when the family made it their home. Her father's abiding devotion to England was to have a tragic ending: he had not become a British subject because he would not believe that war would come, and when the situation darkened he applied for naturalisation. But the formalities were not completed when war was declared between England and Germany in September 1939. Herr Fischer was not interned, but he was not allowed contact with his factory and lost all his shares in the Nottingham business. He died of a heart attack in the following year.

At the beginning of 1935, however, the family were living in one of Nottingham's large handsome houses and Helga, having begged to be allowed to stay in Hamburg, was living there with friends. She wanted to go on the stage and had persuaded her father to give her a dramatic training. This had started with some classes in London while she was living in Leicester. In Hamburg her father knew Ernst Leudesdorff who agreed to take her as a private pupil. In 1935 she had been accepted as a student actress with the Thalia Theater, and it was as a reward for good progress that Ernst Leudesdorff had invited her to the ball, an event which unknown to them both would shortly put an end to her career so recently begun.

Hans and Helga were both very young, although he was already a name in the musical world. They met and danced and talked, and for a time she held to her aim of becoming an actress. But it was not a very strong ambition. He with his own deep dedication to music and at last a real commitment to opera perhaps took her stage ambitions more seriously than she did, and was determined not to obstruct her career. But in any case when they became privately engaged she made him a gift of her intentions for a career of her own, renouncing it to devote herself to him and to his artistic life.

Both families were far away and had still to be won over to the engagement. Hans met the Fischer parents at Wiesbaden where they were staying for a holiday, and Helga's father, though anxious about his daughter's prospects with a professional singer immediately fell under the young man's spell. Hans took Helga to stay with his mother in Munich while he went to Barcelona for a concert, and Crescentia Hotter initiated her into the art of Bavarian cooking!

At Christmas time 1935 they went over to England to meet the rest of Helga's family and the official engagement party was given there. They were married six months later.

The wedding was not in England. It was divided between their two home towns, the civil ceremony

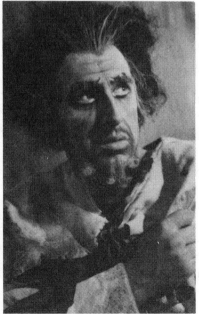

13. *(Above, left)* As Basilio (a favourite role) in *The Barber of Seville,* Hamburg 1937

14. As Pizarro in *Fidelio,* Munich 1945 (photo Sabine Toepffer)

15. As Amonasro in *Aida,* Munich 1938

taking place in Hamburg and the church service near Munich, where Hans' brother married them in the beautiful church of Blutenburg. All the Fischer family gathered there for the occasion.

Two years after coming to Hamburg Hans was a married man, settled in a home of his own, and with more responsibilities ahead. Their son Hans-Peter, now a gifted painter living in Munich, was born in the following spring of 1937, and the family was completed by a daughter, Maria Gabriele, born just before the outbreak of war in 1939. With this young family and an already famous husband Helga Hotter had a very full life with no time to regret her acting.

When Hotter came to Hamburg he had a repertoire of between twenty and twenty-five operatic roles. His first performance as one of the company was as Pizarro in *Fidelio*. The conductor was Eugen Jochum, Martha Geister sang Leonore, Paul Kötter Florestan and Theo Herrmann was Rocco. The newcomer created a sensation, 'We can expect greatness from him,' wrote one reviewer. A week later he sang Macbeth opposite Sabine Kalter making her last appearance at Hamburg, and despite the ovations for her in the house and in print the new Macbeth also made his mark.

Quite soon after his arrival he was cast as Dietrich in Hans Pfitzner's opera *Der arme Heinrich* and this was to mark the beginning of his personal knowledge of Pfitzner. The opera is not very well known but the part is rewarding. Pfitzner conducted himself, and produced. Hans was excited to meet and work with him, for he had known and admired his other operas, especially *Palestrina*, his oratorios and other music from his Munich boyhood. He had heard a good deal about him, not always in praise. Pfitzner was a rather contentious personality, difficult with many people, a perfectionist who demanded total dedication from himself and others with whom he worked.

With Hotter, forty years his junior, a ready sympathy

84

sprang up, and Hans came to know and understand him better than most. He calls Pfitzner a humanist in the best sense. A man with a deep love and understanding of many arts. Words probably meant as much to him as music (he wrote his own libretto for *Palestrina*), and he had an enormous knowledge of German literature and delighted in quoting long passages of Goethe from memory. Words in themselves fascinated him, and his word games were well known, and also his sharp, ironic humour. He enjoyed good wine and after dinner his eloquence would flow in discussion, in quotation, in what was considered the art of conversation in a more leisurely age. But he demanded the whole attention of his audience.

There was one occasion in late 1939 when Furtwängler conducted a concert with several Pfitzner works in Berlin; it included the world première of his Sinfonetta and Hotter was there singing Dietrich's great Rome narration from *Der arme Heinrich* as well as Schubert lieder. Afterwards there was a party at the Adlon, Gieseking was there and Elly Ney, and a number of famous artists. Twenty or thirty of them were sitting at a long table. At one end Pfitzner was sitting talking, reciting and delivering wisdom in one way or another and surrounded by an attentive group. At the other end people were talking among themselves, and then someone laughed. Pfitzner broke off, bounded to his feet and shouted 'Silence!'

Born in Russia, he had all the patriotic devotion to Germany of one who started life as an expatriate and it has in a way infused his work. Pfitzner's music, so widely known and appreciated in his own country has never quite achieved the wide fame that it deserves. I remember discussing this years ago with Erik Maschat, then archivist of Bavarian Radio and formerly personal assistant to Clemens Krauss. He agreed, and aptly compared Pfitzner with Elgar in that respect. Each is so deeply identified with and rooted in the nature of his own country and people that the music does not transplant as successfully as the work of many other composers.

Hans Hotter's voice delighted Pfitzner, both in his own and other music. Immediately after *Arme Heinrich* he recommended him to sing Borromeo in *Palestrina* in Vienna under the baton of Bruno Walter, in 1935. Hamburg refused to release him on that occasion but Pfitzner also invited Hans to sing in several broadcasts which he was giving at the time in Hamburg. One of his best Pfitzner stories relates to one of them.

'He asked me to sing for him, with himself as accompanist, in a programme partly of his own songs and partly of Loewe's ballads. He was very fond of Loewe and had orchestrated some of them. He would choose his own songs for the programme but he asked me to select the Loewe pieces. Here was I, a young singer, being given a free hand by a famous composer. I thought — what would please him? and decided to choose the songs he had orchestrated because he would probably feel near to them. Among them was *Odins Meeres-Ritt*. It is for me a very rewarding ballad, and the accompaniment is exciting. Loewe of course was himself a singer and an accompanist. He was a really perfect pianist and a connoisseur of voices who knew exactly how to write for them, which is why singers enjoy his songs so much. But this accompaniment has some technical problems. The day before the rehearsal there was a phone call in the late evening — I had some friends with me. It was Pfitzner, and without any introduction he said "Are you crazy? I am not Backhaus! I cannot play this!" So I said, "I am terribly sorry, but we don't have to give this one, there are plenty of others". "No," said Pfitzner, "Its in the programme. I asked you to choose it and you have made this mess for me, and now I have to cope with it. See you tomorrow at 9 o'clock", and he slammed down the receiver.

'I thought — my God, what is going to happen? I

knew he was always early, and so I would get to the broadcasting station well before 9 o'clock. I arrived about twenty to 9 and asked the doorman if Dr. Pfitzner had arrived. He said "Is that the tiny man with glasses? He has been here since 8 o'clock and insisted on having a practice room. You will find him there." I could hear him as I went up. Imagine, a famous man in his late sixties and all this for a young singer's choice!

'I came into the studio nervously and he jumped up in an excellent mood, "There you are, come in, now we will rehearse this." I said "Shall we do your songs first?" "No, we will do the Loewe first, and first of all *Odin*, but before it all I will play you this last section with its difficulties which you have given me." He sat down like a child and gave the passage all the intensity of Odin's celestial horse and the pursuing eagles. He looked up at me, "Fabulous!" I said, "*Isn't* it?" cried Pfitzner. He was so happy. He was in a better mood then than perhaps I ever saw him.

'In some ways he had great humility, the dedicated humility of the true artist. In others he expected absolute deference and obedience. He was always ahead of schedule, so eager to start on rehearsals or planning that he would come to a place before anyone else arrived, and then feel affronted because the others were not there. There were many occasions like that. Once he went to some town in the middle of Germany and as usual he was a day too early. He stayed in a small hotel and had a room on the first floor. Quite early, probably about 6 o'clock he woke and as he could not sleep any more, got up and started composing. But by 7.30 — you know what the Germans are — workmen started breaking up the road outside with a drill. He was enraged, jumped up, threw open the window and shouted "Quiet! Pfitzner lives here!"

'In 1944 I gave a complete Pfitzner recital in Munich in honour of his 75th birthday. It was very difficult to find a hall then because so many buildings had been bombed. I think we had it in the University. And I sent him a telegram and invited him to come. He refused — because the Munich opera was not going to perform *Palestrina* to honour his birthday! The company no longer had a production — sets, costumes, anything of *Palestrina* at that time, and in any case their programmes were nothing to do with me, but he was so angry that he would not come to my concert. Happily five years later there was a *Palestrina* there to celebrate his 80th birthday. That was in 1949 only a few months before he died, and he was very old and frail and nearly blind, but his hearing was not affected. We almost carried him onto the stage after the final curtain, and he was very happy.'

The Hamburg years were full and exciting ones. During 1935 Hotter sang the title part in Handel's *Julius Caesar* and the Wanderer in *Siegfried* among many other roles. In early 1936 he was made a Kammersänger of the 'Free Hanseatic City of Hamburg'. At that time the title was bestowed by the Bürgermeister on behalf of the city, and it was the first of many such honours he was to receive in later years.

Also in January that year he played Boris, 'my first great character undertaking', in Germany's first performance of Moussorgsky's original score of *Boris Godunov*, dating from 1868-9 without Rimsky-Korsakov's later emendations. Eugen Jochum conducted. The performance was an overwhelming success, placing Hotter firmly in the front rank as the star of a new and historic performance. By his dramatic and vocal command of the role he was hailed as the definitive Boris and it remained always one of his great roles and among his personal favourites. These performances were also a triumph for Jochum and the *Boris* forged a close friendship between conductor and singer which has continued through the years.

At the end of the 1936 season Hotter took over another very different but interesting role, that of Kaspar in Werner Egk's *Die Zaubergeige*, an opera which he was to produce more than thirty years later in Dortmund.

Among his other roles during these years were Falstaff, Iago, Escamillo, Tonio, the Count in *Figaro* and the *Rheingold* Wotan which he first performed in 1938 in Hamburg. In the same year he recorded the second act of *Die Walküre* in Berlin with Martha Fuchs as Brünnhilde and Bruno Seidler-Winkler conducting, but he did not sing the *Walküre* Wotan on stage before 1941 in Munich. Although the *Siegfried* Wanderer was one of his very first roles it was more than ten years before he completed the trilogy of the character.

At the same time he was beginning guest appearances in other German houses and abroad. In February 1937 he went to Cologne to repeat his Dietrich in Pfitzner's *Der arme Heinrich*, but his first visits to Belgium were even earlier. In April 1935 he had been to Antwerp to sing Amfortas in some *Parsifal* performances with the Royal Flemish Opera. He was there again in October the same year to sing Kurwenal, and in October 1936 he returned to Antwerp as Pizarro. In December 1939 he went to the Paris Opera for the first time to sing the Wanderer, Furtwängler conducting, and in 1939 he also sang the Wanderer at the Scala, Milan. There were also other guest appearances, and he sang at several concerts in Holland.

Walter Legge, on behalf of Beecham, invited him to Covent Garden in 1938, but by the time he had arranged his release from other commitments Covent Garden had engaged another singer. They repeated the invitation in 1939 but in that case they themselves were too late, Hans having a full schedule. After that the war ended communication and it was another eight years before he made his London debut.

For nearly five years Hotter had no direct contact with Clemens Krauss. During that time Krauss left Vienna and went to Berlin as musical director of the Staatsoper where he followed Wilhelm Furtwängler. Then in 1937 he became intendant and musical director of the Bavarian Staatsoper in Munich.

Shortly before, when Hans was in Berlin for a concert he had a telephone call from Krauss' secretary asking him to come to see him.

When Hans arrived Clemens Krauss looked at him and said 'Would you like to go to Munich?' This of course had been Hotter's dream ever since he embarked on an operatic career but there seemed to be a cruel irony in the timing. He explained that he had just signed a new contract with Hamburg which committed him to that company for the next five or six years. Krauss said 'Perhaps we can find a solution. You may be able to shorten this contract and at the same time you could sing guest performances at Munich.'

Overjoyed, Hans said he would consult with Hamburg's director Strohm. In the meantime, he added, he had brought some music as it was a long time since Krauss had heard him sing. 'I don't need that,' said the imperturbable Krauss, 'I have my spies, and I know everything about you. But I have to introduce you to the Munich public, even though it is your home town.'

So he sang his obligatory contract *gastspiel* there, the Wanderer in *Siegfried* on April 12, 1937. It is one of the dates he will never forget, for the performance was a tremendous success. The Munich public took him to its heart, and he has remained one of its most personally beloved and honoured artists ever since.

There had been an earlier suggestion to appear there which came to nothing. He had been invited to sing the Wanderer in Munich in December 1934 by the director of that time, Wallek, but a few days before the date he received a telegram saying that his *Siegfried* appearance was for the time being not possible.

Afterwards it was revealed that Hans Knappertsbusch who was to conduct had been accused of anti-Nazi remarks and the director knew that a demonstration against Knappertsbusch was likely (it did in fact take

place, and another conductor had to finish the performance) and he did not want the young Hotter to be
subjected to this at his debut, so he cancelled the
engagement. Unhappily Knappertsbusch was not told
of this and for years believed that Hotter had withdrawn
as a gesture against him. It weas not until Hotter sang
under Knappertsbusch in Vienna in 1939 that each
discovered what had really happened.

But in 1937 there were no undercurrents at the vital
performance. The contract situation had been resolved
happily. The Hamburg contract was revised to allow
him to sing some 20 guest performances each season in
Munich, but his main contract remained with Hamburg
until 1940. Then the position was reversed and his
principal contract was with Munich and a guest one
with Hamburg. In 1939 he signed an additional contract
for about 10 performances a year in Berlin, and another
with Vienna for a limited number of guest appearances
each season. That was the beginning of an association
with the Vienna Staatsoper which lasted more than
thirty years. During the war years nearly all his operatic
singing was at these four houses.

The first months at the Munich opera were not quite
as warm hearted backstage as the welcome from the
audience, but Hans had the trust and liking of Clemens
Krauss, an outstanding musician whom he admired
greatly, and very soon came the association with
Richard Strauss and a remarkable range of his operas.

'I met Strauss for the first time when I was rehearsing
for the first new production in which I appeared in
Munich. It was *Salome* in the spring of 1937, very
shortly after I made my introductory appearance on
April 12. The famous Hildegarde Ranczak was Salome,
Julius Pölzer sang Herod, Patzak was Narraboth and
Clemens Krauss conducted. Rudolf Hartmann was the
producer and it was the first time I had worked with
him (by the way he was no relation of Georg Hartmann,
my director in Breslau, who also came to Munich later).

Rudolf Hartmann was first a singer (when he studied with Willi Wirk) and later became a producer and director.

'Those first rehearsals were like rehearsals anywhere else. I did not yet know the ensemble, had no real contact with them. Any everyone was very suspicious. The Munich opera always had the reputation of being very conservative and traditional. However Krauss had just come to Munich in 1937 and he was new too, and the opera organisation was just about to be changed into the system which he created. I was very conscious of a strange, distant atmosphere against this young 28-year-old singer who dared to come and sing in the holy temple of Munich! I often remembered this later when I got to know the others better. I felt so lost at the beginning. Afterwards a colleague of mine, Georgine von Milinkovic, who came to Munich a few years later, told me a similar story about her early days. It must have been a very typical atmosphere in Munich, this sort of withdrawn, uncommunicative attitude. In that way the Bavarians are very like the north Germans; they can be so reserved. And of course there was a number of elderly singers in the house, some of them in the same range I was, so it was quite natural they should be suspicious.

'Anyhow that was the first production and there was Richard Strauss himself, and his wife Pauline who occasionally visited rehearsals and made comments in her own way. Of course there was great shyness on my part, but Strauss was very understanding, *he* was communicative, helpful and inspiring.

'I was struck then and many times later by his enormous personality which one would not connect with the idea of a world famous composer. It was much more the character of a very wise man of the theatre. Practical about everything in the house. He would know and explain details which nowadays I think young singers have no opportunity to learn because

16. With Viorica Ursuleac in *Mona Lisa*, Berlin 1938 (courtesy Willot)

17. As Jupiter in *Liebe der Danae* at dress rehearsal, Salzburg 1944

18. As Don Giovanni with Hilde Güden, Munich 1941

nobody is around to tell them. It is partly their own fault too — its a two-way thing — they do not always want advice.

'Anyhow I learned so much from this man Strauss, who was then 73 years old, though he always gave the impression of being a very youthful person. He was extremely demanding in what he wanted. Very firm on that. A strong personality. I would not say a dictator, but so strong that you would not dare to voice or even think something against what he said.

'That was, I felt, for me the whole importance of this change from Hamburg to Munich. Krauss said to me 'We are planning to do new productions of all the Strauss operas in the next ten years, and I need you for that.' Now I appreciated what he meant, because I could feel the enormous mental co-operation between the two men. I think Richard Strauss was the only man to whom I ever knew Clemens Krauss yield an opinion. Not in words but by saying nothing. Normally Krauss was a very dangerous man to get into discussion with, unless you could prove what you meant. I never saw him give in to anyone except Strauss. That impressed me. From the first moment I saw them together I could see that Strauss had a strong influence and that Krauss had a very high opinion of his powers and gifts. It proved later on to be a most fruitful association for many years.

'Richard Strauss was the complete opposite of Pfitzner, a man with a very easy social manner, sometimes almost too smooth and polished but in work always practical and often witty.

'For example in one rehearsal Strauss came over and said "This is what we want: don't make that note too long because the expression is much better if you do it — so," I said, "Yes, but Doctor you wrote a whole note — four beats," "Did I? Give me your score. We'll change it. Its just half a note, I forgot to mark it." He made the half note on the spur of the moment. He had

94

just said something which did not fit with what he had written, so he changed it. He was always like that.

'Another time he said, "At this moment the orchestra is so loud you will not be heard. Just open your mouth, but don't forget to breathe otherwise people will recognise that you are not singing." That was very clever, because now when you see a synchronised performance on television and you watch the singers synchronising — some forget to breath! Everybody ought to see that its false. Perhaps a lot of viewers do not know, but any practical musician can see that they are not singing. That is why Strauss said "Take a good breath!" But it was so different from Pfitzner who would have been horrified at the idea of telling an artist not to sing something that was written in the score simply because they would not be heard.

'There are many famous sayings of Strauss such as "Speak forte and sing piano," "Piano in making music is soft not holding back; forte is not loud but firm and strong. Both are relative." All practical advice. He was always proud that he was a conductor in the first place, rather than a composer.

'It was a very exciting thing to sing with the help of the greatest opera composer of your time, but to be given that sort of advice by him — things which go very much into the details of the singer's profession — was something tremendous. He was always present at rehearsals of new productions of his operas and he would often come for repeat performances. And he conducted. I sang two performances of *Salome* and one *Fliegende Holländer* when he was the conductor.

'Then I also met Krauss' working team which remained more or less constant for all his productions. So unlike today when directors always want new conductors, new designers. At that time Krauss worked in his own very conservative way. It was modern in style, but conservative in execution. He had as his producer Rudolf Hartmann (later he became assistant director to

95

Krauss) and Ludwig Sievert the designer. They were on the spot for all discussions and so new productions could be planned far ahead. There was no waiting until the last moment to get the key people together. Everything followed a well tested routine. Perhaps some young singers may have felt this a little restrictive, but it was a great help to be able to rely on regular methods.

'This working team impressed me very much also, although I had been quite spoiled at Hamburg where there was a very good ensemble atmosphere. But this was a still higher standard, and there was a musician and a theatre man of the highest degree as its chief.

'The *Salome* production was a great success. I remember I was accepted right away. They were already very enthusiastic at the Wanderer performance. Then a few weeks later in the 1937 festival time — the festival operas were still given in the Prinzregenten Theater then — I remember a *Tristan* conducted by Karl Böhm. That was the first time I sang with Böhm, and there were more *Salomes*.

'From that time I remember the travelling between Munich and Hamburg, on and on and on. Mostly by train, four or five times a month. I was still a Hamburg resident. Of course it helped me in Hamburg to be a member of the Munich company. At that time too I was asked to go to Holland and Belgium to sing opera and concerts and there were the first invitations to Berlin. I sang in many concerts, oratorios and opera arias, but not lieder.'

In Holland he sang in several concert performances of *Mathis der Maler* and after one, in 1937 in Amsterdam, Hindemith wrote on his score 'To Hans Hotter, the first and ideal personification of Mathis, for whom this part seems to have been written without knowledge or permission!'

Professionally these years from 1937 to 1939 were glowing ones. In 1937 he was Escamillo in a new *Carmen* in Munich, and that year he made his first

96

appearance as the Grand Inquisitor in *Don Carlos* — a role which he has sung more than four hundred times, second only to Wotan in the number of performances.

In 1938 there was the world premiere of Strauss' *Friedenstag* when Hotter sang the lead opposite Clemens Krauss' wife Viorica Ursuleac. The opera was impressive and the première received enormous publicity. Hotter was acclaimed as an artist of the highest rank and it was the real opening to an international career.

Through it he got to know Strauss more personally, for the composer invited him to his house in Garmisch where he played the *Friedenstag* music to him and Hans had his first experience of the Strauss' domestic life and charming home, which he was to know so well in later years.

During the same year he sang Morone in *Palestrina* in Munich in the presence of Pfitzner, though Krauss conducted, and his first Munich *Rheingold* Wotan, following the Hamburg one.

In Munich in later years he alternated in the role with Hans Hermann Nissen 'A fine, noble colleague, rather distant but always kind. Krauss was very clever and diplomatic and did not play us off against each other. He would come and say "Now this is the older colleague, he has his old rights and I think it is right he should sing the first *Walküre* and *Siegfried* performances, but you should be present and take over later. Try to be here and watch the rehearsals."'

1939 marked Hans' thirtieth birthday, and he had already reached full fame, at least in the German-speaking operatic world. In one week in June he conquered Vienna, making his debut there as Jochanaan in a *Salome* conducted by Knappertsbusch (June 4), then appeared in the title role of *Julius Caesar* with the visiting Hamburg company (June 7) and finally sang in the Austrian première of *Friedenstag* (June 10), a gala occasion in honour of Strauss' 75th birthday in the presence of Hitler and Goebbels. The whole German press featured the occasion. That year he also appeared in a new production of Schillings' *Mona Lisa* in Berlin.

There were some problems in this fame. Winifred Wagner invited him to sing the Dutchman at the 1939 Bayreuth Festival, but Hans wished to keep away from the political associations of Bayreuth at that time. It was rather a risky thing to refuse, but Clemens Krauss helped him by 'blocking' the dates with Munich commitments, and as Winifred could not comprehend that anyone would refuse on grounds of political conscience she assumed it to be a personal vendetta of Krauss against Heinz Tietjen who was then artistic director at Bayreuth. But she did not forgive Hotter.

Happily there are also some hilarious memories of his Vienna debut. Although Hans already knew Knappertsbusch, that particular *Salome* was the first time that he had sung under his baton. As usual there was no rehearsal, and before the performance the conductor walked into Hans' dressing room and barked 'Good evening. Do you know the opera?' 'I, I believe so,' said Hans. 'I too. Auf Wiedersehen,' said Knappertsbusch and stalked out again.

Hans' mother Crescentia was in Vienna for that performance and after it she overheard two teenagers enthusing about the new singer. The girl said 'Have you heard that man, the naked one (Jochanaan was clad only in a camel skin) with the huge voice?' 'I don't know about the voice,' said her young man, 'but did you see those great arms which he stretched out when he was pronouncing the curse? My word, he would be the right member for our Danube rowing club!'

Vienna has produced a harvest of Hotter stories including the famous turkish bath one, which actually happened much later, shortly after the war. There was then only one place in Vienna where turkish baths were available — it was of course long before the international fashion for saunas — which was the *Janner Bad* where both ordinary swimming and steam baths were provided. It was clean and well run and from time to time many singers went there. In the strangely levelling situation of the men's section where all the bathers were stark naked Hans came out of the steam to go to the cold water pool and was met by another nude who came up and said 'Aren't you Mr. Hotter?' For the moment Hans was so taken aback that he was speechless, then he stammered 'Why?' His interlocutor realising the rather bizarre situation hurried to explain, 'Well I saw you last week as the Dutchman, and I recognised you *at once.*'

If it had been Jochanaan it would be understandable as Hans remarked later, but swathed in the long black costume of Wagner's tortured hero, hat, beard and all, where was the likeness?

Arabella was the next of the Strauss canon to have a new production in Munich in 1939 and Hans was the Mandryka. There were more *Salomes* and *Friedenstags.*

Offers from the Metropolitan, Covent Garden and other international houses rolled in. The Hotters' daughter Maria Gabriele was born in August, during the Munich Festival.

Then came the war. The political situation had over-shadowed life for a long time beforehand, the span of war was ten years rather than five to those who lived under the Nazi regime, but with Septmber 1939 came the actual beginning of the declared state of war.

Hans Hotter was a young healthy man of military age. Like other leading artists on both sides of the conflict he was exempted from military service, but this was not without its own problems. A civilian who appeared to have opted out of the fighting was no more popular on overcrowded trains full of soldiers in Germany than in Britain, and might also have been a Nazi informer. 'I could not always explain that I was an artist, and they were suspicious.'

He is the first to declare that he never had any serious trouble with the authorities either in trying to involve him in political affairs or to penalise him. Nor does he attempt to dissociate himself from the faults of his country. He was and is a German, however much he inwardly condemned what he knew of Nazi activities.

In the years just before the war there were one or two offers to get him out of the country. One was from Bruno Walter when they were together for a concert in Holland in 1937. Walter said that he could help him to get away and settle in the United States. Hans said that he had a wife and small child, mother, and a brother who was a catholic priest. Could he hope to take them all, and support them in America? No, said Bruno Walter, he could not undertake that. So Hans stayed.

His own position was in fact more precarious than he knew until the end of the war. He was a catholic, his brother a priest, who though not actually persecuted suffered many problems, indignities and delays to his teaching career. In Hans' dossier this was included, and also it was noted by the Nazis that he was 'politically unsound', the records showing that he had been watched and reported on even in the Prague days. But against this was written 'No action to be taken — he is under the personal custody of the Führer.'

Hitler admired his voice, had heard him sing several times and met him once or twice. When Hotter was screened by the Americans after the war this raised more doubts on the other side. Why had he been 'protected?' why were some of his gramophone records in Hitler's collection? 'I believe the Pope has a few also!' said Hotter when interrogated.

He consistently refused to make concert tours sponsored by the Ministry of Propaganda during the war. 'It was tempting though, when you had a young family to support. If you were sent to other countries by Goebbels' organisation you could keep foreign currency. You could bring in food without being searched. But if you were invited, as I was, by Switzerland or Holland you were only allowed to keep enough money for living expenses while you were there. The whole of the rest had to be changed into German money. There were times when one wanted to say — to hell with politics, I will go and get some food for my children.'

And there were all the other strains of wartime life. Not so bad at the beginning but getting progressively harder. The travelling on packed trains, halted sometimes during bombing or gunfire. The smaller trials — no porters to carry luggage made heavier because there were no laundry facilities, clothes could not be bought, so the concert artist had to travel with enough dress shirts and linen to complete his tour.

Forty years later the oppressiveness of the blackout still remains with him. 'It sounds silly, perhaps, but for an artist it is terrible when everything happens in darkness, because he lives in public, he needs the public.'

They were grim years. Hans Hotter did not have to suffer the worst horrors of war, but for a long time the blackout of freedom darkened his career.

PART THREE
International Career

THE END OF the second world war was a focal point in history. Both for better and worse nothing could ever be quite the same as before. For the individuals who had lived through it on both sides of the conflict adjustment was first of all a personal matter, the opening up of new ways of life full of hopes and doubts in an environment psychologically and often materially battered.

Few of those who have grown up since that war can conceive either the sense of new possibilities or the problems among which we strove to launch out on what we hoped and believed would be the seas of peace and justice. Because of the magnitude of that war there was no parallel from the past to guide us, and being ourselves the fabric from which the new world was to be built it was hard to find perspective in our present, let alone to foresee the future.

An artist such as Hans Hotter had to face an exceptional role in this new life. His international career had been retarded at least ten years by the war, but within his own German speaking world he had come to full artistic stature. He was one of the great names of the operatic firmament in countries where opera was indigenous, a pride and joy and solace to a very wide section of the public.

When the time came to go forth into what had so recently been an enemy world it was performing artists and sportsmen who were the first to be invited, the first to meet a foreign and possibly hostile public on the neutral ground of art or sport. It was they who would create the first human impressions of a people obscured by the inevitable 'enemy' caricature by which men and women are enabled to fight each other.

As an artist Hotter had not been compelled to military

19. As Mandryka in *Arabella*, Munich 1939 (photo Hanns Holdt)

20. With Ruth Michaels in *Faust*, Munich 1944

21. In the film *Seine Beste Rolle*, 1941

service, but as a famous artist he could and did meet the world as a German, as a man, as a musician. With the hindsight of those who did not live through that time it is easy to see only the glowing success of those encounters when Hans Hotter and other leading artists were received with honour, admiration and delight, the public taking them to its heart, the reputation of their gifts and charm and personalities spreading like a flame from land to land.

But it was not always so. There was hostility sometimes, and humiliation, often — and understandably — from German emigrants who had fled from the Nazi regime and resented honour being paid to their countrymen who had stayed, however unwillingly. And at first who knew where this hostility might show itself? On stage and even more on concert platform the artist is totally exposed, under fire whether it be of adoration, hatred or derision.

Hans Hotter and those others who first crossed the psychological armistice lines were ambassadors in the field of understanding. They had to be good as artists, for art was the gift they bore, personality and integrity alone were not enough. And they succeeded, many of them. For their gifts and courage and obvious humanity we came to love them and they, perhaps, to find us responsive. They crossed the bridges to meet us and we learned much about the rest of their countrymen from them. I wonder how many of the early British post-war visitors to Germany went, as I did, at the call of music.

The later war years though darkened by the intensity and horror of the conflict were not without strong musical life in Germany and Austria, born of the need to provide entertainment and relief for the people and the close-knit camaraderie of artists working together under great difficulties.

One of the highlights was the world première of Strauss' *Capriccio* in Munich in October 1942. Hotter sang the young poet Olivier, and found the rehearsals productive and exciting. 'Strauss himself was there almost all the time, and Clemens Krauss with his skill and experience had written the libretto and was very insistent about its importance. 'You must pronounce the words; they must be heard, otherwise it gets boring!' And Strauss in his jovial way would say 'Well if some music can be heard now and then I wouldn't mind!' *Capriccio* is of course very much an opera of and for theatre people — the balance between words and music — and we all wondered if it would succeed with the public. Yet ever since it has proved one of Strauss' most attractive works just because of that.'

Two years later there was another — the last — occasion when Hans worked personally with Richard Strauss on a new creation. This was *Die Liebe der Danae*, which Strauss began before *Capriccio* but only completed in 1944. The role of Jupiter was written for Hotter, and the world première was planned for August of that year in Salzburg. All the preparations were carried through and the dress rehearsal in the presence of a sizable audience took place, but the first night was cancelled when the Nazis closed all theatres following a plot to assassinate Hitler. As a result the opera was not given a public performace until 1952, and then with a different cast. That dress rehearsal has since been regarded as the true première, and Strauss' speech at the end of it when he said the closure heralded an end to true culture among them marked a dramatic and poignant occasion. It was also the last performance which Hotter sang before the end of the war.

Hotter also did some film work, chosen for his good looks and personality rather than voice, for singing was only incidental in all of them.

The first film offer came just before the war when Hans was making his Vienna debut in June 1939. A Berlin script writer saw a notice of his Caesar in Handel's opera with the Hamburg company in Vienna and telephoned the film producer to say Hotter seemed to be the type they wanted to play opposite Käthe Dorsch in *Mutterliebe*. The role was a handsome country boy. But the producer, an Austrian, particularly wanted a south German accent for the part and as Hotter was a member of the Hamburg opera he thought he was likely to be a northerner. Nonetheless his assistant telephoned Hans and found he was a Bavarian, so he was invited to come for a film test.

Hans has happy memories of the kindness and charm of Käthe Dorsch, then a middle-aged actress considerably older than himself. The first test take of a love scene between them was not a success. There had been no rehearsal and it was his very first experience of working before film cameras. When he saw the result he was only too conscious of his shortcomings in contrast to the actress' poise. He felt sure he would not be offered the contract, but much to his surprise he was asked to do another test of the scene. Later he discovered that it was Käthe Dorsch who had urged the producer to give him a second rehearsal take of that scene but with a much younger actress. That time it worked, and when the actual filming was done with Käthe Dorsch that wise and generous lady won his lasting regard and friendship by whispering 'Sorry its me again, but imagine I am the other one!'

Other films followed, among them *Seine beste Rolle* in 1941, *Brüderlein fein* in 1942 and *Sehnsucht des Herzens* in 1950.

There were wartime festivals at Salzburg also, when Hans sang the Count in *Figaro* and the Speaker in *Die Zauberflöte* and during a German Italian art week in Hamburg in 1941, he sang in Malipiero's *Julius Caesar*.

With the end of the war came the first adjustments into the peacetime life of a vanquished country controlled by occupying forces. Bavaria was in the American zone and the Hotters got to know music-loving members of the US forces and their families. It was not a time when classical singers could afford to be pedantic about their work, and Hotter and his family were glad enough to go to Salzburg and for him to sing *Old Man River* and *Deep Purple* for the troops, and to appear in an hilarious skit on *Carmen* in which Hans played the name part. It meant badly needed money and food.

One day a British military staff car drew up outside their house on the edge of the Englischer Garten in Munich. This was unusual because there were no British in the area.

An officer came to the door asking for Hans Hotter, and having found him, said 'The great Hans Hotter! Your name is sacred in the musical world and we have come to take you back to sing for us in Hamburg!' At that time Hotter had not even been through the de-nazification screening, but he was passed from one military zone to the other.

It was on that visit to Hamburg that he first met Walter Legge who had been in touch with him on Beecham's behalf before the war, and was to become such a deus ex machina for international artists in later years. Legge, still in uniform, was there organising ENSA performances of *Madam Butterfly* with Victoria Sladen in the title role, and his secretary was a young lady named Joan Ingpen.

Also in Hamburg at that time he got to know Ferdinand Leitner, then a gifted accompanist, and it was at Hotter's instigation that Leitner was first invited to conduct in Munich in 1945. Later, again at Hans' suggestion, he became for a time musical director of the Munich opera.

Through Walter Legge Hotter got his first post-war recording contract. The fee was only 1000 Swiss francs but it was good hard currency, and a gateway to the new life.

First however there was the de-nazification procedure, which presented no problems in Hotter's case in view of the Nazi records about him, despite Hitler's admiration. It even produced one of life's odd quirks in transposing relationship. Among his interrogators was a German-speaking American with whom he maintained a lasting friendship both in America and Vienna. At the time of the cold war between America and Russia this man said, half joking, but half in earnest: 'If the Russians took over, and I had to be de-Americanised, would you be willing to give me an affidavit that I treated you well then, at the end of the war?!'

England was the real starting point of Hotter's international life. Joan Ingpen on behalf of Legge arranged for him to give a live recital of *Die Winterreise* on the BBC at Easter in 1947. This was Hans' first trip to England since the engagement party in Nottingham more than eleven years earlier, and it was his very first professional visit.

It proved to be a momentous one. Joan Ingpen was anxious that he should meet the impressario Jan Pomeroy, then presenting opera at the Cambridge Theatre in London. That did not materialise, but she also got into touch with David Webster, then general administrator of the new opera company at Covent Garden. This was the successful beginning of a long professional association between Hotter and Joan Ingpen. Webster came to the BBC to hear Hotter's *Winterreise* recital, and offered him a contract for the 1947-48 Covent Garden season.

But first he returned to London when the Vienna State Opera ensemble visited Covent Garden in September and October 1947. After a total hiatus in the life of the great German-speaking operahouses at the end of the war, rebirth came quickly, with the support of the occupying powers. Even when the buildings were severely damaged, improvised stages and seating were created. In the old British phrase 'the show must go on' and opera came back very rapidly in 1945, first in Vienna, then Hamburg and Munich in the autumn of that year.

The Vienna company that came to London was a

111

brilliant one. Clemens Krauss and Josef Krips were the conductors, and the singers included Elisabeth Schwarzkopf, Irmgard Seefried, Sena Jurinac, Ljuba Welitsch, Hans Hotter and Erich Kunz, all making their London operatic debuts, and Maria Cebotari, Hilde Konetzni, Julius Patzak, Paul Schoeffler and Ludwig Weber who had sung here before the war. *Figaro, Don Giovanni, Cosi fan tutte, Fidelio* and *Salome* were given. Older operagoers still remember Hotter's elegant, dynamic Giovanni, a role which, alas, he never sang again in England.

In January and February 1948 came Covent Garden's first post-war Wagner: *Tristan und Isolde, The Mastersingers of Nuremburg* and *The Valkyrie*, the two latter being sung in English translation.

This was because of Webster's determination to establish opera in the vernacular. The visiting stars were accustomed to this in their own countries, Italian opera being habitually sung in German in Germany and Austria, and vice versa. Opera in the original language only developed on the continent in post-war years. It was, however, a heavy assignment for artists to relearn their long Wagnerian roles in English for a few performances. There is a well known story of the trick Webster employed to achieve this.

Coming to Hotter he said, 'I know you won't mind learning Wotan in English when Madam Flagstad is so keen to sing Brünnhilde in English for us.' Hans naturally agreed. Later, during the rehearsals Flagstad said to him 'Why were you so anxious to sing this *Walküre* in English? David Webster urged me to sing in English to please you.' Webster was always a brilliant strategist.

That was the beginning of many Flagstad — Hotter performance both in London, where they appeared together until her retirement from the Wagner stage in 1951, and in other parts of the world. She was the reigning world Brünnhilde and Isolde, he wherever he

22. As Borromeo in *Palastri-na*, Vienna 1955 (courtesy Fayer-Wien)

23. As Pogner in *Die Meister-singer,* Vienna 1962 (courtesy Atelier Dietrich)

24. As Gianni Schicchi, Munich 1961 (photo Sabine Toepffer)

appeared was acknowledged as the new world Wotan.

She of course belonged to an earlier musical generation, and Hans regarded Kirsten Flagstad with the
reverence he felt for some of the older great artists with
whom he had already worked such as Max Lorenz and
Ludwig Weber, but she was even more an international
name, and something of an idol to Hans.

'Flagstad was a dear kind colleague. Very helpful on
stage. She was not the greatest actress, but compensated
for that with the expression of her face — and her poise.
Despite her stoutness — and it was all muscle, no fat —
she had such dignity, and a marvellous face. She
radiated personality: the personality of the role, by her
face and her voice. Singing with her one had a constant
wish just to listen to this glorious voice during a
performance. Some artists sing certain phrases in such a
way that you always associate that music with one
singer. That is true for me about some phrases of
Isolde's music; they are always Flagstad.'

She was also very practical. A producer wanted her to
make a swift ecstatic rise from her knees at the point
when, in the third act of *Walküre*, Brünnhilde entreats
Wotan to guard her helpless sleep with magic fire 'Auf
dein Gebot entbrenne ein Feuer . . .' 'That may be all
very well for a young girl,' said Flagstad to Hotter, 'but
I am an elderly housewife. So will you, as a very young
father, step in front of me and give me your left hand to
lean on?'

Kirsten Flagstad was not of course his only female
partner of generous proportions. His very first *Walküre*
Brünnhilde back in 1941 in Munich had been Erna
Schlüter, then in her prime and a fine colleague, but
physically massive. When Wotan came to embrace his
daughter he could not quite get his arms round her —
'not even my long ape-arms!'

At the third or fourth performance of the same series
there was a cast change and Helena Braun took over as
Brünnhilde. 'Sometimes with changes you forget the

114

small practical things. I opened my arms to receive the beloved daughter. But Helena was very slender. My arms crossed behind her and my hands seemed to get lost, waving in the air . . . After that I always studied the size and shape of my Brünnhildes!'

Another well known story dates from those first London *Valkyrie* performances in early 1948 — that of Hotter's falling from the rocky scenery at the back of the stage, due to a change of lighting. 'It was very dark, with the only light coming from above. Flagstad and I had to climb up a ladder at the back for the final scene when Wotan puts Brünnhilde to sleep. It was not easy for her, and at the top there was only just enough space for me to lay her down and stand beside her. We managed fairly well at the rehearsals, but on the first night they changed the lighting plan without telling us, and there was one brilliant light immediately over our heads. The effect was that you could not see the contours of the rock — normally the edges are whitened. I could not see anything, and in those days Wotan had to wear a long cloak, armour and an enormous winged helmet which did not help. Anyhow I laid her down, sang the last phrase and was trying to get down, feeling with my feet for the edge when I stepped into nothing and fell — armour, spear and all — about six feet.

'Luckily I fell in front of the rocks, behind it would have been three times as big a drop. Nothing happened except that I tore my little finger a bit, but down I went with a great crash and the audience gave an audible gasp. I got up, raised my arms in an enormous gesture to the audience, and went off stage. There was tremendous applause at the end, and the next day the papers were full of it. Some of my colleagues declared I did it on purpose to make the front pages!'

Afterwards David Webster told a rather malicious story about one of the Covent Garden governors related to this. Said the governor: 'Are you sure Hotter didn't suffer any real injury? I saw him in another performance a few days later and he had a patch over his eye.' To which Webster replied: 'I think I had better give you a score of the opera!'

But it also brought a very charming enquiry from the Queen (now Queen Elizabeth, the Queen Mother) who with Princess Margaret was in the audience that night. A few days later Hans received this letter from Webster's secretary.

'Her Majesty the Queen's Private Secretary telephoned to Mr. Webster this afternoon to say how much her Majesty had enjoyed the performance of *The Valkyrie* on Wednesday evening, and she also enquired how you were after your accident, and hoped that you had not hurt yourself.'

Three months after that Covent Garden season Hotter with his wife and 11-year-old son left England for South America on a four-month contract at Buenos Aires where he sang Günther in *Götterdämmerung* and Kaspar in *Der Freischütz*. Their little daughter Gabriele was life in the care of friends in England.

That season was extremely successful and, life in Germany still being very difficult, they thought seriously about making their home in the Argentine. At the end of the season Helga Hotter and Peter stayed on in Buenos Aires, while Hans returned to Europe to fulfil his commitments in Vienna. He collected Gabriele en route and father and daughter spent the 1948-49 winter together in Vienna. In the following June they went together to Buenos Aires for another three months when Hotter appeared as Sachs and Giovanni. The money was good, but Peron's regime was a fascist one, and they realised that they might have survived the Nazi disaster only to exchange it for another totalitarian state; and in the meantime the situation in Germany had improved a great deal. So the whole family returned to Munich in the autumn of 1949. Hans did not go back to Buenos Aires until 1960 when he gave several recitals there, and 1962 when he sang in the *Ring*.

1949 saw the onset of a vocal crisis which constituted a problem in the middle of his career. Very many singers experience a comparable time of difficulty after some twenty years of singing. Some never overcome it Others like Hotter use it as a time to learn more of themselves and their art and so to re-establish their careers more securely.

In his case there were several reasons for the crisis. From his teens Hotter had suffered from hay fever, a complaint which wins little sympathy from non-sufferers but is relentless to its victims and diabolical for a singer. Although for most sufferers there is a regular season for it, the attacks can strike without rhyme or reason. At noon you may be clear, at seven p.m. a sneezing, gasping wreck, and vice versa.

All through his singing career Hans avoided engagements in June whenever possible. That was not infallible, for the hay fever could start in May or extend into July, and from time to time through the years he was forced to cancel appearances for this reason, but on the whole he knew and could cope with it.

Hay fever was a contributory factor in the crisis, but the real cause was a psychological one: delayed reaction to the strain of war and the stresses of its aftermath. Years of undernourishment and the tensions of wartime life take toll on even a young healthy constitution, but they were counterbalanced to some extent by working in what Hans calls the 'nest' of ensemble artistic life. The problems were so very great that all those working together to overcome them artistically were drawn together.

When this wartime pressure ended the whole world changed. The possibilities were enormous and so were the demands. Tall, powerful, masculine, Hans Hotter like all real artists has extreme sensitivity to the reactions of others. Mostly he was received in other countries, countries which were former enemies, with gratitude, friendship, even adulation, but that in itself makes demands. And there were other reactions, sometimes hostile, and no doubt a good deal of jealousy among strangers and colleagues as well as foreign audiences, all combining with the first pressures of the international circuit.

England and later America presented few problems, nor did he ever find any real animosity in France where the Vienna company also gave a Paris season in 1947. Belgium and Holland, perhaps naturally, harboured their anti-German feelings much longer.

At the age of forty — *mit vierzig Jahren* like the Brahms' song — all this built up in an artist with two decades of stage life behind him and infinite possibilities ahead.

By 1951 the crisis was past, though Hotter's summer season at Covent Garden was afflicted with hay fever, and afterwards he suffered some vocal unsteadiness for a time.

It was during what Hotter himself calls the crisis period that he made his debut at the Metropolitan, and the specacular success which he achieved is proof that he was then in good form. 1950-51 was Rudolf Bing's first Metropolitan season, and he brought in nine non-American singers, among them Fedora Barbieri, Cesare Siepi and Hotter.

He sang the Dutchman — that was when Virgil Thomson compared his stage presence to that of Chaliapin — and also the Grand Inquisitor in *Don Carlos*. Cecil Smith, writing on that season in *Opera*, described both performances as unforgettable and Hotter as perhaps the most striking of the newcomers, welcomed by Met audiences as one of the finest additions to the roster of male singers for many years.

In the *New York Times* Olin Downes went into greater detail: 'In the second *Don Carlos* Hans Hotter, who made his debut as the Dutchman in Wagner's opera in the second performance of the season, alternated with

Mr. Hines, as the Inquisitor, and made a sensation.

'This was not surprising, for Mr. Hotter, in Wagner's opera, had given the most moving and impressive portrait of the Höllander that we had ever seen. He is a first-class musician and a tragedian of exceptional powers. He has a voice of remarkable range and power, yet he made his effects more often by limiting and shading his tone than by challenging the sonorities of Wagner's orchestra. With half of his natural equipment as a singer he could have made an equally eloquent interpretation of the role... Mr. Hotter's Dutchman is a thing to see and hear and study.'

From then on New York audiences were always devoted to him, and he appeared at the Met during four consecutive seasons. In 1952 he sang Jochanaan, Orestes, Günther in one *Götterdämmerung* and repeated his Grand Inquisitor — 'giving perhaps the most overwhelming single performance to be encountered at the Metropolitan today' (Cecil Smith again).

In the following year he appeared as Wotan in a new production of *Das Rheingold* and as Amfortas in *Parsifal*. Jay S. Harrison in his notice in the *New York Herald Tribune* wrote, 'Hans Hotter is a ringing, a superb Amfortas, a figure of pity made all the more pitiable by its cutting solemnity. Personal projection, moveover, is Mr. Hotter's shining glory, and his first act cry 'Erbahrmen! Erbahrmen!' spoke of suffering as unmerciful as it was unrelieved.'

Other parts that year were in the bass rather than the baritone range; Pogner in *Die Meistersinger* and King Marke in *Tristan und Isolde*. Both are roles which he sang in later years as his voice became fuller and darker, Marke indeed being one of his great characterisations. But at that point his gifts and fame were chiefly focused in the dramatic baritone or bass-baritone fields. The Met casting was a sign that Bing was trying to divert him into other channels.

Still, in 1954 he did in fact sing one or two *Walküre*

Wotans, alternating with Ferdinand Franz and singing Hunding to Franz's Wotan.

That year he was chosen as the Met's 'best actor of the year' and Bing seized on this as a pretext for offering him lesser roles. When discussing renewal of the contract he suggested that Hotter should not sing big leading roles but should choose the secondary parts — 'this is where you can show your gifts much better than with major ones.'

After that, in Hans' own words 'There was separation!' He has never sung again at the Metropolitan, though some years later after an ecstatic reception of his Wotan in Chicago, Hotter received a telephone call from Rudolf Bing asking him to produce *Die Walküre* at the Met and perhaps to sing in one or two performances. To which Hotter replied, 'Mr. Bing I think you must have read the Chicago press notices, or you would not ask me!' The matter was closed.

From the earliest days of its festivals, to sing or conduct at Bayreuth was to receive the accolade of greatness in the Wagnerian field. Glance through the programmes of the past and one finds a galaxy of famous names. They all considered it the highest honour they could win and came, in the old days, for very low fees. Artistically and professionally the Bayreuth hallmark ensured engagements wherever an operahouse aspired to the best, and with that came big money.

But there was always more to it than the gateway to professional and financial success. The Wagner festivals on Bayreuth's green hill were something of a cult, often mocked in the past few decades, but nonetheless they focused a genuine passionate love for the music of this unique, maddening genius.

It affected artists as well as audiences, and this aura of reverence is the main reason why Cosima Wagner was able to maintain implicit obedience to her long-dead husband's stage directions for so long, and why even later under the direction of Siegfried Wagner, and then Winifred, so few changes were made in the presentation of the operas. It was Bayreuth, it was Wagner: the unquestioned authorized version of something which for its devotees ranked almost as a religion.

When the festivals were revived in 1951 much of this aura remained, though it was assailed by doubts and prejudices in some quarters because of the Nazi stigma which was attached to Bayreuth in the '30s and '40s due to Hitler's patronage and enthusiasm.

Still, when the Bayreuth phoenix rose again from its ashes, all established and budding Wagnerians longed to appear there. Hans Knappertsbusch was an outstanding example of this. He regarded conducting at Bayreuth as the climax of his musical life. He refused to accept fees, though he was of course paid expenses and generous ones for his Bayreuth seasons, and his whole approach to working there was that of an idealist, if a somewhat theatrical one.

The revolution of style which marked the post-war festivals and became known as New Bayreuth is now too well known to need detailed comment here. In brief, Siegfried Wagner's widow Winifred who held absolute control was debarred from restarting the festivals because of her Nazi associations. She therefore resigned in favour of her two sons Wieland and Wolfgang and they, young men in their thirties, purged the memory of Hitler and overcame the problem of elaborate renewed staging (for all sets and costumes had been looted) by the masterly artistic stroke of introducing an entirely new type of production. It was simple, it was static, it depended for its effects on inspired lighting — and on the music itself.

New Bayreuth was therefore a re-embodiment, and a very ethereal one, of the true Wagner spirit. Visually it was new and exciting, musically the aura remained. It was some years before first Wieland himself, and much later other producers, began to treat both the music and the stories of the opera as little more than a plinth on which to build their own fantasies. But it was Wieland's early work at Bayreuth that gave a completely new importance to opera producers. Today although singers and conductors are still noted, discussed and admired at the Bayreuth festivals, and the Bayreuth cachet remains present to a limited extent, it is the producers who claim three quarters of the pubic's attention, their adulation or their boos.

By 1952 Hotter's vocal crisis was past and at the age of forty-three he was just coming into his prime, as a complete artist. I saw his Wotan in Bayreuth that year and it was overwhelming in its impact, both in *Walküre* and as the Wanderer in *Siegfried*. Hermann Uhde sang the 1952 *Rheingold* Wotans. Joseph Keilberth was the conductor, Astrid Varnay the Brünnhilde, Bernd Aldenhoff sang Siegfried. But Hotter's actual Bayreuth debut was as Kurwenal in Wieland's new *Tristan*, conducted by Herbert von Karajan, the second and last year that Karajan appeared at Bayreuth.

That was in fact the reason why Hans did not sing the *Rheingold* Wotan: it would have meant four consecutive nights of singing at the beginning of the festival, as Bayreuth then performed the *Ring* with only one day's break between *Siegfried* and *Götterdämmerung*. Later Hotter persuaded Wieland to introduce a free day after *Walküre*.

So began the great post-war years of both Bayreuth and Hans Hotter. Like many pre-war newcomers among Bayreuth artists he was fully established internationally before this debut, but he has always admitted its importance in his career. 'It was the main point of interest when one was being interviewed by press or radio or television, and of great importance for other engagements.'

The enthusiastic and cricket-minded English contingent who scraped up their foreign currency allowance and came to Bayreuth in growing numbers in the next

25. As Kurwenal in *Tristan*, Bayreuth 1952 (photo Liselotte Strelow, courtesy Festspielleitung Bayreuth)

26. As The Holländer with Leoni Rysanek, Vienna 1955 (courtesy Fayer-Wien)

27. With Evelyn Lear and Thomas Stewart after a performance, Bayreuth 1960s (photo Wilhelm Rauh)

few years called the leading singers of these festivals in the '50s the Wagnerian First Eleven, and certainly they set a magnificent standard both there and in operahouses all over the world. Hotter was the acknowledged king of them all, or simply 'the god'. By experience though not in age he belonged to an earlier generation. Others such as Astrid Varnay, Martha Mödl, Ramon Vinay, Wolfgang Windgassen, Josef Greindl, Gustav Neidlinger, and much later Birgit Nilsson and Fischer-Dieskau came to fame in those years and, apart from Fischer-Dieskau, largely through their Bayreuth appearances.

There were also some of the pre-war older giants like Ludwig Weber, and the conductors were all fine musicians, some very great ones, each in his own form: Knappertsbusch, Karajan, Keilberth, Clemens Krauss, Eugen Jochum, André Cluytens, Wolfgang Sawallisch. There is always a danger of idolising past performances in the warm glow of nostalgia, but the complete Bayreuth *Ring* recording conducted by Knappertsbusch, taken from live performances in 1957 and issued only a few years ago is evidence not only of the splendour of the whole, but also of the amazingly high standard of almost all the singers.

From 1953 until 1958 (the last year of Wieland Wagner's first *Ring* production) Hotter sang the Wotan/ Wanderer in all three operas of all *Ring* cycles.

Those were the years when at Bayreuth and other operahouses throughout the world he was at the summit of his powers in this particular role. The fruit of more than twenty years of musical and acting experience ripened into what became the definitive interpretation of perhaps the greatest and most complex of all operatic characters. Hotter was the world Wotan, not only of his generation but standing for comparison with his predecessors, and creating a standard and a legend by which later singers are still judged.

I have seen between fifty and sixty complete *Ring* performances in many countries during the last three decades and I have seen and heard other fine Wotans, but none which could stand with Hotter's for vocal splendour combined with profound psychological and emotional insight.

This was particularly noticeable in *Das Rheingold*, dramatically the most difficult of the three parts. Here he was the young god, patrician, imperious, selfish, but his pride was that of a highly sensitive nature. Modern politically orientated productions overlook this, relating the characters of the *Ring* to types and symbols, but Wagner created real characters; that is why, with the potency of the music, the operas can enslave generations of operagoers.

Wotan is one of the most complete of all Wagner's creations, and the performer has it in his power to touch the audience on two levels. First the essence of Wotan's story is that he stoops to gain his ends by an unworthy trick and when he seeks to right the wrong becomes ever more deeply enmeshed in tragedy as his own understanding and suffering develop. There is no human being who has not at some point taken the nearer way of selfishness and experienced remorse and helplessness in the outcome, and so we feel nearer to Wotan than to the simpler characters of Brünnhilde or Siegfried.

But there is another quality in Wotan, for he is in Wagner's conception truly a god although an erring one. Like a king in past, less democratic, days Wotan is set apart from the lesser inmates of Valhalla and the mortals and semi-mortals. Not even Brünnhilde can enter fully into his mind and suffering. It is the utter loneliness of Wotan and through it his final recognition of truth that makes the god so poignant. And Hans Hotter revealed this, not spasmodically but time after time with the technique of the great professional, without which any amount of artistic inspiration is a matter of uncertain glory.

It was in the supreme musical and emotional scenes of

125

Die Walküre that his Wotan touched its greatest heights. The second act narration, opening almost in a whisper, was spellbinding where it can often prove a bore, and the farewell to Brünnhilde at the end gave some of Wagner's most profoundly moving music all the tenderness of a father's love. In *Siegfried* his Wanderer was wise and humorous till the final tumultuous encounter with Erda, and the poignant quiet moment when Siegfried has shattered his spear and power.

At the same time there were his other performances which now bore the Bayreuth hallmark. In 1952 he was Kurwenal in the *Tristan* conducted by Karajan. In 1953 he sang his first Bayreuth Amfortas when Clemens Krauss conducted *Parsifal*. It was one of his earliest Wagnerian parts which he had first sung in Breslau.

For the next two years Hotter's Amfortas remained one of the outstanding performances of the festivals. Vocally it was not perhaps his best role, for the intensity of his portrayal produced some unsteadiness in the singing, but the character was complete, agonizing. Here was the ascetic knight who had sinned, the consciousness of remorse and the selfish introspection of guilt. This Amfortas in its stark personification of suffering always reminded one of an El Greco painting.

Wieland Wagner's first Bayreuth *Meistersinger*, popularly known as *Die Meistersinger ohne Nürnberg* — the mastersingers without Nuremberg — because the town's streets and houses were transformed into an insubstantial dream world, came in 1956 and with it Hotter's Sachs. Here is the antithesis of Wotan, but Wagner's other most complete character. Hotter's Sachs was warm, human, humorous, very tender in his love for Eva but with a robust understanding of himself and his fellow creatures. Some singers concentrate on the simple shoemaker aspect of the role but Wagner's Sachs is a leading poet and one of the best loved and most influential burghers of Nuremberg, and it was as a wise and powerful personality that Hotter played him, singing the music with rare beauty. He appeared as Sachs in Bayreuth in 1956 and once or twice in the following year. In 1958 he was the Bayreuth Pogner. Although he was extremely fond of the role and character of Sachs he found the part did not suit him vocally as well as others.

One of these was the Dutchman which was always among Hotter's most famous roles and which he continued to sing in Vienna and Munich for many years. At Bayreuth, however, he sang it only in 1955 and 1965 and then not at every performance. Unfortunately I did not see him in it. In 1955 which was Wolfgang Wagner's first *Holländer* production he shared the role with Hermann Uhde, and in Wieland's later production he shared it with Thomas Stewart. Anja Silja was by then the Senta.

When Wolfgang Wagner's first *Ring* production opened in 1960 there was a general cast change for all the leading roles and it was in that year that Hotter first appeared at Bayreuth as Gurnemanz in *Parsifal*, and established another unmatched identification with a Wagnerian character.

By then his voice had deepened and he had turned more to the full bass range. Gurnemanz is the longest part in the opera although he does not appear in the second act, and it is the central though passive one. All that happens, all the suffering, all the faith are reflected in Gurnemanz's words and music.

On the singer who plays this part depends a great deal of the opera's meaning. He can be a nonentity. He can be a bore. As Hotter played and sang him he had the wisdom and understanding of a saint, and also perplexity and sorrow disciplined to patience. Every movement, every facial expression, every inflexion of the great, luminous voice conveyed the man, aged but still vigorous when Parsifal returns to bring redemption to Monsalvat. His singing of the great paean of joy at Parsifal's mission 'O Gnade! Höchstes Heil!' and the anointing and the exquisite description of creation's joy in Christ which follow, made this music, for many of those who heard him, as wholly transcendent as was his Wotan's Abschied.

For seven years from 1960-66 he sang Gurnemanz at Bayreuth and there was a wonderful continuity in the series. The production was Wieland Wagner's famous one dating from 1951 and his greatest artistic achievement. Hans Knappertsbusch established himself as the Bayreuth *Parsifal* conductor, bringing to it his unparalleled sense of mystic dedication. His tempi may have been slow but they were never lifeless. With the exceptions of Krauss in 1955 and André Cluytens in 1957 Knappertsbusch conducted all *Parsifals* at Bayreuth from 1951 to 1964; he died the following year. The 1965 and 1966 *Parsifals* were conducted by Böhm and Boulez respectively.

The Parsifals, Amfortas and Kundrys varied during those years and included Jess Thomas, Wolfgang Windgassen, Jon Vickers, Thomas Stewart, George London, Régine Crespin and Astrid Varnay. But the Wieland — Knappertsbusch — Hotter triumvirate formed the core of the greatest years.

Wieland's especial gift for grouping and stillness was shown at its best in *Parsifal* when, particularly during the first half of the '50s, the singers were lit so that they stood out like statuary. The audience marvelled and praised this, the singers did not. 'He nearly ruined our eyesight' says Hans drily, 'forcing us to stand for hours with spotlights directed onto our faces at eye level.'

One year, 1964, he sang King Marke in Wieland's memorable Böhm — Nilsson — Windgassen *Tristan und Isolde*.

In 1966, the year of Wieland Wagner's death, Hotter sang one more complete *Ring* cycle Wotan/Wanderer in Wieland's new symbolic and controversial production which had been launched the previous year, as well as Gurnemanz. It proved to be the last year he was to sing at Bayreuth, but in 1968 and 1969 Wolfgang Wagner invited him to direct Wieland's *Ring* production, a somewhat thankless task, but one which earned him the gratitude of both Wolfgang and his mother Winifred, who while holding no official position was still an indomitable figure in the shadows of the past.

Even more than Salzburg, Bayreuth is an intimiate festival. During the first cycle of performances, rehearsals for the later productions continue and artists are constantly in and out of the Festspielhaus stage door, providing a focal point for devoted followers and fans. The artists like other mortals eat and even like to drink and so they frequent the hotels, restaurants, *gaststätten* of the town and its surroundings. Hans Hotter, his two-metre height towering above the heads of smaller folk, is not difficult to recognise and he was always a familiar — if elusive — figure in Bayreuth, sometimes accompanied by his wife, his daughter or his mother. But on the whole what is so delightful to the public is less enjoyable to the object of attention. Munich and home were happily only some 250 kilometres away, and once rehearsals were over he seldom lingered in the holy city of Bayreuth.

In retrospect he sees the Bayreuth time as one of the major influences in his professional life, often difficult but enormously stimulating.

'Wieland Wagner was not easy to work with, everyone knows that. We all had our problems, especially when he would change his mind about productions at the last moment. But looking back I see it all more positively. Wieland was a great influence in the way of acting. At the beginning he was not an experienced producer, and he always made the point that old hands like Ludwig Weber, Josef Greindl and myself helped him. He used to say, "I owe you so much." On the other hand he would say "now try to get rid of this ballast of the old tradition."

'It was hard for me at first to change, to give up things one had esteemed, cherished in one's memory of the great Wagner singers of the past. We accepted the artificiality because we believed it had to be like that. In one way, as I have said before, I rejected it; that was why I was doubtful about becoming an opera singer. But having seen Chaliapin, having learned what could be done with artistic understanding, and with some success myself perhaps, I had accepted the traditional form. It was in me, although I was still not happy about the old bombastic "ham" style, and that was why I was getting rather tired of singing Wagner

'Then I came into contact with Wieland, and although I did not agree with all he did it was he who brought about an important change in my outlook on operatic acting and especially Wagnerian acting.

'At first it was so difficult to stand still and do nothing, and to have an empty stage. He used to say "an empty stage helps you, there is no distraction."

'There were practical problems too. Standing still for long spells on a steeply raked stage puts tremendous strain on one's back and feet — a totally unnatural posture, especially for singing. And the glare of the spotlights at eye level was blinding. The effect may have been marvellous, but it was at the expense of our health! And we did it all for very little money. As at the Metropolitan in the old days what counted was to have sung at Bayreuth — that in itself raised our fees elsewhere.

'Prophetically, as we see now, Wieland used to say, "maybe what I am doing now will become outdated, but it may lead to something else. I have not invented a style. I just want to get the dust of Wagner, to get rid of the stilts."

'One of my own discoveries through this simplified approach of Wieland's is that diction in singing is a stronger interpretive medium than visible acting. Where there are few movements diction can take over. It was a new dimension. But of course when one went back to other operahouses and the old style of production it meant going back to traditional ways of acting. I remember a number of us agreeing about this — Astrid Varnay, Greindl, Gerhard Stolze. The new style did not fit into old sets.

'Yes, I enjoyed Bayreuth in a way, but it was hectic, there was always tension. Bayreuth is a podium for international artists. Many who excel elsewhere do not succeed there, so there is always anxiety. Competition was very strong because success in Bayreuth meant so much. It was the complete opposite to the ensemble opera company where there was a "nest warmth", such as during the years at Munich under Clemens Krauss.

'Wieland created a clash of temperaments, and a specially excited audience responded to his spell. The results were often positive and sometimes achieved a superlative performance.

'Wolfgang Wagner had from the beginning the unrewarding task of keeping a clear head for all the business and financial organisation of the festivals. He always took very seriously his grandfather's insistence that one of the family must be in charge. He felt responsible, and it was a great responsibility — the only major private operahouse in the German speaking world. Later Wieland came to understand more of the business side, and it was good that Wolfgang had artistic experience in his own Bayreuth productions during Wieland's lifetime, starting as early as his *Lohengrin* in 1953. Wieland had the more inventive new ideas, but Wolfgang developed in the new form too, though in a quieter, more conservative way. I think it was a good thing that there was this balance between the two brothers' work, or the public might have found Wieland's style too extreme in the early days. But Wolfgang's productions developed in a more personal, creative way after Wieland's death. And now he certainly tries to bring in new ideas, revolutionary producers and designers. They may not be popular with everyone, but I think we owe a debt of gratitude to Wolfgang Wagner for keeping the vitality

131

of Bayreuth so strong, and even controversial. After all there is controversy about most festivals. There are still people who feel that Salzburg should have kept solely to the music of Mozart.'

Within the electric atmosphere of the Festspielhaus the relationship between fellow artists was naturally a matter of great importance. Some were already old friends, others met there for the first time. Probably the very tensions, excitement, anxiety and triumphs did much, both to make and to mar personal friendships, and a sense of humour often proved the essential safety valve. It is interesting that so many of those artists who stayed the course and became a lasting and integral part of the festivals were gifted with the power to laugh kindly at themselves and each other.

One whose ready sense of humour Hans recalls happily was Gustav Neidlinger. Their friendship dated back to Hamburg in the mid-1930s, and now twenty years later Neidlinger sang Alberich to Hotter's Wotan, Klingsor to his Amfortas and Gurnemanz, and many other roles. It was Hans who suggested Neidlinger to Wieland Wagner and he became one of Bayreuth's most famous artists, both in character and dramatic roles, bringing a fine and distinctive voice and rare acting ability to all he did.

Wolfgang Windgassen was one of the singers who came to Bayreuth almost unknown and reached his world fame through singing virtually every leading Wagner tenor role there. He too had a ready gift of laughter and also the ability to separate all the artistic demands and problems from his private life. To Hotter he was an absolutely reliable colleague — almost the highest praise an artist can give — and a skilled performer who developed steadily through the years. He eventually reached such a quality of acting, that on stage he ceased to be Windgassen; he became the character he played, and this by Hotter's own exacting standards.

Brünnhildes naturally figure largely in his memories

28.   Hans Hotter, 1959

of singing round the world, and not least in Bayreuth.

'When I have been asked — and have refused — to write a book of my memories of fellow artists I have often said that such a book ought to be called *My Thousand Daughters!* But it is too difficult, one cannot talk about them all. And a thousand is not an over estimate, it may well be nearer two thousand.

'There are nine valkyries in every *Waküre* performance so in five productions there would be forty or fifty, and there have been *Ring* productions in Bayreuth, London, Vienna, Munich, Hamburg and single *Walküre* performances in so many other places and over so many years. In fact I have sung about four hundred *Walküres* altogether, not quite so many as the *Siegfrieds*, but enough!

'Mostly of course I think of the Brünnhildes, large, small, young, old, great artists or beginners. But many of the singers who appeared as the other valkyries graduated to Brünnhilde or became famous in other leading roles.

'At Bayreuth in the '50s there were only two Brünnhildes, Astrid Varnay and Martha Mödl and they were perfectly contrasted. You simply could not compare them because each excelled in her own very different way. Astrid was always for me the great actress. Her acting was so good that you could not decide whether she was trying to be the character or whether she actually *was* the character. She has such a dynamic quality that she was able to project and to fire the onlooker's imagination, to create contact. That for me was her great quality — the performer, the actress, the personality. And she was always a helpful artist, very controlled. She was a really refreshing colleague, relaxed, understanding — though one had to try hard not to laugh at her jokes on stage!

'Martha Mödl had a very unique personal quality. Her presence created an aura. Her poise, her stance, her manner were intensely feminine and seemed simply to become the character she was playing. Her's were always deeply emotional interpretations, and she is a very charming person. Everyone loved her.

'My stage partners have always been important for my own performances. There are two ways of making a success. Some artists seem to prefer to stand out alone. But for me the colleagues mattered a great deal, and I do not say this from any particular modesty. I knew that with the right partners I could sing and act better. I needed the response, understanding, a human liking. With a lifeless or unsympathetic partner the performance became a chore.

'Much of the success of those Bayreuth *Ring* cycles came from a real understanding between colleagues.'

During the whole span of Hans Hotter's international career England was the scene of some of his greatest successes. For more than twenty years he came to London almost every season and sometimes several times a year, for opera performances, for concerts, as producer of the *Ring* cycles conducted by Georg Solti, and later for teaching and master classes.

If Munich has always been his true home in every sense, Vienna an adoptive home where the public claims him as their own in a very special way, and Hamburg the background of his first real graduation as one of the great singers of his age, London must rank at least fourth among the cities where he came, saw and conquered.

From the beginning London audiences and British critics have held him in a very special regard. He has always had great rapport with them, and regarded them as some of his most loyal public.

London has welcomed him, even inadvertently. One of his favourite stories is of arriving in London in the early days to be met with banner headlines 'Hotter in London — and more to come!' Even though that journalist was concerned with one of Britain's freak heatwaves the message was no less true of his career.

After that first operatic visit with the Vienna company in 1947 and the following seasons at Covent Garden with Wagner in English, the Royal Opera House mounted what was virtually a Wagner festival in 1951. That was the year of the Festival of Britain, a nationwide celebration designed to focus Britain's emergence and purpose in a post-war world. The arts figure largely in it, and ranged from performances of Shakespeare and Marlowe in the quadrangles of Oxford colleges and special productions in famous little theatres like the Maddermarket at Norwich to major events in London.

In retrospect it is interesting and quite impressive that Covent Garden should have decided to devote a great part of their celebration to so emotive a composer (at that time) as Richard Wagner. It bears out Hotter's experience that there was very little anti-German prejudice at least among the musical public, and it is evidence of David Webster's ebullient artistic courage and assurance.

Two complete cycles of the *Ring* were given and several performances each of *Parsifal*, *Tristan und Isolde* and *Die Meistersinger* and all were sung in German. Karl Rankl was then musical director of the Royal Opera and he conducted the *Ring*. That was Kirsten Flagstad's last Covent Garden season. She sang Brünnhilde only in *Götterdämmerung*, but also Isolde and Kundry. Anny Konetzni and Astrid Varnay sang the *Walküre* and *Siegfried* Brünnhildes, Set Svanholm was Siegfried, Sylvia Fisher Sieglinde, Gottlob Frick Hunding, and Otakar Kraus Alberich — a role in which he was to become as famous in London as Neidlinger was in Bayreuth, where Kraus also sang the part later. Ludwig Weber, Peter Klein and Benno Kusche were others in that very international company.

Hotter was the Wotan, and the second cycle of those *Ring* performances in May 1951 were the first times I

136

saw and heard him in what was also my very first *Ring*. After thirty years it is difficult to give a balanced description, but I remember the effect of the operas on myself and the extraordinary revelation, dramatically and musically, of Hotter's performance. Wagner is heady stuff; it was days before I was sober again.

The production was a pre-war one with the old type of sets and costumes. Wotan, heavily bearded, wore the great winged helmet beloved of Wagnerian caricaturists, a long blue robe, scarlet cloak and broad metal bracelets. And he carrried a nine-foot spear. Costumes have changed greatly over the years and we now accept frock-coated Wotans almost without comment, but the spear cannot be eliminated. Hotter was always famous for the perfect naturalness and mastery with which he carried and used Wotan's symbol of power. A quarter of a century later I watched him explaining and demonstrating its use and balance to a student. An expert trout fisherman has the same command of a fly rod.

That season he also sang Sachs in German at Covent Garden, but hay fever intervened and he was only able to appear in one performance. That was sad, because it was the only time when he sang under the baton of Sir Thomas Beecham. Although his voice was far from its best that evening I still have a vivid impression of his characterisation which could be more fully revealed in this traditional production than in Wieland's disembodied *Meistersinger* at Bayreuth a few years later, and the enchantment of Beecham's conducting remains unforgettable.

Hotter admired and respected him, 'It was often said that he disliked or despised singers, but he certainly did not show that to me. Like Clemens Krauss he was essentially a gentleman.'

In 1951 the London Siegfried, Set Svanholm, also sang Loge and Siegmund. He was a fine Heldentenor with a powerful rather astringent voice whose intelligence and gifts as an actor overcame the handicap of lack of height. He and Hotter had sung together in Vienna during the war years and later in South America and the United States and Hans always found him a charming and rewarding colleague.

That year's *Ring* cycles marked the passing of an era, the last appearance of the complete pre-war production, though *Walküre* and *Siegfried* were given again in 1953 and Hotter sang in them with a new Brünnhilde Margaret Harshaw, and Fritz Stiedry conducting. It was after those performances that Harold Rosenthal writing in *House and Garden* remarked 'Hans Hotter ranks with Van Rooy and Schorr as one of the greatest Wagnerian baritones ever to have come before the public.'

The following year, 1954 the Royal Opera House launched a new *Ring* production by Rudolf Hartmann in a transitional type of staging designed by Leslie Hurry which was somewhere between the old style and the gradually spreading influence of Wieland Wagner. Hotter did not sing in the London *Ring* that year, but returned in 1955 to sing Wotan throughout the first cycle, and for many older operagoers his performances and the conducting of Rudolf Kempe are remembered as its outstanding features.

That partnership in the same production continued in 1956, 1957 and 1958 (when Hotter also sang Günther). In 1959 Franz Konwitschny and Reginald Goodall conducted, Kempe returning in 1960, the last year of that production. Hotter sand one cycle in both these seasons.

During all these years his musical life in London steadily developed. There were lieder recitals first in the Wigmore and Kingsway Halls and later in the Royal Festival Hall, broadcasts and recording work.

It was during the *Ring* revival of one of those years when Peter Potter took over Hartmann's production that the first thoughts of Hotter producing in London germinated.

He had been helping Potter, unofficially, with directing some of the acting and stage grouping. Lord

Harewood, who was watching, came to him afterwards, saying he did not know that Hotter was interested and gifted in that way. Would he consider producing the *Ring*? Hans explained that he did not want to take over an old production but would be very interested in handling a completely new one. Nothing more was said at the time, but with Georg Solti's incumbency as musical director a new *Ring* was high on the list of priorities, and probably George Harewood added his persuasion to Webster's. Hotter finally produced a *Ring* cycle which appeared in instalments from 1961 to 1964 and was the forerunner of the famous 'Golden Ring' complete recording also conducted by Solti.

In the meantime Klemperer was also in London. As mentioned earlier, it was one of the sad things for British audiences that despite his many visits Hotter sang so few roles here: no Dutchman, no Amfortas, no Gurnemanz, no Grand Inquisitor, no King Philip, no Boris, no Scarpia, no Schigolch or Schönberg's Moses. Indeed considering the size of his repertory in German speaking countries the London range was minimal largely, no doubt, because of the towering fame of his Wotan.

But early in 1961 there was a new production of *Fidelio*, conducted and produced by that great Beethoven master Otto Klemperer. The cast was an outstanding one: Sena Jurinsa as Leonore, Jon Vickers' Florestan, Gottlob Frick as Rocco, Forbes Robinson as the Minister, a charming young Jaquino and Marzelline by John Dobson and Elsie Morrison and Hotter's first London Pizarro.

This was a mighty, spine-chilling performance, though one so intense that he sometimes did violence to the vocal line. *The Times* critic described it as 'a Lucifer incarnate whose evil towers over goodness.'

He had a great admiration for Klemperer and always enjoyed working with him.

'His name and fame had been familiar to me since I could think, and I had the real privilege to be liked by him. With great conductors — if you are yourself a musician — you either agree with them, go with them, or you fight them. There is no way of compromise. I was very happy with Klemperer, He was a character, and lived up to it in an amusing way. He was famous for his outrageous remarks and was perhaps the most amusing conductor I ever worked with. He was a man of tremendous personality, and one of the most honest to music. He made no detours, did nothing for personal effect. He was simple, straightforward, absolutely true to the heart of the music. He could be very hard, like most great conductors, but you can get on with the greatest dictators if you are positive yourself, and know your own mind musically.'

A year later — the opening performance was on January 4, 1962 — came a new *Die Zauberflöte* also produced by Klemperer, and Hans Hotter was the Speaker. Neither of these productions was outstanding per se, but both were examples of Klemperer's self effacing honesty and faithfulness to the work. *Zauberflöte* has been restaged at Covent Garden a number of times since the war, and when I later asked David Webster why it was necessary to spend more money on yet another new one his comment was, 'What did you think of the earlier ones?'

Musically this was a very impressive *Zauberflöte*, rather slow in tempi much of the time in Klemperer's own dedicated way, but beautifully played and sung. Again the cast was an outstanding one with Richard Lewis and Joan Carlyle as Tamino and Pamina, Geraint Evans a delightful Papageno, and Joan Sutherland as the Queen of the Night. The Speaker's role is a very short but vital one which Hotter had sung many times in different houses. Here it proved one of the superb passages of the evening: noble, wise, authoritative, sung with exquisite vocal quality and colour.

In the meantime the *Ring* had been launched with *Walküre* a few months earlier, in October 1961. The first choice of designer was Herbert Kern whose sets were very simple, spacious and — or so it seemed to many of us — a happy marriage of old and new ideas in Wagnerian staging. It was an admirable framework for Hotter's own art as producer which was embodied in acting, character and diction, in the unfolding of the story as Wagner created it. This was a very subtle approach, not one which catches the sensation hungry eye of the publicist, and it was not one which could be fully achieved in that year's short series of performances because it depended on teaching and developing the interpretations of each individual singer, and some of the company were new to their roles.

Hotter himself sang Wotan, thereby holding together the drama and musical depth of the opera. Solti conducted with tremendous enthusiasm, fire and passion which rather too often engulfed the voices but received much excited praise. A greater contrast to Kempe's sensitive, beautifully shaped and classical *Ring* could hardly be imagined, but Solti welded the blood and tears and primitive emotions into an overwhelming experience. Later his reading was to develop enormously in style and meaning; at that time he was something of a magnificent bully, but no one could have called it dull.

There was a new young Finnish Brünnhilde, Anita Välkki, a splendidly dramatic Fricka in the person of Rita Gorr, a warm and vocally lovely Sieglinde by Claire Watson, and Jon Vickers as a fine Siegmund. Other names who were to become famous in London and abroad were Michael Langdon who sang Hunding and Marie Collier and Josephine Veasey among the valkyries.

Unfortunately that particular production from the scenic point of view did not succeed. Although well received by some critics, others found the staging unimaginative. One complained of the absence of a door in Hunding's hut in the first act, a comment which now has a certain piquancy after years of *Rings* where doors have become the exception rather than the rule. In one way and another censure fell on those *Walküre* designs and the result was that Kern did not complete that *Ring* although a further series of *Walküre* performances in Kern's sets was given in December 1962.

A new designer was appointed in the person of Günther Schneider-Siemssen then quite famous on the continent but still almost unknown in England apart from an effective *Erwartung*. It was he who created the great adjustable circular disc, nicknamed the pineapple ring, on and round and under which the Solti-Hotter *Ring* of the following years was to have its being.

This time they began with *Siegfried* which opened on September 7, 1962, and a new Wanderer received the cloak and spear of the chief god: David Ward. Few artists have been so generous in ascribing their debt to a teacher as Ward has been about Hans Hotter, and certainly in those early days the success of his performance was rooted in Hotter's conception of the part and his patient coaching. Otakar Kraus had by then been London's definitive Alberich for a number of years, and there were three famous Bayreuth artists, Wolfgang Windgassen as Siegfried, Gerhard Stolze as Mime and above all Birgit Nilsson's Brünnhilde. It was a very strong cast, Schneider-Siemssen's decor and costumes had a good reception, Solti developed his tense, dramatic orchestral reading, and Hotter continued his own style of breathing life into the beings of the saga.

In the autumn of 1963 came *Götterdämmerung* with Birgit Nilsson and Windgassen, Thomas Stewart as Gunther, Marie Collier as Gutrune, Gottlob Frick a granite tower of evil as Hagen. And there was Josephine Veasey singing Waltraute, a role which she was to make especially her own, excelling vocally and dramatically and with marvellous insight into the nature of the

142

29. With Astrid Varnay and Joseph Keilberth, Bayreuth 1953 (courtesy Presse-foto-gebauer)

30. With Gré Brouwenstijn in *Die Meistersinger*, Bayreuth 1956 (photo Siegfried Lauter-wasser, courtesy Festspiel-leitung Bayreuth)

31. With Toni Blankenheim and Wieland Wagner, Bayreuth 1955

143

valkyrie maid. 'She is truly Wotan's daughter' as one member of the audience said. Two other names later to become famous appeared in that cast: Rita Hunter as the Third Norn and Gwyneth Jones as Wellgunde.

The Times headed it notice: 'Mr. Hotter's Impressive *Götterdämmerung*', and the production in general received an enthusiastic press. Many of the leading singers were world names and all the more able to profit by Hotter's knowledge and perception, while the newcomers were shaped by his experience and understanding. The result had a wholeness, an impact which is rare because it was created from the characters and their interplay out of which sprang the action, instead of a manipulation of the individuals to achieve a particular overall interpretation. There were some wonderful scenic effects with lighting and the varied use of the great disc.

Siegfried's death had a spiritual beauty and poignancy, his youthful figure lit almost as if by inner radiance among the menacing surrounding shadows, and the dark wondering company of the Gibichungs. I heard and saw Windgassen sing the part many times and in many different operahouses but never, I think, with greater inspiration than in this production. Wilhelm Pitz, for so many years Bayreuth's famous chorus master, coached the Covent Garden chorus and achieved wonders.

Except at Bayreuth where festival conditions demand that a new *Ring* must be born complete, most productions of Wagner's magnum opus are created by staging one opera at a time, and since the three later ones stand alone better in repertory the order of separate productions is often not chronological. Hence the pattern of this *Ring*: *Walküre, Siegfried, Götterdämmerung*. Finally in 1964 came *Das Rheingold*, then *Walküre* restaged in the Schneider-Siemssen sets, followed by *Siegfried* and *Götterdämmerung* and all given in two complete cycles. It was the culmination of long, patient, often difficult work for both Georg Solti and Hotter with new singers coming into the casts. The whole was a remarkable artistic achievement, enormously exciting and satisfying to many of us who found in it a true presentation of Wagner's work, inspired by new insights, using modern techniques and artistic expression without violating the spirit of the music or the composer-librettist's intention. It was not perfect, certainly not in Hotter's own estimation, much remaining to be polished and fulfilled in later performances, but the overall concept was presented to the public.

It did not, however, meet with universal approval from the critics, probably because of its intrinsic faithfulness to Wagner. Critics — and I have been one for many years — are always in danger of being satiated by seeing too many operas. A radical new approach provides matter either to rave about or to pillory. Critics, contrary to the belief of many artists and operagoers, are human. They take sides in any controversy and defend their standpoint with enthusiasm. Where a production and performance are what one might call classical you either accept it with delight or, in order to be critical, pick out minor defects, assess their number and effect and in some cases administer reproof on the principle of death by a thousand cuts.

There was no wholesale slaughter in the press reaction, indeed there was a great deal of warm praise both musically and dramatically, but there was division over details. Some found the Schneider-Siemssen decor a delight. For others the visual theme of the disc hampered the action. Some were excessively irritated by the absence of a rope for the Norns, others damned the costumes.

But all who stopped to consider the psychological insight, the immediacy of the emotional and dramatic characterisation paid tribute to Hotter for this result. For once gods, dwarfs, giants or mere mortals in the saga were real, sentient people, each in their own form,

145

with whose sufferings or joys the audience could identify and that is what carries a performance into the realm
of creation, a living, poignant experience. Many great
artists can do this individually. To achieve it with a
whole cast, or the majority of a cast depends upon a
producer who knows not only what the stage characters
are but a good deal about the gifts and problems and
inhibitions of the artists who have to play them.

Was that enough? It depends on whether success is
equated with sensation. Donald Mitchell writing in the
Daily Telegraph the previous year said 'Hans Hotter, to
my mind, is the perfect Wagnerian producer. He
eschews fussy movement and concentrates on statues-
que stage groupings which almost always very tellingly
clarify or emphasise the dramatic action.' A great many
people agreed with Mitchell and still remember those
qualities. But the general published opinion was luke-
warm.

Hotter sang Wotan in the second cycle, and that was
what the public preferred. They were ready to accept
him as a producer but above all they wanted him on
stage. Few knew what those performances cost him in
physical endurance.

All through that summer he had been suffering from
disc trouble which had caused acute pain in his back
during the long hours of standing in Bayreuth performances. Then came the weeks of intensive rehearsals of all
four operas of the *Ring* in London, and finally when all
was completed there was the second cycle where he
appeared as a singer. He manager *Rheingold* and *Walküre*
but by the *Siegfried* night the pain was too bad. Helga
came over from Munich and took him home to rest and
David Ward sang in his place.

Yet despite the pain that *Walküre* Wotan was one of
the finest I ever heard him sing, musically superb and
acted with a depth of feeling that made the character's
tragedy almost unbearable. What was in fact a quite
different form of physical suffering was transmuted into

Wotan's psychological anguish. I remember talking about this with him later, and he said 'The pain was so bad I could not think about my performance at all, but sometimes it works better that way.' It was several months before the back trouble was completely cured.

For the next two years he returned to direct rehearsals of the *Ring*. In 1965 he sang Wotan in one complete cycle, and in 1966 in *Rheingold* and *Siegfried*.

By 1965 the whole production had fully developed and received wide acclaim from critics and public, and Hotter was in top form vocally. Andrew Porter writing of *Walküre* that year in *The Financial Times* said 'Hotter was in voice. And those four words are as much as to say that the greatest, most moving Wotan of our day was with us again.' And Alan Blyth in another notice: 'Hans Hotter reappeared last night in his own production of *Die Walküre*. He proved, if proof was needed, that he is still the greatest actor-singer of his generation.'

It was under his direction that two British dramatic sopranos first came to fame in Wagnerian roles. Amy Shuard was the new Brünnhilde, appearing first in *Siegfried* and *Götterdämmerung* in 1964 and in the three operas the following year. And in 1965 Gwyneth Jones, having spent two weeks in Munich for special coaching with Hotter, appeared as a lovely, fresh voiced Sieglinde, a performance which really launched her international career.

Once more Hans Hotter returned to his London *Ring* in 1967 when the production was rehearsed by Peter Potter with whom he had worked on the earlier *Ring* in the '50s. He was to sing a whole cycle and it was announced as his last London Wotan. Sadly, ill luck wrecked what was to have been a series of great evenings and a personnal tribute of gratitude and honour from Hotter's devoted London public.

He developed a throat infection which affected his singing to some extent in *Rheingold* and grew worse after the performance. As a result he was unable to sing in *Walküre* or in *Siegfried,* and so the farewell was never made, as he did not sing again at the Royal Opera House.

Opera, however, has been only one part of Hans Hotter's life, and in the '60s and early '70s as he sang less on the operatic stage his professional and artistic life experienced almost a renaissance in the field of lieder singing which in turn led to more teaching and a place among the judges at international competitions.

From the very early '50s he had sung recitals in London. These continued, and he sang in two memorable performances of Beethoven's 9th Symphony conducted by Klemperer at the Royal Festival Hall in 1957, and another, also under Klemperer in 1963.

Outside London he gave a lieder recital at the 1965 Edinburgh Festival and another in Bristol in 1967. Between 1973 and 1976 he gave a series of lieder recitals all over the country, singing mostly Schubert's *Die Winterreise* with which he became almost as closely identified as with Wagner's Wotan, ending with a masterly performance of the cycle in the handsome setting of Fishmongers' Hall, one of the historic livery company halls in the City of London, on March 16, 1976, which was his last public concert in London.

At the same time there were master classes, talks, broadcasts, and from time to time he gave classes and special coaching to students at the London Opera Centre and to soloists under contract to the Royal Opera.

His first visit to Aldeburgh was not as an artist but one of the panel of judges for the Benson and Hedges Gold Award competition for concert singers in 1977, and he was there again in 1978.

If Hotter's Wagnerian *Abschied* in London was cut short and an occasion of sorrow and disappointment, probably much more deeply felt by his admirers than by himself, his continuing relationship with Britain through all the later recitals and teaching commitments

148

has been and remains a relaxed and happy one. He always found British audiences responsive and loyal and once during his producing work at Covent Garden a colleague declared him to be wholly English in his calm, untemperamental way of tackling the work in hand. By then he was of course completely bilingual, and his command of English idiom and exact appreciation of the wide ranging English vocabulary often amazed his friends in Britain and America.

One official gesture of recognition of his services to music in this country came in 1972 when he was made an Honorary Member of the Royal Academy of Music. It was in July, one of England's rare hot summer days, and an occasion which also marked the 150th anniversary of the RAM itself. Eugene Cruft, John Denison and Hotter all received their Hon. RAM from the Duchess of Kent that day at a ceremony in the Duke's Hall of the Academy before the annual prize giving to students. There was a delighted, well mannered audience, a happy formal informality. Indeed it was all very, very English and the only surprising aspect was the Mediterranean temperature.

During the two decades from 1950 until 1970 the principal centres of Hotter's career were four cities: Munich and Vienna at both of which operahouses he was on the regular roster of leading singers, Bayreuth and London, but he also went much farther afield. Over those years he sang on every continent.

The 1948 season in Buenos Aires made the Argentine his very first distant country. North America followed the southern continent with the New York seasons which started in 1950.

His connection with Chicago also began in 1950 with a Wagner concert. Then in 1952 he returned for Beethoven's Ninth Symphony conducted by George Szell. The other soloists were Frances Yeend, Martha Lipton and Eugene Conley. This concert was received with great enthusiasm, and Elmore Bacon wrote with typical American fervour in the *Cleveland News* that Hotter's 'deep-seated basso was a flashing brand of fire in the recitative.'

There have been long gaps between his visits to Chicago, but never any lack of enthusiasm for his singing there. In 1960 he appeared in some performances of *Walküre* (those which were the cause of Bing's tardy effort to get Hotter to return to the Metropolitan), and in 1961 he went back for *Fidelio*. The production had a brilliant cast. Birgit Nilsson sang Leonore. Jon Vickers was Florestan, and among the others were William Wilderman as Rocco, Irmgard Seefried at Marzelline and Walter Berry as Don Fernando. In the '70s he came again to sing the Speaker in *Die Zauberflöte*.

Most impressive and dramatic of all perhaps was a series of concert performances of Schönberg's *Moses und Aron* in 1971.

Georg Solti was by then the musical director of the Chicago Symphony Orchestra and was keen to give Schönberg's massive unfinished work. Moses is virtually a spoken role with only a few lines which are actually sung, but the speaking is as it were floated on music. Schönberg here created another operatic giant of Wagnerian stature, and Hotter had appeared as Moses in Frankfurt the previous year, later in Nuremberg, and had already made the part his own. Solti knowing his dramatic gifts and musicianship, a combination of which would be needed to convey the great Biblical drama in the static conditions of a concert platform, wanted Hotter for his performances.

I was a link in this particular transatlantic drama. *Moses und Aron* was to be given three performances in Chicago and another in New York, and they would use an English translation by David Rudkin which had been used for a stage production by Peter Hall at Covent Garden six years earlier. The Royal Opera therefore had the text and would lend it to Hans. But this was not enough. Being a perfectionist he wanted to be coached in the enunciation and stresses of the English words and he wanted this from an actor rather than an elocutionist. A leading, modern actor with classical experience.

As it happens, Donald Sinden is an old friend of mine, and he had enough spare time to do this coaching and was intrigued by such an unusual task. I put them in touch with each other. Hans came to London and spent intensive hours at the Sindens' home, and later went to Chicago where I heard and saw him give an immensely authoritative and deeply moving performance, beautifully balanced with Richard Lewis' Aron on the platform of the Orchestra Hall. Then indeed the fruits of that study were apparent. Hotter's enunciation, his feeling for the quality and colour of the English words infused the deeper meaning of the work. They sounded like original inspiration, not a translation.

Quite recently he returned to Chicago as producer, when he directed *Fidelio* for the Lyric Opera in 1981, just twenty years after singing Pizarro in the same house.

In 1954 he made his first visits to San Francisco appearing as the Dutchman and as the Count in *Figaro*. He sang there for two or three seasons and gave there his only performance sung in Russian, as the Jesuit Rangoni in *Boris Godunov* when Christoff took the title role. There were also *Walküre* performances with Nilsson. Although Hotter's San Francisco seasons were few they created a tremendous impression in America's west coast musical world, and opera enthusiasts followed him east to Europe for performances in Vienna and Bayreuth. A nostalgic echo of those seasons was celebrated in November 1978 at the silver jubilee of Kurt Herbert Adler as general director of the San Francisco Opera. Many stars who had appeared there during his reign were invited from all over the world and Hans Hotter was an honoured guest among them.

On the other side of the world he made several

concert tours of Australia between his first visit in 1955 and the most recent one in 1975, when he gave a series of master classes.

In 1967 there was his only concert tour of South Africa. In Cape Town he sang a programme of mixed lieder: Schubert, Brahms, an English group which included Peter Warlock and Vaughan Williams, and also some Afrikaans songs; his accompanist was Walter Klien. In Durban he sang operatic arias — Handel, Verdi's 'Il lacerato spirito' from *Simone Boccanegra* and Philip's 'Ella giammai m' mane' from *Don Carlos* as well as Sach's *Fliedermonolog* and Wotan's *Abschied*. There were other concerts too, during the tour, but it has remained his only visit.

Of all the far flung places the country which has always shown greatest devotion and honour to Hans Hotter is Japan. He went there first in 1962 and returned many times over the years.

The Japanese are an extremely musical people and their love and appreciation of western classical music is phenomenal. This creates enormous sales of classical records there, and of course their own brilliance in producing hi-fi equipment has focused much musical reproduction into a Japanese context.

Their own music is so different that it is fascinating to know how they became so absorbed by and sensitive to, for example, the songs of Franz Schubert. There is a very large Japanese public for these. I remember on one of Hotter's later tours he sang *Die Winterreise* eight times, plus one mixed lieder concert in various cities of Japan in a three weeks' tour. The halls were large — sometimes too large for such intimate music — yet they were virtually always full. I wonder how many European countries could fill eight large halls for *Die Winterreise* in the space of some eighteen days, even for Hans Hotter or any other top singer?

He made one operatic visit there when the Bayreuth company went to Japan in 1967, the year after Wieland

Wagner's death. They were taking part in the annual Osaka Festival, held in April. Like so much of Japan's musical life this is closely linked with the west, and for many years Osaka has been a kind of extra-mural member of the European Association of Music Festivals.

That year Bayreuth took two of Wieland Wagner's productions to Osaka, *Die Walküre* in which Theo Adam and not Hotter sang Wotan, and *Tristan und Isolde* with Birgit Nilsson, Windgassen, and Hotter as King Marke. The *Tristan* conductor was Pierre Boulez. It was the only time that his Japanese fans actually saw Hotter in a Wagnerian role in their own country, though very many Japanese visitors have for years flocked to Bayreuth, Vienna and other European and American operahouses.

That year he also sang in Hong Kong, a concert of Handel arias and mixed lieder.

Twice when my own writing work took me to Japan I was able to arrange my visits to coincide with Hans' concert tours. The first was in the spring of 1969 when he sang in Tokyo, Nagoya, Sondai, Fukuoka, Sapporo, Osaka and Yokohama; it was the year of the eight *Winterreise* performances, and I was able to attend two of them, an electrifying one at Osaka and another, the last of the series, in Tokyo. His accompanist that year was Hans Dokoupil.

The Japanese are much less vociferous in their applause than westerners, but audiences were extremely intent, deeply absorbed in the music.

Three years later the Japanese edition of a book of mine on the Bayreuth Festivals was being published in Tokyo, and I went out for the launching of it. Hans was making another of his extended Japanese recital tours with Helga and the Dutch accompanist Tom Bollen.

We were all staying at the New Otani, then one of Tokyo's newest American type hotels, large, luxurious, but not absolutely efficient in details. One night the central heating got over enthusiastic (windows were hermetically sealed) and pumped hot dry air into some of the rooms to an uncomfortable extent. Mine was not bad, but Hans and Helga, sleepless and dehydrated rang for the night manager and clad in dressing gowns and carrying their books were solemnly led by an apologetic little Japanese along miles of corridors to an alternative room.

The Japanese are, generally speaking, small in stature, and we probably noticed this especially by contrast. Hans stands some six feet four inches, and Helga and I are both tall for women. Wherever we went together we seemed to move like a little fleet of tall-masted ships among the small, neat speedboats who were our Japanese hosts. I remember this very clearly at the reception for my book which was given by the British Council. We towered above our fellow guests, easily identified but all too conspicuous.

That tour was not without its anxieties as Hans got bronchitis — probably partly due to the hotel room atmosphere — and for twenty-four hours there was some doubt as to whether he would sing the first Tokyo recital. In fact as so often happens after a crisis of worry all went without a hitch, and apart from a slight lack of breath support it was another faultless *Winterreise*. There was a really enthusiastic audience that night, and we all left the hall among waving crowds.

Two days later we went by train to Niigata, a delayed journey during which the Hotters taught me scrabble, their favourite pastime on railway journeys, and at which I was singularly bad. It is deflating to be beaten at word games in one's own language by friends born to another mother tongue!

Niigata is a busy town on the north-west coast of Japan, and here again there was an immensely keen audience and obvious knowledge and appreciation of Schubert's music as well as the singer. They cheered at the end with few inhibitions.

There I left the Hotter entourage for my own commitments in other lands; they had another seven cities before the tour was over. Two years later he made another extensive Japanese recital tour, his last, but not for lack of invitations from concert promoters or eagerness on the part of the audience. Several years later he was still receiving offers from Japan, at which he remarked rather wryly 'I think they would want me till I'm ninety!'

Like most professional travellers who are constantly moving on from one country, city or hotel to another Hotter has learned the mechanics of travel by long experience. He does not particularly enjoy this nomadic life any more than the rest of us do, the novelty wears off very quickly, the physical and mental stesses remain, but everyone blessed with commonsense learns to reduce it to a science as far as possible, and not to moan about it.

Despite the fact that for most of his international travelling career Hans has had agents, concert promoters or operahouse representatives to make the arrangements for him, he is one of the most practical and knowledgeable travellers I know, quick to grasp the facts and time schedules, and able to plan and explain these to others. I do not know a more thoughtful and thorough person in making arrangements for people to visit him at home or in other cities. Probably it stems from those early days of weary wartime travelling when there was no one at hand to shield the artist from the slings and arrows of outrageous transportation.

No doubt he has occasionally been late, or missed trains, but I have never seen or heard of it. His timing for travel or appointments is as acutely judged as his artistic timing on the stage or concert platform: neither late nor — the mark of the inexperienced — excessively early. Perhaps this too is a legacy from Clemens Krauss who used to say 'If one takes talent for granted I would add that you cannot achieve anything above average

155

without diligence and a sense of order.'

Still things can occasionally go wrong with the most careful and well organised planning, as I remember on the 1972 Japanese tour. Hans dislikes dim lights. Perhaps it is still a memory of the claustrophobic darkness of wartime blackout, but especially when working with scores or simply reading he often found hotel bedrooms ill-lit and so devised the plan of carrying a set of high powered electric bulbs with him. As we settled down on the train to Niigata Hans remarked to Helga as a confirmation of good team work, 'I packed the bulbs,' 'So did I,' said Helga. They looked at each other. 'Well its too late to do anything about it now,' said Hans after a slightly horrified pause, and we all laughed helplessly as we wondered who would discover that some of the New Otani's most celebrated guests had decamped with a set of the hotel's electric bulbs. Perhaps they would conclude that great German singers had an eccentric taste in souvenirs.

In Europe there were the regular seasons at Vienna and Munich and guest appearances at many other opera-houses as well as the summer festivals. Having so large a repertory Hotter did not essay many new parts in those years. His regular public saw him as Scarpia, Borromeo, the Grand Inquisitor, the Speaker, Pizarro and various other roles as well as the great Wagnerian leads. In 1960, however, he made two notable debuts, both in Vienna.

One was when he sang Galitzy in Borodin's *Prince Igor*. Unfortunately the opera is seldom performed, and he never sang it again. The second was in a new work, as Thomas Becket in Ildebrando Pizzetti's *Murder in the Cathedral* based on the T.S. Eliot play. It is a fine role, but the opera is not as good as the play, and this production did not survive either.

Those were the years of Herbert von Karajan's *Ring* in Vienna, produced and conducted by the maestro and for long the city's Wagnerian pivot and Hotter their idolised Wotan. His contact with Karajan went back to 1936 when the conductor heard him as Iago in Hamburg, came round to his dressing room and said 'Because of the way you articulate I want you to sing in Brahms' Requiem for me.' Karajan was then musical director as Aachen. Later he sang under Karajan in Berlin and Milan and in 1947 they recorded the Brahms' Requiem in Vienna, and Hans sang in his concerts.

There was a pause in their work together for a few years, but when Karajan became musical director in Vienna the *Ring* and *Parsifal* performances were times of happy musical collaboration. 'I had great inspiration from Karajan in those performances, and he had a rare instinct of how to do things on stage. Not necessarily the whole production, but his musical stage sense. We had a very happy relationship which continued right up to the time he left the Vienna opera.'

Elisabeth Schwarzkopf was the soprano soloist in that Karajan recording of Brahms' Requiem. She and Hans were both stars of the Vienna company which came to Covent Garden in 1947, and she was one of the first artists to record for Walter Legge. Through him she went to Australia, as did Hans. In Vienna they often sang together in opera and sometimes on the concert platform, and he knows her as one of the hardest working musicians with whom he has ever collaborated, 'she would work for eight or ten hours a day, on and on, just to perfect two or three songs.'

In the Vienna *Ring* his great partner was Birgit Nilsson. On stage there was her magnificent, tireless, diamond bright voice. Behind the scenes she had another more human quality and one which has endeared her to many colleagues — absolute reliability.

'She always appeared, she was always vocally secure, never a handicap or an anxiety. And she has a splendid sense of humour too. Normally Birgit is not very communicative but when she does talk it counts all the

32.   As Gurnemanz in *Parsifal*, Vienna 1960 (courtesy Fayer–Wien)

more, is all the more worth listening to, and her viewpoint is really refreshing or amusing. One can always laugh with her.'

1963 was an important year in the history of the Bavarian Staatsoper, for it saw the opening of the rebuilt National Theatre, with all its magnificence, as a proud symbol of Munich's place in the musical world of the new Germany and a memorial to Bavaria's long artistic heritage dating from the Wittelsbachs. Rather surprisingly Strauss' *Die Frau ohne Schatten* was chosen for the opening performance, but this also was a tribute to a composer who was one of Munich's most famous citizens. There was enormous demand for tickets for the first night, which were said to have been sold on the black market for the equivalent of £50 each, a fantastically high price thirty years ago.

The opening ceremony took place in the morning on November 21, 1963 with speeches by Dr. Alfons Goppel, Bavarian first minister, and Rudolf Hartmann the general intendant. Before this Hans Kanappertsbusch (musical director there from 1922 to 1934) conducted Beethoven's overture *The Consecration of the House,* and later came choruses from Handel's *Messiah* when the conductor was Robert Heger, whose connections with the company went back to the days of Bruno Walter.

All the state dignitaries and a galaxy of great musical personalities were present including Paul Kuhn then in his 90th year, a famous Mime and David before the first world war, as well as later stars such as Viorica Ursuleac, Maria Ivogün, Delia Reinhardt and of course the existing company, Hans Hotter among them.

That evening came the *Frau ohne Schatten* in which Hotter sang the Spirits' Messenger. Dietrich Fischer-Dieskau was Barak, Inge Borkh Barak's Wife and Jess Thomas and Ingrid Bjoner sang the Emperor and Empress. Martha Mödl was the Amme and Joseph Keilberth conducted. Two days later came *Die Meistersinger* with Hans as Pogner.

That year was also the 150th anniversary of Wagner's birth and thus the occasion for a number of new productions and special revivals in many cities. In Milan the Scala mounted a new *Ring* cycle conducted by André Cluytens and produced by Heinz Tietjen with Hotter and Birgit Nilsson as Wotan and Brünnhilde. Naples also saw him that year in a Wieland Wagner production of *Die Walküre* with Anja Silja and Windgassen.

In the spring of 1964 I went to Geneva to see some performances of *Parsifal* which really belonged to the 1963 celebrations. Herbert Graf had the idea of producing the opera with decor and costumes based on the notes and designs of Adolphe Appia and dating from 1912. He offered the idea first to the Zürich opera who turned it down, and afterwards to Geneva who responded enthusiastically, but it was then too late for staging in 1963.

Hotter was the Gurnemanz, Windgassen Parsifal, Thomas Stewart Amfortas, Anton Metternich sang Klingsor and Isabelle Strauss was the Kundry. Leopold Ludwig conducted and Graf's production followed Appia's wishes closely, using scenery and costumes 'realised' by Max Röthlisberger.

There are often suggestions of putting the clock back to show us what 19th century audiences really saw. This has been mooted at various times, especially for the *Ring*. Probably that *Parsifal* was as near to a reincarnation of past staging as one is likely to see, and it was not wholly successful. Some things were beautiful, but we are now unaccustomed to a solid dungeon for Klingsor, whose costume and lighting were rather too suggestive of a demon king.

But sometimes a different production inspires some special facet of an individual performance. When Gurnemanz finds the unconscious Kundry at the beginning of the third act he tries to revive her (according to the stage directions) by rubbing her hands and temples, or rendering first aid in any way which commends itself to the producer. Very often Gurnemanz merely makes some sort of magic gestures over her.

On this occasion Hotter passed his hands lightly and slowly over the whole length of her body using the palms and not the fingers. The gesture was very slightly different from the way I had seen him play this elsewhere and it was so exactly right, so perfectly indicative of the occasion and the characters that I remembered it vividly afterwards and came to the conclusion that this particular effect came from the position of the hands. Sensuous touch is always rendered by the fingers; here the palms were used in a kind of healing benediction. I am not sure whether Hotter had thought this out, or whether it was instinctive.

Hotter's personal endowments of voice, stature and features marked him out from the beginning for commanding roles and his success in these resulted in the public identifying him with majesty and demanding that it was as such characters that he should appear.

He had to be greatly good as with Gurnemanz or Wolfram von Eschenbach, or greatly suffering as Amfortas and the Dutchman, or ambivalent but projecting suffering on an heroic scale with Wotan, King Philip and Boris, terrifyingly powerful as the Grand Inquisitor or evil in a powerful way as Scarpia and Pizarro.

In the early days there were of course some frankly romantic roles, but although his gift for humour infused to some extent all his characters, as it must in any true delineation of human nature, he was allowed few roles in which to be frankly funny.

There were two striking ones, however. First came Gianni Schicchi which was in his early repertory, and later Falstaff. He had first sung Shakespeare's fat knight in Hamburg in 1938, well before his earliest *Walküre* Wotans. Hans Schmidt-Isserstedt was the conductor and there were some sixty rehearsals before that *Falstaff* was presented to the public. In the following year he sang in a Leipzig radio recording, later issued on disc. Falstaff was a role he really enjoyed, and he has always stressed the importance when playing him of knowing the character as Shakespeare created it, for Falstaff, like Baron Ochs, is a gentleman for all his follies, and not a boor.

Michael Langdon once said to me with characteristic modesty 'It was lucky for me that Hans did not make Ochs one of his roles!'

There was what one might call a borderline case in Sir John Morosus in Richard Strauss' opera *Die Schweigsame Frau,* which was given a handsome production at the Salzburg Festival of 1959. Böhm conducted, Günther Rennert was the producer and the scenery and costumes were designed by Teo Otto. This is a boisterous comedy freely adapted from Ben Johnson's *Epicoene or the Silent Woman* about a noise hating, miserly retired admiral who disinherits his nephew for joining an operatic troupe. His barber and the nephew trick the old man into a mock marriage with a 'silent woman', who is actually the nephew's wife. There are many of the overworked devices of classic opera buffa, and it ends with the usual reconciliation all round.

Die Schweigsame Frau is not Strauss at his best or anywhere near it, though there is plenty of vitality and a certain amount of beautiful vocal writing for the leading character, but it is this character which unbalances the opera. For Morosus is a 'real' person: difficult, fractious, laughable, but capable of suffering, of thinking, of having an identity of his own. All the rest are stock pasteboard characters. When Hotter sang and acted Morosus the contrast was even more marked than it might have been if the character was played by a lesser artist.

The result was that the deceptions and pranks played on Morosus had a much more cruel undertone than when the whole is an obvious charade. Hotter gave a

162

delightful and well judged performance, balancing the humour and pathos and never putting more into the character than it can carry, but the imbalance is there in the writing of it, and Morosus does not really qualify as a comic role.

It was not until Hotter was beginning to unload some of the weight of the great leading roles that he was able to indulge in two character parts which were, psychologically, little men: weak, mean, laughable or pitiable. One of these was Schigolch in Alban Berg's *Lulu*.

Berg's bitter unfinished tragi-comedy was first performed at Zürich in 1937 and just thirty years later was produced by Günther Rennert as part of the 1967 Munich Opera Festival. Evelyn Lear sang Lulu and Hotter was received with surprise and delight by the public as the comic, despicable Schigolch.

I did not see that production, but the following year I saw Vienna's version. Although *Lulu* had been taken up gradually by a number of countries and operahouses Vienna had only flirted with it by concert performances in 1949 and 1960, and a 'scenic' presentation in the Vienna Festival of 1962. At last the Staatsoper decided to give it a full-scale staging, which opened on December 16, 1968, with Karl Böhm conducting and in a brilliant production by Otto Schenk. Günther Schneider-Siemssen was the designer.

The success of *Lulu* depends upon the singing actress who takes the name part. Here it was Anja Silja, and she was superb. Surrounding her were many familiar artists: Ernst Gutstein as Dr. Schön, Waldemar Kmentt as his son. Hilde Konetzni appeared in a small role, and Martha Mödl also renouncing past beauty and dignity was the lesbian Countess Geschwitz. And Hans Hotter, shabby, spectacled, bewhiskered, wearing a greasy felt hat as the crafty, lecherous time serving beggar Schigolch! He revelled in it, and gave a brilliant and very amusing performance. It was in fact a role which gave him enormous personal enjoyment in the characterisation, the singing-acting. The whole of this *Lulu* was hailed as a triumph by many critics and much of the Vienna public.

Some three years later Vienna was first in the field with another modern opera in many ways comparable in its satire and bitter humour — Gottfried von Einem's *Der Besuch der Alten Dame*. Based on Dürrenmatt's play (in English *The Visit*) the opera was a joint creation, Dürrenmatt himself working with von Einem to construct the libretto and the world première was at the Vienna Staatsoper in May 23, 1971. In this case Horst Stein was the conductor, but the producer-designer team was the same as that for *Lulu*: Otto Schenk and Günther Schneider-Siemssen.

Christa Ludwig was the monstrous Old Lady who returns to the little provincial town of her youth to exact revenge on the early lover who had betrayed her. Eberhard Waechter was this unfortunate man, and there was a strong cast, in which Hotter was the schoolmaster. Joseph Wechsberg described his performance as 'a perfect miniature portrait of a sanctimonious, demoniac teacher.' I saw this production a few months later with the inimitable Astrid Varnay in the lead.

This time Munich followed, four years later, and there again I saw this immensely effective and horrific piece; horrific in its remorseless revelation of the worst of human nature as the moderately decent townspeople disintegrate morally under the blackmail of the Old Lady. In Munich she was played very skilfully by Kirsten Meyer, and Hans repeated his tragi-comic, completely integrated study of a nonentity.

There was to be one other assumption of a great role, greatly performed on the former scale of nobility — Moses in Schönberg's *Moses und Aron,* in which Hotter appeared in Frankfurt in 1970 and again in 1975. Schönberg's great uncompleted, unwieldy, masterpiece is an appallingly difficult work to stage, and to perform. At that time it was suddenly embraced by Frankfurt,

164

Nuremberg, and Stuttgart, having been given earlier in Berlin and Düsseldorf. London saw it in 1965 when Solti conducted (the forerunner of his American concert performances) and Peter Brook then described it as 'the only great tragedy this century has produced.'

If Covent Garden's staging was more arresting, especially in the golden calf orgy scene, Frankfurt was far more memorable and moving. Christoph von Dohnányi was the conductor and brought a remarkable sense of dedicated spirituality to the playing. And there was Hotter. It was Schönberg's idea that Moses should be a spoken role to symbolize God having denied him the gift of communication. Aron his spokesman is a tenor part, in this case sung by Václav Kaslik. But Hotter with his deep musicianship spoke the words over the orchestral flow in such a way that, as one critic put it 'one imagines to hear their secret melody.'

His make-up was modelled on the famous Michelangelo statue (without the beard) and his whole performance was spellbinding by the very truth and anguish of its simplicity, the simplicity which only a very great artist can achieve. Here was Moses, the servant of God, alone in his human inability to transmit the vision which he had been vouchsafed: 'O word, word that I lack . . . '

The later concert performances in America were perhaps more musically and more textually electrifying. One could hear every word which is rarely possible on the musical stage. But Hotter's acting on stage at Frankfurt was something which a static concert cannot convey. I saw the 1975 Frankfurt revival as well as the original production, and those performances will always rank with the greatest of Hotter's Wagnerian roles.

May 5, 1969 was the centenary of Hans Pfitzner's birth, and Munich's Staatsoper which had disappointed the composer on his seventy-fifth birthday and retrieved his satisfaction on his eightieth, did not fail to honour him again then, almost twenty years after his death.

There was a memorable performance of *Palestrina* in which Hotter appeared as Cardinal Borromeo. He was in noble voice and this profound personification, always among his most impressive, held us enthralled by its realisation of Pfitzner's dramatic form of a great historical figure who was eventually to be honoured as a saint. Meinhard von Zallinger conducted that performance, Richard Holm sang Palestrina and Gottlob Frick appeared in the small role of Pope Pius IV.

Through the later 1960s Hotter gave fewer opera performances. Those were the years when he was doing a good deal of producing, and more and more lieder recitals. There was no less work, indeed in many ways his professional life became more demanding, but its artistic form changed gradually and wisely.

He is by nature a very sane, well balanced person. Not without the temperamental fluctuations which are inherent in almost every sensitive artist, but conscious of them, and a realist.

Official honours had come to him at diferent stages of his life: Hamburg's title of *Kammersänger* in 1936, the same honour from the Bavarian Staatsoper in 1956, the Bavarian Order of Merit in 1966 and the British RAM 1972. On his 65th birthday in 1974 he received Germany's highest honour *Das Grosse Bundesverdienst Kreuz*, being nominated for this by Bundespräsident Scheel. In 1978 he was created Honorary Professor of Music by the city of Vienna, and in the following year he received Vienna's *Goldener Ehrenmedaille*. These entailed official presentations, but not allied with a performance.

He did not covet dramatic stage farewells and much publicised ovations. He wanted to phase out his opera singing by easy stages, though the public always prefers something more spectacular from their idols; partly of course because they yearn to perform themselves in an extrovert expression of their gratitude and devotion. In

Hotter's case time produced a compromise. The public had in fact two occasions of demonstrative acclaim. Fate and Hotter himself made the rest of the transition from one musical form to another almost imperceptible.

For one thing, unless caused by accident or serious illness, there is no exact point in the life of any singer when he or she ought ideally to retire. The fact that physical aging must affect both singer and dancer in a way which other artists are spared is something which all must realise and face from the time of their professional zenith. For each individual it will be different, and there are the qualities of technique and experience which play an enormously important part. When the unintelligent singer has lost the natural youthful beauty of voice which gave him the opportunity for a career, there is no future but a steady decline, and one which develops all the more speedily because they lack the understanding of how to use and conserve the natural gift. With the real artist the position is exactly the reverse: with the years their musicianship continues to grow and deepen with their own broader knowledge of life and of themselves. It never stops; there is no point of saturation. Therefore in the case of all really great singers their finest performances are given some years after the voice has actually passed its natural peak of beauty or quality.

With Hans Hotter, by the time he had reached the age of sixty with some forty years of constant singing behind him, his voice was not, of course, the instrument it had been a quarter of a century earlier. The evidence of this can be heard in some of his early records made in the 1940s which show a breathtaking beauty, a very rare vocal translucence and colour. But they are still a young singer's work.

The performances and recordings of the late '50s, the '60s and lieder recitals even later in the '70s revealed a musicianship no young artist could possibly possess; technique, experience, diction, dramatic sense. Those may sound rather cold intellectual qualities, but with

33.   As the Grand Inquisitor in *Don Carlos*, Vienna 1962 (courtesy
Fayer-Wien)

Hotter the lifeblood that infused them had always been his own quite simple love of music for its own sake. That, with his experience, has never ceased to grow.

The voice grew darker and, apart from much exquisitely coloured and ravishing lieder singing, harder. He overcame the tendency to unsteadiness almost completely in later years, but the vocal texture became harder as it was more perfectly focused. Here was the mature man of music.

Where then was the professional break to be made? For the physical vocal quality is never wholly stable. At any age it is liable to health hazards and fatigue and as the individual grows older these problems inevitably occur more often. One night he might feel marvellous and the voice be in every way as powerful, flexible and beautiful as it had been ten years earlier. I heard many performances like that towards the end of his opera career. On the other hand there was growing likelihood that his voice would play up. So he phased out opera. Some of his public would have liked him to go on for ever; 'Just let him stand on the stage and act.' A folly which is remorselessly condemned by others who see artists trying to repeat their former triumphs with declining resources.

Did Hotter go on too long in opera? I do not think so. He chose to appear in smaller character parts like those in *Lulu* and the *Alte Dame* or in the spoken one of Moses. He sang a few Pogners and Grand Inquisitors, sometimes a Gurnemanz which always lay well for his voice. But there remained the golden burden of Wotan. Somewhere, somehow the public had to share in their Wotan's Abschied.

Viennese operagoers used to say that Hotter had on a number of occasions sung his 'last' Wotan there, and each time to their delight he appeared in the role again, I doubt whether Hans himself ever said or intended that any of those performances should be a decisive finale. Neither the Vienna Staatsoper authorities nor those in

Munich seem to have made any special effort to mount a farewell performance in this role by one of their most famous and long standing company members. London tried, in that *Ring* cycle of 1967, and it was the misfortune of Hotter's illness that prevented its triumphant fulfilment.

Any one of those three operahouses would have been an obvious setting for the god's farewell. Instead it was Paris that was to provide the venue.

In the autumn of 1971 the Paris Opéra put on some performances of *Die Walküre* in Wieland Wagner's Bayreuth staging. Bernard Lefort was then already the musical director of the Paris Opera and Hans Hotter was invited to re-produce it. Lovro von Matacic conducted and the Wotans at those performances were Hubert Hofmann and Franz Mazura, with Berit Lindholm and Margaret Kingsley as Brünnhilde, Régine Crespin as Sieglinde, and Jean Cox and Ernst Kozub sharing Siegmund. Out of this came the suggestion that Hotter who had then not sung the role for about four years should return and make his farewell appearance at a further performance the following summer.

This time the occasion succeeded. The Paris Opéra gave it much publicity and the word went out far and near. Operatic celebrities, critics and the many Hotter devotees gathered there from most parts of the world.

It was on Thursday, June 29, 1972 and Hans Hotter was then in his sixty-fourth year. Lovro von Matacic was taken ill and none of the conductors with whom Hotter had sung Wagner for so many years being available, that *Walküre* was conducted by the then young Alexander Gibson from Scottish Opera, and well he did it, especially the final act. Almost all the leading singers were colleagues with whom Hans had appeared or whom he had directed in his own productions: Berit Lindholm was Brünnhilde, Regine Crespin was Sieglinde, Jean Cox sang Siegmund and Michael Langdon was Hunding. It was decided that Hans should sing in the third act only, so Franz Mazura appeared as Wotan in the second act.

Once more the great figure came, fearful in his wrath with the disobedient valkyries, imperious then wonderfully tender with his favourite daughter. The poignant spell of that miraculous music was on us. Gently he laid Brünnhilde down, called up the rampart of flames, and then passed slowly from a scene which had enshrined his charismatic musical glory some four hundred times.

Perhaps the voice was not quite as we had heard it in this role a few years before, nor as we were hearing it in glorious lieder recitals at this time, and for obvious reasons. The occasion was far too emotionally charged, both for the artist himself and the audience. But the splendour of the whole performance was undimmed. Harold Rosenthal writing in *Opera* said, 'When Wotan came to the passage, beginning with the words "Der Augen leuchtendes Paar," as he gazed fondly on his beloved Brünnhilde for the last time, the voice was again meltingly beautiful and his tender singing infinitely moving. It was one of those great moments in the opera house that those present will never forget'.

Many of the audience wept. Flowers and laurel chaplets though not presented on stage poured in at the stage door (many of them never reached Hotter at all). Bernard Lefort made a charming speech in which he said that Hans Hotter was honouring the Paris Opéra by having chosen to make his Wotan farewell there. Two medals were presented to him, one from the Opéra and the other from the Paris Wagner Society.

After that the emotion-charged atmosphere relaxed in an operahouse reception and later many of us went on to supper at the Grand Hotel where the celebrations continued well into the small hours of the morning. The hero of the occasion left the party by 2 a.m. Characteristically, he was up soon after 7 the next morning to leave for another musical commitment in Holland.

Thus he resigned the Wagnerian godship with no

little sense of relief — and continued his musical career. To a certain section of the public it must have come as something of a surprise to find that Hotter the artist was not immolated in Walhalla. Having given and received the dues of greatness in one field he was finally free of the yoke of the *Ring* and able to continue in what had long been his greater love, lieder singing, and to devote himself more and more to teaching.

There was however another stage farewell, far less formal, more spontaneous, and therefore less onerous for Hans. He had ceased singing at the Vienna Staatsoper without any official final performance, though he retained a second home in the city and still gave recitals there. Then at last in 1978 the Staatsoper authorities invited him to return to the scene of so many of his triumphs for one more Grand Inquisitor. There had been much sorrow and regret among the Vienna public that they had had no chance of giving him a personal final ovation. He knew this, and agreed, provided that the occasion should be kept unofficial.

The news of course was soon known, and leaked to the Vienna press, but few of us in other countries heard in time to make the journey. So the Viennese had that *Don Carlos* on December 10, 1978 for their special personal tribute. The conductor was an old colleague who had shared many performances with Hotter, Berislav Klobucar; the Philip was a new singer just coming to fame, Simon Estes, Giacomo Aragall sang Carlos and Gwyneth Jones Elisabeth. But it was for Hotter that the public came that night and from all accounts he was in remarkably fine voice, his total performance more electrifying than ever. The audience gave him their hearts as perhaps only Viennese can — when they are really moved.

Between those two farewells there was a dramatic debut. In 1977 came a request to fly out to Los Angeles in April to appear with the Los Angeles Philharmonic Orchestra under Zubin Mehta in a performance of

Schönberg's *Gurrelieder*. This was given on a mighty scale at the Music Center Pavilion with an augmented orchestra, three choruses and six soloists. I was not able to be there, but the event captured the Californian musical public and created considerable excitement with some criticism. For Hans Hotter alone there seemed to be unmixed praise.

Martin Bernheimer, music critic of the *Los Angeles Times* wrote 'For at least one observer, however, the evening belonged to Hans Hotter, the great Heldenbariton who was making a belated Philharmonic debut, at 68, in the "Summer Wind" narrative. He always was a towering, charismatic figure on the stage, and an actor of incomparable grandeur and refinement. Nevertheless, one was not prepared for the shattering experience he made of the poetic finale — the idyllic hush he brought to a line like "Still! Was mag' der Wind nur wollen?" or the lyrical shock of his sudden resonant tone at "Frühlings blaueweisse Blütensäume . . ."

'Hotter offered an object lesson in dramatic concentration, expressive poignance and musical logic. He also gave the evening a radiant climax with his apostrophe of summation: "Erwacht, ihr Blumen, zur Wonne" (Awake, you flowers, to bliss).

'Hotter also did a strange thing. He actually sang some of the time, ignoring Schönberg's explicit instructions regarding the Germanic parlando known as "Sprechgesang".

'But when he sang, he sang with such overpowering poignance that the stylistic liberty did not just seem justified. It seemed inevitable.'

PART FOUR
Opera Producer

'I THOUGHT — it's an adventure I am jumping into. I will take a chance. Take up the challenge.'

For a dozen years from the later 1950s opera production formed an important part of Hans Hotter's artistic professional life. Those who saw his productions remember them in different ways depending on their approach to the stage presentation of great and familiar works. For people with a jaded appetite, looking for a new piquant sauce to make the same boring old dish palatable, then Hotter's way will have left small impression, and has probably been dismissed as the work of "the singer-producer" which he himself acknowledges as implicit criticism. There was much that was different in Hotter productions, but the changes were subtle and likely to pass unnoticed by the sensation seeker.

To those of us who actually love the operas, their music and drama, and do not need to have them dressed up so that they appear to be quite different, there were, as I have said in relation to the London *Ring,* fresh revelations at the heart of each work: a peeling away of the onion skins of stereotyped presentation to reveal the real life that the composer and librettist intended, a bringing out of the basic inspiration instead of superimposing a new meaning on it. One must, of course, admit that there are many opera libretti which do not have great dramatic or emotional heights or depths to reveal, which use stock characters and stock situations as a framework for the music. But most of Hotter's productions have been of Wagner operas and all Wagnerites will claim that these music dramas are certainly not hollow, and none of the other operas he produced lacked a core.

34. As The Holländer, Vienna 1955 (courtesy Fayer-Wien)

35. As Scarpia in *Tosca*,
Vienna 1968 (courtesy Fayer-
Wien)

36. As Pogner with Clair Watson in *Die Meistersinger*, Munich
1963 (courtesy Felicitas, Munich)

Apart from all this, however, in an assessment of Hotter's life as man and artist, what is most interesting about his production phase is not what he did but why he did it. Production for him was focused on the two main themes of his life, the strands which, developed and woven together ever more strongly through the years, form the character of the man: his devotion to music and the need and power to give to others.

Personal life is a blending of the divine and the earthly, of spiritual and human elements. Music in most of its forms is a kind of spiritual experience, indefinable, very individual and personal. It is something which as far as our inner joy in it is concerned can scarcely be communicated, even though musicians spend their lives imparting music to others. It can therefore be something which makes the music lover solitary at heart; an extra personal dimension of life which is sufficient in itself. Hans Hotter was born with a deep natural love of music and a desire to make music for its own sake, which influenced his life long before he adopted a professional commitment to it. But the fulfilment of life, true maturity and the continuing satisfaction of growing understanding needs human contacts. Giving is more important than taking. For Hans this has found its expression in teaching, in handing on his own art, and the fruits of his own professional and musical experience. Its final and most satisfying form is now in his musical teaching but it was this aspect of producing which was particularly important to him, and that is something which makes his role as a producer unlike that of most stage producers whose names spangle the entertainment world. He was an unselfish producer not because of an excessive conscious modesty but simply by reason of his own priorities, of what made the work interesting to him.

This is best shown in his own thoughts on how and why he took up producing, and equally the reasons why he has not pursued it, but first it is worth looking at the scope and type of work he has done in this field.

The first opportunity came when he was invited to re-produce *Siegfried* in existing sets for the Strasbourg Opera in 1954. This particular opera has played a curiously important part in Hotter's stage life: the Wanderer was the first of the Wotan roles which he sang and continued to sing for a number of years before he essayed the *Walküre* Wotan, and it was as the Wanderer that he made his first appearance at the Munich opera on that memorable April 12, 1937, so it seems fitting that *Siegfried* should have been the first opera he produced. He sang the Wanderer himself in those Strasbourg performances and there were several old friends in the cast, among them Bernd Aldenhoff as Siegfried and Gustav Neidlinger as Alberich. The conductor was Frédéric Adam.

It was after this that his unofficial assistance at *Ring* rehearsals in London inspired Covent Garden to invite him to undertake their complete new *Ring*.

Before that, however, came the offer of a *Walküre* at Amsterdam. This, like Strasbourg, was technically a revival in that the scenery dated from an earlier production but the sets had been modernised: two weeks or more of intensive rehearsals with a new cast made this Hans' own production, and one in which he took much pleasure.

His continuing work on the London *Ring* from 1961 to 1964 and later revivals has figured earlier in this book. It was his first totally new series of productions, worked out with Georg Solti as conductor and musical director of Covent Garden, and with Günther Schneider-Siemssen as designer. It is by that *Ring* that he will be best remembered as a producer, and during the course of the six years that he worked on the premières and revivals of it, a considerable number of singers came under the influence of his direction, some long established world names and familiar colleagues who were to help him with their support and enthusiasm, as well as other younger artists who first made their names in Wagner within the framework of that cycle.

In 1964 he made his production debut at both his 'home' operahouses, in Munich and Vienna. In Munich at the end of October he mounted *Der Fliegende Holländer* with imaginative decor by Schneider-Siemssen. One German critic said that the designer's experience at the Bremen opera must have given him a feeling for the sea, the dark stormy sky and inky clouds which he designed for this *Holländer!* The settings on the huge stage of the National Theatre were very effective, with the Dutchman's ghostly ship (following Bayreuth tradition of that time) a true projection phantom.

Hans Knappertsbusch was the conductor announced, but an accident prevented him from appearing on the opening night and Hans Gierster took over. The Dutchman was Hans Günter Nöcker, Ludmilla Dvorakova sang Senta, Gottlob Frick was the Daland, and the two tenor roles were strongly cast with Wolfgang Windgassen as Erik and Fritz Wunderlich singing the steersman. It was an impressive and happy occasion, and the production remained in the Munich repertory for seventeen years.

At Vienna two months later Hotter made his first production breakaway from Wagner, but there also the opera chosen was one in which he had long been a famous leading singer, Pfitzner's *Palestrina*. Again Schneider-Siemssen designed the scenery, excelling himself with a tremendously impressive hall for the second act Council-of-Trent scene. Robert Heger, old friend and colleague of Pfitzner's was the conductor. Fritz Wunderlich sang the title role with great success after strong persuasion from Hans. They had known each other since the Salzburg *Schweigsame Frau* in 1959, but Wunderlich was still doubtful about undertaking Palestrina which had previously been sung by older, famous artists. Otto Wiener was Cardinal Borromeo, Sena Jurinac appeared at Ighino, Christa Ludwig as

181

Silla. *Palestrina* calls for an amazing number of leading male singers — one of the reasons why so few opera-houses can perform it — and here there was a regular stellar rollcall: Gottlob Frick as the Pope, Walter Berry as Morone, and Gerhard Stolze, Walter Kreppel, Peter Klein, Gerhard Unger among the other parts. It is interesting to see that the three angel voices were those of Mimi Coertse, Lucia Popp and Gundula Janowitz. At some of the later performances Hans himself sang Borromeo and Anton Dermota Palestrina. *The Times* critic particularly praised Hotter's direction of individual singers and the handling of the milling crowd before the council session.

In 1966 he was off to Zürich where he had first sung in a *Walküre* performance under Clemens Krauss as far back as 1941. Now it was to produce *Tannhäuser,* the season's first new production, with Hans Hopf in the name part. Also that autumn, he went to Dortmund to direct a new *Fliegende Holländer* production. This was the beginning of a very happy association which continued with a new production each season for four years. Dortmund's opera might not have the great artistic standing of Vienna, Munich or London, but it possessed what was in many ways more important to Hotter, a permanent company and a stable artistic policy. It was in fact nearer to the ensemble operahouses in which he had worked before and during the war, offering an opportunity to carry out extended rehearsals with soloists who were not only available but accustomed to working together. The musical director of the Dortmund opera Wilhelm Schüchter conducted all four operas so that there was a continuing unity in the work.

I went over to Dortmund for the opening performance of the 1966 *Holländer* and was immediately impressed by its dramatic qualities and the scenic effects, especially in the first and last acts, and at the very end when the masts and spars of the phantom ship formed a cross in the sky, symbolic of the resurrection of Senta and her redeemed Dutchman. The designer was Paul Haferung who had all the facilities of a very modern stage, the new Dortmund city theatre having been opened only a few months before, and had been more or less affectionately nicknamed 'the eggshell' on account of its great curved concrete roof.

Howard Vandenburg was an aristocratic, mystic Dutchman, admirably contrasted with the earthy Dalard of Günther Morbach, and Maria van Dongen was a moving, spiritual Senta. All were members of the regular company.

The following year came *Lohengrin,* designed by Hainer Hill with an oriental flavour inspired by the Japanese Nö-Theatre. Schüchter was conducting again, Maria van Dongen sang Elsa, Vandenburg was Telramund and Karl Ridderbusch, later to become a famous international Wagnerian bass, sang King Heinrich.

For the 1968-69 season Hotter tackled something entirely different: Werner Egk's *Die Zaubergeige,* a fairy tale piece about a magic violin. Years later he said that he had enjoyed the work on this production more than any other, and at the time one German critic described his production as being clothed in a silken mantle of poesy.

His last production for Dortmund was a *Tristan und Isolde* at the beginning of 1970. In this he sang King Marke and at a performance which I saw several months later Wolfgang Windgassen made a guest appearance as Tristan, but otherwise it was a moving ensemble performance, marked by clarity of direction and a touching human quality in the lovers' ecstactic passion, something which is not always expressed.

Two years earlier, other productions had occupied him in both Vienna and Hamburg. In February 1968 there was Strauss' *Die Schweigsame Frau* at the Vienna Staatsoper, not a new staging, but using the scenic framework designed by Teo Otto for the Günther Rennert production in which Hans had sung Morosus at the Salzburg Festival more than eight years earlier. But the work here was completely new: this opera had to wait thirty-three years for its Vienna première. There was a certain piquancy in the event, because the opera was well known in Salzburg, Munich, even London before it came to the Austrian capital, but late as it was, it was well received. Silvio Varviso conducted, and Oskar Czerwenka sang Morosus.

A few weeks later, on Good Friday 1968 Hotter's only production of *Parsifal* opened in Hamburg. He does not himself feel that this was a success, for reasons which he discusses later in this chapter, but for me when I saw it a few weeks later it was an exciting experience. I was accustomed to the Wieland Wagner Bayreuth *Parsifal,* a production which was Wieland's unquestioned masterpiece — incredibly beautiful, mystical, a profound spiritual experience. I had also seen the Herbert Graf-Adolphe Appia *Parsifal* in Geneva and some less than perfect performances in London.

Hotter's production with decor by Rudolf Heinrich was immensely dramatic. Writing of the performance, I said 'Not everyone will like it. On the other hand those who have boggled at the quasi-religiosity which has grown up round the opera will be delighted. This *Parsifal* is not a rite. It is a drama with a deep religious significance . . . Hotter sets *Parsifal* in its mediaeval background. During the prelude to the first act a curtain shows fragments of an ancient manuscript. This rises to disclose a vivid tableau of Gurnemanz and the young squires of the Grail. Light and colour are everywhere; for a moment it is like the simple, colourful grouping of figures in a Christmas crib. Then the drama begins to unfold.

'Instead of a nameless, almost faceless crowd of indeterminate beings, the knights of the Grail are individuals, members of one of the great mediaeval orders of chivalry. In the last act they wear monkish habits, but in the first they are all dressed differently, as nobles, priests, squires. They are men like all others, but striving to remain true to their dedication, and sorely tried by Amfortas' withholding the sacrament. He also is a man, paralysed by the pain of his own sin. Parsifal is a man, learning compassion on the bitter road of experience. These are far more than symbols.

'In the same manner the flower maidens are neither fairy dolls nor a corps de ballet; they are the concubines of an eastern potentate's harem — as accepted in the Middle Ages. In the days of the Crusades evil was identified with the world of the infidel, and here Kingsor in his claustrophobic chamber of mirrors is an eastern magician.'

Hotter sang Gurnemanz at some performances including the one I saw. Richard Cassilly was a fine Parsifal, Theo Adam a moving Amfortas, Irene Dalis an exciting, human Kundry. Leopold Ludwig conducted with feeling if not greatness. Whatever Hans and others may say, I shall long remember that Hamburg *Parsifal*.

For the 1968 and 1969 Bayreuth Festivals Wolfgang Wagner invited Hotter to take over the production of his brother's *Ring* cycles. Wieland Wagner's second *Ring* production was first staged in 1965. By then his artistic development had passed from the stark simplicity of the early '50's to a dramatic symbolism which often did violence to his grandfather's instructions, initiating a fashion for changing the balance of the characters, and down-grading the gods; this has been carried to extremes by later producers in more recent years.

After Wieland's death his *Ring* was supervised by Peter Lehmann in 1967. Wolfgang had plans for a new *Ring* of his own which was given at Bayreuth in 1970, but for the two intervening festivals he handed over the direction to Hans Hotter.

This can have been no easy task. Wieland's work was the most talked of aspect of Bayreuth, and there were passionate feelings both for and against his innovations among the regular public. It was not a case of taking over former sets and creating a new dramatic vision within them; Hans had known Wieland well for many years, valued his help and inspiration and admired much though not all of his work.

In these *Ring* productions he adhered scrupulously to Wieland's overall conception, his decor, symbolism, and most of his stage directions. Hotter added to, rather than changed the whole. For he brought to it his own gifts of enhancing the characters, of helping each individual artist to create a living being.

The result was a very definite enrichment of the meaning of the great saga. Where Wieland's later work had tended to make the characters puppet-like in the development of the story, symbols rather than people, Hotter's hand reinstated them as people, mortal or immortal, and thereby released in the artists concerned and the audience the personal meaning and poignancy of Richard Wagner's music. There was a marked difference in the Wieland Wagner - Hotter *Rings,* but it was a psychological one, not superficially apparent.

It was also in 1969 that Hotter undertook another production of a former staging — this time it was *Arabella* in Vienna. Claire Watson sang her first Vienna Arabella in these performances. Eberhard Waechter was the Mandryka and the conductor was Berislav Klobucar. Again it was the personalities in the story who came through to the audience, more naturally than in any other *Arabella* I had ever seen. They were real people, expressed both dramatically and musically, touching one in sympathy or with laughter with their loves and stupidities, their idiosyncrasies and the sparkle of the Strauss-von Hofmannsthal collaboration.

Then back to Wagner and the mantle of Wieland with the Paris *Walküre* in the autumn of 1971, the production which was to be the setting for Hans' Wotan farewell in the following summer. It was also the ending of that particular production decade, but without the finality of a farewell. In the years that followed there have been

186

other offers. In 1981 he accepted one, *Fidelio* at the Lyric Opera in Chicago: Hans had always wanted to direct *Fidelio* and derived a lot of pleasure from this production which had Johanna Meier in the title role and Jon Vickers as Florestan. I saw it and found again his particular gift for the inner life of the characters and dedication to the intentions of the composer. Hotter may well appear as producer again.

His own views on his producing career are relaxed, regarding it as a sort of sabbatical from the serious life of a musician.

'Producing was something that I had always had in mind, like conducting. Because I studied music conducting was always a cherished dream — something I would love to do. Today it is almost obligatory for a leading singer to conduct! But I think one cannot do everything, though I still cherish the idea of it.

'It was the same with producing, and in a way I am glad that it never became a whole time occupation for me. I often say to students: if you do not find that you are able to succeed as a professional singer accept that, but keep singing as an extra part of your life - for love of it, for fun, almost as a hobby. Often they are hurt and disappointed when I have to say that, but sometimes they come back later and thank me. You can enjoy an art without ambition.

'I suppose producing was rather like that for me. It was not necessary to make a big name in it; to compete with others. There were two reasons why I wanted to produce, and perhaps they were not the usual ones. They came from my experience on the opera stage; from the inside so to speak. I wanted to help singers who were not born actors, and I wanted to present operas in a way that was faithful to the composer and librettist's intentions.

'I had so often felt and said that producers do not go enough into the personal side, the individual needs of

37. With Anja Silja in *Die Walküre*, Florence 1963 (courtesy Foto Troncone, Naples)

their artists. People — very kindly! — do not believe that I was not a good actor when I started, but it is true. I had to learn. And I have always believed that there are a lot of singers who are never "developed" as actors. When I began there were house producers who worked with a regular company and got to know the members' special gifts and weaknesses and could bring them out and help them develop their performances. Now there are few really experienced house producers of this kind. No one cares very much. I felt that I could help singers with their complexes because I had shared them.

'Then of course I had been disappointed in the artistic way that opera was staged in the early years, as compared with the musical performance. I wanted to see if I could overcome the wooden, stereotyped methods of acting by working more closely with the singers. Now producers demand so much, and have little time for working with indivuduals. I thought I could help them with technique and the best way to appear natural on stage.

'But I never really tried to become a producer. The offers came to me and I accepted — some of them. I have never tried to find productions. When the offers came I suspect I accepted partly because of my pedagogic tendency. My mother called me a born schoolmaster! Certainly I love teaching now.

'Wieland Wagner when we got to know each other better urged me to try producing, and when the London *Ring* was offered to me he said — of course you must do it.

'Then there was fidelity to the work. It was often said that I was too conservative, too much a singer-producer, which is already a mild rebuke . . . But it was not that I could not think in modern terms but that I feel one must be loyal to the composer, both to what is implicit in the music and what he actually writes as directions in the score. Wagner was himself a producer. He knew exactly what he wanted his audience to understand, and it was to convey this musical drama not only to musical critics but to the ordinary public that he conceived the form of the *leit motif.* There was a very simple dramatic reason for this, really. Wieland was insistent about his grandfather's wishes, at least in the early years.

'When I was first offered a production I was not sure whether I could cope with the technical side. I thought I could deal with the psychology of the singers, and there would be no problem with the conductor. But how to handle the chorus, the lighting, above all the discussions and planning with a designer?

'The failure of the Hamburg *Parsifal* was due to not following through my intentions. I was over-ruled by the designer Rudolf Heinrich, who was a famous man but who was definitely going a different way. I should have managed that. It was lack of knowledge on my part. I was lucky in London, Munich and Vienna to work with Schneider-Siemssen who is a friend of mine and we were able to collaborate very closely together with a good level of understanding. Somehow this did not happen with Heinrich. Later I talked to Günther Rennert and he said, "but why didn't you talk to him?" I simply did not know how to convey my own conception.

'At the beginning it was a new challenge: that was the main thing. When the Strasbourg offer came, I took it. That was the first experiment. Then in London when I started, that was nice. The singers began to ask my help. When I came to producing there it gave me enormous satisfaction and joy because I felt — here is something new, different from what I had done for so long and a practical opportunity to use and develop my experience of working with Wieland Wagner. Most of the artists were accustomed to the old ways and I could try to bring in the new. And my colleagues, Birgit Nilsson, Windgassen, Thomas Stewart and the others were all very helpful; and Solti too. That is the background of how it all started.

190

'But as I did more producing I came to realise more and more the importance of ensemble, which I had known in all the companies with which I sang in my early career. Today you really only find it in the smaller opera companies. You may have less splendid voices, certainly less famous artists, but you have more interested people who want to learn. Practically speaking you have these singers always on the spot. In Munich or Vienna nowadays leading singers are constantly away. A famous producer may insist in his contract that the singers shall be present for all rehearsals and the administration must compel them to be there. But you often feel their minds are far away.

'That was why I did so much at Dortmund, four productions during a span of four years. It was a permanent company and there was good co-operation between us all. I very much enjoyed the work there, and of all the operas I have produced I think the one which I enjoyed the most was Egk's *Die Zaubergeige* at Dortmund. You may or may not like the work, but it has so much charm and there is scope for working with the many smaller parts. Producing it is like preparing for Christmas — very often most of the pleasure is in the work you do beforehand.

'Although not a permanent ensemble the company for the 1981 Chicago *Fidelio* had the same integrated working atmosphere in the rehearsal time, for example in the discipline and interest of the artistic administration, the chorus and all the backstage staff.

'Today there are few permanent ensembles who can do this real preparation, and most house producers are occupied with revivals of other people's productions, but theirs is a job that counts for very much.

'Operas are now chosen with no relationship to a company and cast with guest singers. In the past the conductor-producer-designer triumvirate would say — what can we put on with the singers we have? I remember very well in the Clemens Krauss days at

Munich saying to him once, "Why cannot we have an *Otello* here? That is what is lacking." And Krauss replied, "My dear friend I would love to do it, but there is not a suitable tenor in the house and I cannot produce an opera with a guest in the main part." Then you built up a repertory to suit the ensemble, and the alternative cast could be present at the original rehearsals. There were great singers within the ensemble; today as artists come to the top they also come out of regular companies because of high payments and economic pressures.

'Everything is so different. I do not say that it was better then, but the difference is so great that one cannot compare producing conditions. There is almost an obligation for someone who has known both to point it out . . .

'Perhaps the singer-producer is a link. He has the advantage that other singers know he will never be against them, which can happen — or the singers feel it happens — with producers from the straight theatre or film work. Film makers are the most dangerous, especially with inexperienced singers. That made it easy for me.

'But the public is suspicious of singer-producers. They say that he becomes a producer because the voice is going down. Which is often true. For me it was not so much that the voice was worse as that I had more time, and the opportunities came.

'People often ask me why I did not go on producing regularly. There were various reasons. One was the lack of ensemble companies. I enjoyed the work in London where we had some continuity, and the Munich *Holländer* and Vienna *Palestrina* in particular. Munich and Vienna were my "home" operahouses; I had good co-operation from the administration and a high quality standard and financial backing. The results gave me a lot of satisfaction. But in general I do not want to work with guest artists who have sung the same role in five or six productions in the past three years. They get so bored. It is like the film companies where you either have a daily contract in which case you want to work as many days as possible, or a total fee when you want to do as little as possible. It is almost the same in opera now. Guest singers never want to rehearse much, and they put in other performances during the rehearsal time for more money.

'Secondly there is not enough time to build up the conductor-producer-designer understanding. The work gets done, but there is little real chance to get to know the other two-thirds of the team.

'I think the main responsibility of the producer is to the author, especially when he makes his intentions clear as Wagner and Strauss did. But the modern fashion is to work away from the author, to make the work attractive in an entirely different way. The more you do that, the more "in" you are. But if one is true to the work one has to accept the lack of inspiration in this sense in some productions. I do not think one has the right to make major changes.

'Of course some of the old fashioned accretions and mannerisms of acting and staging should go and have gone. Wieland said that the old stilted acting was not attractive, and he was right. And there were some things which had particular unhappy associations for him. Back in 1952 he said, "As soon as I hear the C major chord in *Meistersinger* I see the Nazi flags flying. And when I see conventional *Meistersinger* productions I see tins of Nuremberg *Lebkuchen*." There were political and commercial connotations which spoiled for him personally the traditional approach to that work.

'Because of all these changes, not of style but of approach, I did not have any great enthusiasm to go on producing, although there have been various offers. Partly, too, because you have to know more and more technical things which really have nothing to do with the artistic work.

193

'But I enjoyed it all. The work in London was particularly interesting. I learned so much there, not only about theatre work but about human life, of the people of a different country. To understand the English mentality was most informative! On the continent shouting is something you come to accept, and an emphasis on minor problems is something you must live with. But in England you discover that you get better results from quiet speaking! For emotional people this is a good thing to learn. On the other hand when people hold back because they are not supposed to show their feelings, they may also do it so as not to expose themselves. If you show too much interest someone may accuse you later. It's clever, and it serves a double purpose. It is better not to overpraise, because so often the one who praises may have to rebuke later.

'Vienna is the opposite. People are easily enthusiastic and also quick to condemn, sometimes cruelly. I once said to Clemens Krauss, "I know you are devoted to your old imperial city, your fine, cultered Vienna — but look at these reactions and attitudes!" And he said "I know. You do not need to tell me, but you must understand. The city — the people — of Vienna are like volcanic earth. Plant a dry stick and very soon it grows and blossoms. But the weeds grow tremendously too, and very quickly. You have to take both."

'Krauss had a vivid way of expressing things and he was so perceptive, but sometimes you will also get very perceptive comment from unknown people, members of the chorus, stage hands, carpenters, painters. Mostly they do not talk much. Many of the chorus are disappointed about their careers, the dreariness of their lives, belonging to a group where no-one is a person in their own right. Praise from them can mean much more than from a leading conductor who just wants to be kind. There is no reason why they should flatter you, so when they tell you you have done well it really means something. The stage hands and craftsmen are very knowledgeable too. Often they could earn more money elsewhere but they love the theatre, and would rather work in this wild zoo of ours!

'It is very important that a producer should understand all these people, not just the principals. I think a good producer always reveals himself in the way he works with the chorus. Some producers are good with single actors, understanding the psychological counterpoint and so on. Some are good with chorus movements. But it is possible to understand both.

'A certain gift is needed in working with a chorus because they are always primarily suspicious, not jubilant. A crew of people; they have a lot of passivity. They are not eager to do anything. They wait. Cautious; a bit quiet. To treat them as a group is very important in one way, but I think it is most important to see the individuals who have artistic ambitions. It may be just self assertion. But treat them as individuals. Give them what they can afford, or are able to do. *Give* them something as persons, not just as a group you need for something. Then you will get great co-operation from most of them. There will always be a few who will not respond. A conductor finds the same thing; there are always a few in each orchestra who are aggressive, "against", and want to do as little as possible and get the most for it.

'The supers should also be treated in the right way. Sometimes they are much more interested than the soloists! In other words you need to understand quite a lot of psychology. It never works to treat people as a group or a type — "tenors are like that, so lets do this with them".

'I found that I could make these human contacts, but there are also dangers for the singer-producer. People say he only wants to train singers in his own interpretation, or he is only interested in his own type of voice. I used to say — do not imitate me. I can offer you several possibilities in playing this part. Depending on your

195

own appearance and gifts you can do things in a different way.

'Work with the artists is more or less the same with new productions and revivals, though the latter are less rewarding as far as publicity is concerned. But revivals are often more rewarding for your own sake. Apart from the fact that the producer has to know how far he must keep the basic ideas of whoever has done the original production — for example in Wieland's Bayreuth *Ring* — and how much he can do to bring in the new cast, what he must teach them of the original ideas, then it becomes the same, but without the work with the designer.

'People asked why I did these revival productions which they thought so unrewarding, but I said — I don't mind. It gives me a good chance to work to know more about the opera and about how people behave, and all that.

'Now that I have finished my active singing career I can look back more objectively to the work of many famous producers. I had not the chance to work with the big names of today, Jean-Pierre Ponnelle, Götz Friedrich, or Patrice Chéreau. But during my operatic life there were, among others, Oscar Fritz Schuh, Rudolf Hartmann, Günther Rennert and Otto Schenk whom I rate highly. Their work, with all their modern concepts, was still rooted in the composer and librettist's inspiration. There was still respect for the original.'

PART FIVE
Lieder Singing

If producing was a challenge, a variation of art, and an opportunity to hand on the fruits of his own experience, lieder and oratorio singing have provided Hans Hotter's own greatest personal joy as a musician. In these the human voice is used more completely in the service of pure music, without the distractions and sometimes the banalities involved in operatic stage performance. All through his professional singing career he retained some reservations about opera. Probably nothing gave him more happiness than the steady development of his lieder recitals through the fifties, sixties and right on to his *Winterreise* in 1976.

It was a return to one of his first loves in music, going back to boyhood. Long before there was any thought of his becoming a singer or even a professional musician he was introduced to the great German classical songs in the homes of his friends in Munich. It was an intimate introduction; the natural family circles where people met together for the simple pleasure of making music, the development of the early childhood evenings of folk songs with his father into the realm of a classical art.

Looking back, he feels that he owes it first of all to Cilla von Cornides, the mother of that school friend who brought Hans to his home as early as the high school years. The house itself had a musical heritage, belonging to the Oldenbourg family of publishing fame. Brahms had been a visitor there at musical evenings, and the young Richard Strauss with his wife Pauline and some of his early songs were first heard there.

Cilla von Cornides was a daughter of the Oldenbourgs and had inherited the house. Under her influence Hans first discovered the beauty and magic of this

Three modern roles: 38.   Becket in *Murder in the Cathedral*, Vienna 1960 (courtesy Fayer-Wien)   39.   Moses in *Moses und Aron*, Frankfurt 1970 (courtesy Günter Englert)   40.   The Schoolmaster with Kerstin Meyer in *The Visit of the Old Lady*, Munich, 1975 (photo Sabine Toepffer)

particular form of music, and he learned it not from the clinical perfection of modern recordings but in the warm human atmosphere of live amateur performance where technical shortcomings were accepted in the sheer enjoyment of singing and playing, of experiencing songs for their own sake.

In such an atmosphere it was natural for anyone with musical gifts to take part. And it was in Cilla von Cornides' home that someone said, 'This seems to be made for you, as you're musical.' When he decided to take singing lessons with Matthäus Roemer, the practical reason that Hans gave himself was that while it would be a valuable part of his training as a musician, there was also a personal factor — 'to sing lieder well, that would be something.' Not as a professional, but for the sheer joy of it.

And for that Matthäus Roemer was the ideal teacher. He was himself far more an oratorio and lieder singer than an operatic tenor, and although he believed that Hans was destined for the great Wagnerian roles and taught and groomed him for that future, he believed very strongly that the precision, the sensitivity, the fine focus of lieder singing is the best possible training for real understanding of the singer's art on the broader canvas of opera.

So the young Hotter in fact did much more study in the realms of lieder and oratorio than opera in those two intensive years' work with Roemer, not despite but because Roemer saw his future on the operatic stage. An attitude which Hotter instils in his own teaching of students today.

At the same time his personal love of this branch of music took him to professional concerts and recitals. He heard all the great lieder singers of that time who sang in Munich, and he remembers them still.

Then his own first professional appearances were in the framework of concerts. It was Hindemith's oratorio *Lehrstück* in Munich which led to his contract with the

Troppau opera, and a year earlier he had had his real baptism of fire singing in the *Messiah* in the vast Passau cathedral.

But those auspicious beginnings were also the end of concert work for a long time. 'Life is real, life is earnest' and, paradoxically as it may seem to many people, the reality and hard work of having given himself to the career of a professional singer meant for Hans Hotter setting aside his personal musical preference and the respect which were given to lieder and oratorio. He had to learn a large repertory of operatic roles, he had to learn to act, he had to settle into the life of a theatre ensemble and it took all his time and energy. Then as now a young unknown singer had small chance of making a living on the concert platform. His teacher knew he had the gifts for a great career in opera. He got the chance to start at Troppau and graduated through the other companies to Hamburg and Munich.

More and more in the light of the existing situation today he has valued those formative years when he was part of an ensemble, even though it meant an undivided allegiance. Each year he came back to study with Roemer, when he returned to lieder singing in his lessons. Roemer insisted on its importance both for voice and technique, but at that stage there was no real opportunity to put his lieder singing into professional practice.

He gave a lieder recital in Passau, another in Troppau and in the Prague years he sang one or two concerts of mixed lieder, but there was no time to concentrate on developing this side of his music. Already he was typed, 'rubber stamped' as he would say, as an operatic dramatic baritone. He hardly ever even had the opportunity to go to the lieder recitals of other singers.

His chance came quite unexpectedly at a private party in Salzburg in 1940. The Austrian conductor Meinhard von Zallinger was a guest at that party. Someone said to Hans 'You should do lieder singing,' and more or less

202

on the spur of the moment Zallinger suggested that they should try a few songs out of *Die Winterreise*. They did, Hans with no preparation, but the experiment prompted Zallinger and others present to suggest a concert.

Together with von Zallinger he gave his first *Winterreise* recital in Hamburg on November 14, 1941 and the results came quickly. Rudolf Goette, the concert manager who represented Gieseking and the famous 'cellist Gasper Cassado among others, approached him and offered a contract. Here was proof that an experienced businessman of the musical world took his potential seriously, and Hans was impressed.

Two months later in January 1942 he sang his first Munich *Winterreise,* and repeated it the following October, each time with von Zallinger as his partner at the piano, and they worked together on a number of occasions later. That same winter, December 1942, he gave two more *Wintereises* in Berlin with Michael Raucheisen as accompanist.

At the age of thirty-two Hotter was launched on another very important part of his musical career, and also another personal identification with a particular work.

If the whole of his operatic career with its wide-ranging repertory from Don Basilio to Scarpia and from the Flying Dutchman and Gurnemanz to Schigolch is still overshadowed in the public mind by the spear and majesty of Wotan, the fame of his concert singing is coloured by his mastery of Schubert's *Winterreise.*

Apart from those early concerts, this, perhaps the greatest of all the song cycles, was his debut as a lieder singer. Thirty-five years later it was his farewell to public lieder singing at a memorable performance in one of London's ancient livery company halls, that of the Fishmongers' Company, with Geoffrey Parsons at the piano. Between those two dates he took it to most of the continents of the world.

And he added a typical Hotter postscript to his

Winterreise career when in the summer of 1982 he was invited to take over two performances of the cycle at the Austrian Hohenems summer festival in place of the indisposed Peter Schreier. Hotter's voice was in amazing form, his art and technique greater than ever, and he sang with evident joy to enraptured audiences. Franz Endler writing in Vienna's *Die Presse* paid a long and serious tribute to the importance of Hotter's performance in its own right, not just as a happy legacy of the past: and his headline 'The old Lion with new power' was a phrase borrowed from Hans' now famous student Robert Holl, who was also singing at that festival.

He has sung the cycle in public performance one hundred and twenty-seven times, and recorded it four times.

The first of these with Michael Raucheisen was recorded in 1942. Next came one with Gerald Moore in 1955. Then in 1963 he recorded it again, this time with Erik Werba. Finally, and perhaps the most vivid and profound of them all was a *Winterreise* recorded at live performances in Japan in 1969 with Hans Dokoupil at the piano.

The winter journey of Wilhelm Müller's sombre poems and Schubert's incomparable music proved a triumphant one for Hotter, even though to some extent it bound him in fetters similar to those of Wagner's god. The concert public wanted Hotter in *Winterreise* or *Winterreise* with Hotter, and even when they protested that they would like to hear him in something else, the power of this identification still haunted their consciousness.

Because of this he intentionally avoided singing a *Winterreise* in Vienna for twelve years, between 1961 and 1973; yet when he gave it there again one of the critics said it was always a great occasion to hear Hotter sing lieder, but if only he would decide to give us something different from *Die Winterreise* 'which we have heard only a year or two ago'!

This kind of identification is a penalty of superlative art, and though, especially in London, critics often felt it de rigueur to complain of the necessary transposing down of songs originally written for high baritone voice, their praise was genuine and deep.

As far back as 1952 Dyneley Hussey writing in *The Listener* under the heading 'A Great Lieder Singer' said '. . .only great genius could have transformed such a series of verses into great music, and only a great singer could, even then, persuade one to devote an hour and a half to the contemplation of such unrelieved depression. . .For the rest his singing was most deeply moving, and I know not whether it was more moving in the communication of those chill rays of retrospective sunshine that are the only high lights upon this wintry landscape . . . or in the numb and twilit madness of the end.'

Many of us who saw and heard Hotter sing *Winterreise* many times in many lands would echo those words and one American critic's staccato 'tremendous' after a New York performance in 1954.

As with his operatic impersonations no two performances were ever quite the same. With unfailing art each occasion seemed less a repetition of a masterpiece than a new spontaneous creation in the living response between singer, pianist and audience. Hotter eschews the word accompanist, giving equal honour to the partnership of voice and piano. More than thirty different pianists shared *Winterreise* with him over the years, and this of course partly accounts for the variety of inspiration and expression.

Two of Hotter's dicta were illustrated in his *Winterreise* performances. One was that, although the concert singer cannot move about or use gestures, he can and must act with his face as well as his voice, but with considerable subtlety. As the tragedy of the rejected lover unfolds in the songs, his face would reflect all the emotions of despair, remembered joy, self pity, bravura and at the end a quite terrifying madness.

The other is that the singer can be either subjective or objective in his presentation. He can actually identify himself with the character, or he can reveal him with the knowledge and compassion of the creator of the work, as a storyteller. I have heard Hotter sing the cycle from both positions, as it were, and I think he is right when he says that the second is probably the better of the two. Perhaps it is because the central character in *Winterreise* or any other song of this genre is too engrossed in himself to belong consciously to his surroundings. When the singer stands outside the character he is more closely identifed with the flow of the pianist's accompaniment. Together they show us the unhappy and egocentric hero, both as he feels and as he is.

It is interesting to look at the geographical pattern of Hotter's *Winterreise* during those thirty-five years. By far the greatest number of performances, between forty and fifty, were not unnaturally given in his own country, Germany. Japan had an impressive total of thirty-nine performances over a period of twelve years between 1962 and 1974, and it is as a concert singer that he has been known and so greatly loved there. His only operatic performances in Japan were those few *Tristans* during the Bayreuth visit to Osaka in 1967.

Austria heard eighteen *Winterreises*, Britain fourteen and he has given one or two each in the U.S.A., Canada, South America, France, Denmark and Australia. But the tremendous impact of this particular cycle must not obscure the very wide range of composers and their songs which he has performed in concert halls and on record. There were many other Schubert songs, the lovely *Im Frühling, An die Musik*, the deeply spiritual contemplative *Im Abendrot* — all these and many others, including the *Schwanengesang* cycle will remain in the listener's memory as definitive interpretations.

In Schumann too he seemed a part of the music. I first heard him sing the *Dichterliebe* at a concert in London in 1953, and his *Ich grolle nicht* haunts me still.

Then there were the Loewe ballads, *Edward* and *Erlkönig* being two of the most memorable in his hands, bringing out all the Hotter gifts of drama and expression in the different voices of the characters. But it was not all gloom and anguish. There was the delicious child's warning in *Die wandelnde Glocke* and the tongue-twisting *Hochzeitslied* which would set a whole concert hall rippling with laughter.

Wolf was always a favourite with him, and the *Michelangelo* — *lieder* figured in many of his programmes; my own preference was for the humorous philosophy of love in *Nimmersatte Liebe*, and the striding, open-air rhythms of *Fussreise*. Strauss was a composer whose songs he sang with special love and understanding, which he received from the creator in person. Most people who attended Hotter recitals will have heard him sing *Ach, weh mir unglückhaftem Mann*, but probably fewer know his way with the gravely beautiful little *Ich trage meine Minne*, the setting of a poem by Karl Henckell where an older man sings of his bliss and reverence for a girl's pure love in the midst of a dark world.

From Brahms's *Ruhe, Süssliebchen* to Schubert's *Doppelgänger and Loewe's Hinkende Jamben* lie a whole gamut of emotions, but Hotter made them his own, or rather made himself theirs. In all of them it was the blending of drama or emotion or narrative with the voice of music itself which held the listener spellbound, the artist introducing his audience into his own discovery of the beauty and meaning of each song. Sometimes the depths are profound, the heights elysian, sometimes the piece is just a delicate fantasy which must not be overloaded with meaning or subtlety which the creator did not intend. Others are simply a bit of fun. Hotter always seemed to have an unerring judgment about the particular value of each song, born of his equal love for the words and the music.

Some well known singers will distort the musical line

in their emphasis of drama or anguish. This was never so with Hotter whose love for the melody and the pure music of the composition never became stale. He seemed to say to his audience — listen to this, is it not beautiful? Or enchanting, or deliciously funny? Share it with me. The great voice which could ride Wagner's elemental orchestration was scaled down to a concentrated piano which had behind it all the power, volume and range which we had heard in some of his operatic roles, and with a wonderful variety of colour.

Most composers of songs have chosen to write very largely for the higher voices, sopranos and tenors. Sometimes they may have had a specific singer in mind, but one reason may be that the theme of so many songs is youth — young love, or young grief, and the higher voices suggest youth to the listener's ear. It is a convention in lieder as well as in opera.

Among men this presents difficulties and limitations in performance if the composer's keys are adhered to strictly. There are always fewer tenors than baritones and basses, and a smaller proportion of them are of the calibre for superlative lieder singing. In any generation the number of great tenor lieder singers is very small.

Far more baritones seem to become famous in this field but I do not think it is simply a matter of ratio in the type of voice. Despite the composers' predilection for tenors or very high baritones the deeper voices, by the very nature of their instrument and range, often possess a greater ability to colour their singing in mood or feeling; there is a greater scope for interpretation in the finely focused miniaturist art of the song. This is a personal opinion, but one which I think is shared by many concertgoers. But where lower voices adopt songs written in higher keys there is inevitably the vexed question of transposition.

Critics like to have something to be critical about, and this provides an admirable and perennial field for controversy. A critic may say that Mr X the tenor gave an admirable performance of certain songs in the keys in which they were written but lacked something of the fulness of expression which Mr Y, who is a baritone, finds in them. Or one can say that Y sang the songs superbly, but it is a great pity that for his voice they had to be transposed down which spread an unnecessary gloom over them and a rumbling darkness to the piano accompaniment. Much newsprint has been filled over the years with this kind of comment and in the absence of the composer himself the decision must remain one for the musical judgment of the singer and the acceptance or rejection of the public. The fact remains that there are more famous and successful baritone lieder singers than other voices.

Hotter himself feels that it is very much a matter for the individual.

'I think transposition is a questionable thing, but basically I feel that a singer should be allowed to transpose. It depends on the individual's artistic taste and sense to know what he should do — like a producer's in following the author's intentions. Then of course there is the question of whether this is a woman's song or a man's. That is mostly easy to determine, but sometimes it is for your own taste and intelligence to decide, and a woman can often say — I think I can sing this, despite the fact that it is written for a man. Success can prove the decision right. I think a real woman's song should always be left to female singers. A great many can be sung by both sexes. This is a question which always comes up in lieder classes.

'It depends partly on whether you are singing as the person in the song, or describing that person. It is important that young singers should consider this carefully, as some deny themselves a good range of repertory because of being too limited in their choice.

'For myself I always had this matter of transposition to consider. With *Winterreise*, though Schubert wrote it for a tenor-baritone I think it is more a bass key cycle than a soprano key one, though I have often been criticised for transposing it, especially in England! It was interesting, though, that when I found a way to brighten the bottom section of my voice those criticisms ceased.

'Perhaps with Schumann's *Dichterliebe* there is the possibility to have it done by either tenor or baritone. It does not present so many problems as Schubert's *Schöne Müllerin*. I have never sung the *Müllerin* because of this problem of transposing. In this case it destroys the character. The accompaniment becomes too low down. There is, I feel, more description of nature in the *Müllerin* then in *Winterreise*, especially the water; with the mill the water in the music is so important. In lower keys much of the life of this picture of nature is lost.

'Of course I have sung single songs from the cycle, but I never did it complete because I believe it should be sung by a tenor, or at least a high baritone. I would have loved to sing it, but in life there are always some things one must renounce.

'As I said, transposition is questionable anyway, and some composers have had very strong feelings about it. Hugo Wolf for example. I always felt to some extent bound by his well known insistence that his songs should be sung in the keys in which they were written. He was very strict about it. But I did not always obey him in that way. And I am glad that now the Hugo Wolf Society has begun to bring out a complete edition of his songs transposed for middle and lower voices, as has been done for Schubert and Strauss. I this this is right; why should the lower voices be denied so many songs? Although the original key chosen by the composer will probably always be the best.

'I have always had a great love for Wolf. In my opinion he was the first song writer to feel an obligation to the poets, the poetic word. In his case it was more than that — an adoration. We all know, it has so often been written of him, that he really composed his music to bring out the beauty of the words.

'He went round reciting poetry among groups of his young friends and according to the success he had with the recitations he would choose which poems to set to music. He loved the words so much.

'It is interesting to compare him with Schubert in this respect. Schubert did not have the unification of music and words to the same extent as Wolf, but that was not his fault. In Schubert's time some seventy years earlier there was not the interest in poetry in connection with music that came later. It was Schubert who started that. But it is interesting that it was Wolf who went right back to classical poetry, while Schubert took the contemporary verse of his time, whether it was of a high standard or not. He was not a very learned person, his genius lived outside and beyond intelligence and he took in the dramatic impulse of the modern writers of his day. He was of course much closer in time to Goethe and Schiller than was Wolf. Schubert was born only about fifty years after Goethe, but he still chose poets who were his own contemporaries, and his power to express the dramatic strength of words is amazing.

'Wolf on the other hand was moved by the inspiration of earlier times, and the quality of his choice was extremely high. Only for a very few of his early songs did he choose poems that were less than good. In the past — thank God not now — Wolf was often accused of writing mediocre music. Many singers are not keen on him, and I must admit that it was not the beauty of the music that first drew me to him, but his enormous gift for using the natural diction of the language in his songs. You can almost recite them in the same rhythm as the music. I always make my students recite the words of a song before singing it.

'Wolf was there, deep in my love for music always. He appealed to the musician in me because for him there was no "singer and accompanist" approach. The importance of the piano part is so evident that one knows from the start that this is a partnership.

'You cannot sing a Hugo Wolf song without being musical. That is a general statement. A lieder singer should if possible try to be an opera singer and vice versa. Certainly one finds that an opera singer *can* be good at lieder, but not always. More often the lieder singer can succeed on the operatic stage. The difference seems to me to be that an opera singer has less responsibility. In an opera there are other singers, an orchestra, conductor, costumes, make-up, lighting, acting: all to create one whole performance. Your responsibility as a soloist is of a different kind, to be part of a team. You are a link in the chain.

'On the recital platform the singer has to carry at least fifty per cent of the total responsibility, and you can also choose what you want to do and how you do it. In opera work, very often you have to do what is written into your contract, and what the conductor wants.

'There are certain things you cannot compare. This may sound rude, but an opera singer can be very successful even if he has only average technique, is an average actor, an average artist — provided he has a really beautiful voice. It is the voice that does it, and as long as the singer knows how to use it he can get to the top without being great in other ways.

'The lieder singer must be a musican. The technique is the same but in lieder it is more detailed. The power of imagination, your sense of fantasy, taste, intelligence to grasp the quality of words, all these are so important. As an opera singer one cannot always be interested in the quality of the story. No one will expect that of you! But in lieder even if the poem is nothing very special, the composer is able to raise it with his music. The singer must be interested in it.

'The singer and his partner at the piano have to create the whole story. It is often thought, quite wrongly, that the recitalist must be as immobile as a church chorister. Simply because you cannot move about and gesticulate

41. Hans Hotter, 1976

does not mean that you cannot convey drama. You have a story to tell, and you have to make up for the absence of acting and orchestra and all the rest. It must all be done musically in a concentrated way, and in a few minutes; with interest and power, or pathos or humour, and with intensity and dramatic challenge. That is why it is so good if a lieder singer sings opera too, because he has the experience of the broader canvas, he knows exactly what has to be controlled.

'Control does not mean to cut off a part of the power or volume. It means — have it but do not show it. Have the dramatic power and the emotional intensity but make it effective in a concentrated way. In order to understand that you have to sing opera.

'By performing under Wieland Wagner's direction at Bayreuth I learned how important diction is in acting. The best kind of modern opera acting is a good exercise for lieder singing. Again, the modern opera performer learns from the concert platform that he can create a character without running about and being exaggerated. It works both ways.

'Films and television teach one about economy of movement too. I found that in my early film work, and to a small extent in television though that came rather too late for me. You have to learn the meaning of control. In closeups if you move five inches you may be out of focus. Nowadays they are skilled at correcting that sort of thing, but a good film producer will teach you how much can be expressed in the face. You do not have to move continually. That is very similar to the effect you use in lieder singing.

'One of the most interesting things one learns is programme making. Should one stick to a single composer for a group of songs? Probably one should, anyway usually. Should there be serious songs in the first half, lighter ones after the interval? Or should the whole programme be mixed, changing quickly from mood to mood. This is something which is always a good discussion subject for a class, and something for young singers to learn.

'As the artist becomes a famous name he may actually have less freedom of choice; the music may have to be at least partly what the public wants to hear him sing. Sometimes a singer will say — I choose only by my own sense of artistic responsibility. But artistic responsibility can be a dangerous phrase. Once a singer becomes well known he may also become egotistical, and other people will be afraid to advise him.

'The singer certainly has a responsibility, to the composer and so on, but he may end up overrating his own judgment. There is also a service to the audience which must be balanced with one's own artistic integrity. There is a much more personal and direct responsibility in concert work.

'Designing a programme is most important. I say to students — try to find your own limits. No one will tell you when you are famous. Don't be too narrow, but learn your limits.

'I myself would have loved to sing Hans Sachs more often — the part of parts! — but I had to realise it was something not completely written for my voice compared with other roles. For me to sing *Die schöne Müllerin* would have meant transposing it so far that the music would be damaged. That is what I call acknowledging limits. Therefore to know what to sing. That does not always mean adher to rigid rules. There are times to step out, to experiment, to venture into something different.

'The choice is very wide, even when one is considering only the most famous composers of songs. Schumann ranks among the great ones, and Brahms, Strauss, Pfitzner, Mahler. Its hard to say one is better than another. A composer lives not only by what he does but by what he is, his personality. There is great personality with all those who have written classical lieder. There are songs of Schumann which no one else could have written. He had a special gift just as Schubert had in his own way, only Schubert's range, radius is larger. But they were essentially different. Schubert had the gift of continually giving birth to anything that was music with almost no limits. Schumann although he wrote a lot of other music was less all embracing in his approach.

'Obviously a singer who devotes himself to a lot of lieder singing has his own personal favourites, but these change from time to time. For example any singer who attempts *Winterreise* will have a favourite song, but I have found that over the years all twenty-four have been my favourite at one time or another. One's taste in composers and their works changes. It is not fair to single out one as a permanent favourite.

'Recently at a one-composer competition, where I was among the judges, I found myself wondering if we should be bored by hearing only one man's inspiration, and the same songs over and over again. But it was not so. The music was so attractive, and I noticed that often the other judges would murmur — now comes my favourite! We enjoyed the music as well as seeing if the young singers could live up to expectations. That one changes one's personal classification of favourites shows how rich is the composer's range.

'Strauss' songs of course mean a great deal to me because it was only with him — and Pfitzner — that I had the opportunity of being instructed by the master himself. That is an immeasurable privilege, and I realise it even more now when my students listen with such excitement to anything I can tell them of those composers.

'I had the chance to work whole programmes with Strauss in his house. And he would "mark" even with his 80-year-old voice in an incomparable way. He was very particular about what he wanted, very strict, but — and this was typical of Strauss — because he was so experienced and practical and had been a performer himself and had accompanied in concerts he knew that it is impossible to do things twice in exactly the same way. He himself would sometimes be different in the interpretation, and provided you were a serious musician he did not expect you always to follow his ideas slavishly. This is something very subtle which you cannot express or explain, but the fact that he himself varied emphasis or expression gave one the possibility to use a certain amount of one's own artistic judgment if it stayed within certain limits.

'Strauss used to say "Lieder is a different part of my life". But some of them, the *Four Last Songs* for soprano for example, are clearly very close to opera in a lyric way, and to me they should only be sung with orchestra. His special gift was his ability to characterise. Many of his songs which describe moods are built on a legato line, cantabile line, and they are the more interesting ones. Perhaps a link with opera.

'Everything he saw or heard found an inner expression in music for him. I once asked him why he was so fond of the card game skat. He said "for me everything sounds. Only at my age the transformation into the notes on paper does not always work as it did; so many of the melodies I have already written. It can be frustrating to feel the thing you want to do and not be able to do it. The only thing which does not 'sound' for me is cards. Its a great relief!"

'It made his songs especially interesting when he showed how to do them in different ways, and his vitality when he was already around eighty years old was extraordinary. As a young artist one was so impressed by his authority and the practical experience he could impart.

'Pfitzner the dreamer was quite the opposite of course. He was constantly unhappy because people had too human and imperfect an approach to artistic things. The music of Pfitzner is often on the same level of quality as that of Strauss, but in the way he put it on paper it seems more complicated. Strauss had the personal gift of making things seem easy; simple.

'There is a well known story about a time when Strauss visited a Pfitzner rehearsal. Strauss was genuinely impressed and afterwards said "Pfitzner you have done something really splendid here. You can be proud of it." But Pfitzner instead of being pleased with such a tribute from his rival felt compelled by his honesty to say "Yes, but I had enormous problems with the second act. I found it very hard." To which Strauss remarked "If you find it so hard to compose, why not give it up?"

'That was so indicative of the two men. Pfitzner was brilliant and serious, but always suffering and gauche. Strauss had the poise which appeared effortless. But both shared a passionate devotion to Wagner's music. For Strauss personally there were only two composers: Wagner and Mozart.

'Karl Loewe's songs seem to me somewhere midway between opera and most other lieder. The ballad is an intermediate stage between the two. It brings in the dramatic technique of various persons speaking to each other, quoting people. A great gift for characterising in different ways is needed, a very special technique. Ballads are most important and Loewe was a master of this form of composition. He devoted his musical life to it. Ballads may not always be the most exalted form of musical writing, but often they are the most telling. It is the simplicity which leaves room for the beauty of the words.

'As Loewe was himself a singer and accompanist the songs show an enormous knowledge of what you can ask a voice to do. What you can do with the words and diction, and what the piano can do, is to help create atmosphere in a similar way to that used later by Wagner. I would love to have sung more Loewe. He is often misprized.

'Looking back now I regret that I did not do more concert singing altogether. I am not complaining about what I was able to do and what has come out of it, but it would have been a joy to give more time to lieder. Those singers who can devote a good proportion of their time to lieder are lucky because it is more satisfying. I should not have wished to sneak out of the responsibility of being a link in the chain of opera performance, but a singer who is not just a voice but a musician with a love for making music is better off in lieder. There is no doubt about that, and I have proved it.

'To me it is a dreadful, a ghastly thing for an artist to say — I still have time for lieder singing when I begin to lose my voice. That is wholly wrong, and disrespectful to a very special art. Sometimes it is said without thinking, but the idea that a lieder recital is less effort is ridiculous.

'Perhaps from the point of view of sheer sound it may be more straining to sing a long operatic part, a Wagnerian role, but anyone who knows anything about technique realises that piano does not mean singing with half your voice but to sing with the whole voice in a more concentrated way. What one needs most is support — this concentration of air which is the living part of sound. You use this always, whether you sing piano or forte. So a recital is at least as intensive as singing in opera. Especially when it means creating a whole story in three minutes or less, and up to fifteen or twenty stories like that in the same performance. And then one is singing for one-and-a-half or two hours; very few operatic roles are so long.

'It is silly to say — you can easily sing the Dutchman or Gurnemanz on that date — *you have only a recital the day before*! But is was often said to me. It is true that it is better to sing the recital first because it needs everything you can give in your best form, and to attempt that immediately after an opera can be dangerous. But the effort and the concentration required are at least equal.

'Oratorio is something different; the instrumental

way of using the voice. I always felt very close to oratorio. Matthäus Roemer was a master of oratorio singing. He really knew, and had sung under great conductors. Being my teacher, and as much a musician as a singer, he could tell me the difference.

'I would say the way of using the voice instrumentally in oratorio is very helpful in lieder and opera singing. In order to find the line, think of oratorio and you will see the way.

'Then my first public appearances were in oratorio, Hindemith's *Lehrstück* in Munich when I was only twenty-one, and the *Messiah* at Passau.

'Later I sang the Christ in Bach's *St. Matthew Passion* many times in my Hamburg days, and I also sang in *Elijah* and the *Missa Solemnis* . Brahms' *Requiem* was always a great love of mine. There was not much chance of concert singing during the war. From 1940 to 1950 I was restricted in all fields, but particularly concert singing. I did a little more oratorio after the war but then it ended. Now I am sorry, as I am sorry that I could not give more time to lieder. But one cannot always know, or have the opportunities to plan a career as one would wish, and perhaps it is better not.

'There is also the link with opera. Handel's operas are very close to oratorio, and Mozart's *Requiem* and also Verdi's play an important part in relation to their opera work.

'Oratorio and the great choral works always satisfied my musical heart. I can remember vividly many that I heard in Munich when I was in my 'teens, especially a Ninth Symphony conducted by Bruno Walter. We did not live with radio and records then and certain performances stay with you for a lifetime.

'I suppose in a way it is almost a natural human consequence of being obliged to devote so much of my life to voices, my own and others, that I prefer what I call the honest, pure music without vocal part! When I am teaching it does not worry me, but when I am alone

220

and listen to music I avoid singing. Oratorio is a step towards absolute music, the real classical sound. And those oratorios in which I sang were all great classical music. It was for me real music making.'

PART SIX

Teaching

A BORN SCHOOLMASTER, Hans Hotter's mother had called him, half joking but with a clear perception of his nature, and he acknowledges it now in the same spirit. All the study, the delight in music, the triumphs of a long and brilliant career and the struggles, disappointments and anxieties which have been inevitable components of his professional life have found their final fulfilment in the role of teaching others in the service of music.

From the beginning Matthäus Roemer had urged him to teach as and when he could, knowing that to hand on any art or science one must focus one's own knowledge. The real teacher continues to learn as he teaches, not only from a deeper understanding of the subject but also of human nature in its diversity and complexities. There is the human bond but also all individuals are different, and at the simplest level Hotter always says that he often has to find different words, varying means of expression to bring a particular point home to students.

In the Hamburg period he already had a few pupils and this continued during the war years. Afterwards in Munich came the first Americans, members of the US forces or their relatives and friends. That was the beginning of many friendships and also brought home to Hans the importance of learning English really well. It was something to which he set himself with his usual thoroughness, aided by a remarkable trained memory and a musical ear. In England too his command of the language was a great asset, without which he could not have later undertaken production.

But his present bilingual fluency was not achieved at once. In the early days, after his first visit to the States, Hans asked Norman Feasey, Covent Garden's well loved musical coach, how he thought his English was progressing. 'Oh it's not bad,' said Feasey with a twinkle, 'only I notice a slight sprinkle of coca-cola in it!'

At that time he was also helping English singers, unofficially, with their German. Edith Coates, who had been a ready friend to Hotter in helping him to understand British ways and customs, asked him to correct her pronunciation when she was singing her first Fricka in German, and this gave rise to one of his favourite stories of her ready wit.

Fricka taunts Wotan for having equipped Siegmund with the magic sword, and adds 'Dare you deny it, when night and day I have followed at your heels?' — 'Willst du mich täuschen, die Tag und Nacht auf den Fersen dir folgte?' But the English tongue finds it hard to sound the difference between 'ch' and 'ck' and this irate Fricka seemed to say that she followed her spouse 'Tag und Nackt'. 'Edith be careful,' said Hans, 'because you may be misinterpreted. You are saying that you followed me in the nude.' 'Ah,' replied Miss Coates with perfect composure, 'not very advisable in this weather!' It was mid-winter.

On another occasion the positions were reversed. At a party Edith asked Hans if he had seen any shows while in London. 'Oh yes,' he said, 'as a matter of fact we went to see *Diamond Lil*,' and wondering how he should pronounce 'Mae West' decided to try a linguistic compromise. He murmured, 'Have you seen My Waist?' 'Unfortunately not yet,' said Edith Coates.

Between 1945 and 1950 Hotter always had two or three students who came to his house in Munich for singing lessons, both German and English speaking, and during his seasons at the Metropolitan he also gave lessons, some to well known American singers. Gradually more and more students came to him in Munich. One of his early successes was with the soprano Elisabeth Lindermeier who was later married for a time to

Rudolf Kempe. Hans supervised her first operatic stage development. She became a tremendously skilled singing-actress, and he always took a great pride in her successes with the Munich opera.

She also taught him something about himself. 'I remember when Elisabeth Lindermeier sang her first Butterfly, I was rather worried because I thought it was too heavy for her; prior to that she had only sung much lighter roles. Before the first performance I was helping her with her make-up and costume and trying to make things easy for her, but I was anxious. Years later she said to me "You know the reason why I was not so frightened before that Butterfly was that *you* were so terribly nervous! I almost wanted to laugh, but I had to fight to prevent you from making me nervous!"

'One always tends to worry more on behalf of other people. I hardly ever suffered from stage fright myself, unless there was a special cause, for instance if I had a cold. I used to see other artists round me suffering from nerves and that made me feel that someone on stage must be steady and quiet. But as on that early occasion with Lindermeier I still feel nervous for my students. I must say that some of them are very safe and reliable, but even today I often suffer for them when they give a performance much more than I ever did for myself!'

For a couple of years in the 1950s he did some teaching at the Munich Hochschule für Musik, though on a small scale with only a few students, and he gave this up because he had to be away so much that continuity was difficult, and he felt it unfair to young singers in the early stages who needed regular sessions.

The private lessons continued, however, with many coming from overseas. There were Australians even before his first visit there, and more afterwards, British, Americans, French, Japanese, Dutch, as well as Germans and Austrians. Two of his outstanding pupils in more recent years have been the Dutch bass Robert Holl and the Scottish soprano Margaret Marshall, both of

227

42. With Wieland Wagner
and Anja Silja, Naples 1963
(courtesy Foto Troncone, Naples)

43. *Left to right*: Mr & Mrs Ramonvinay, Hans Hotter, Kurt Adler
and Mrs Hotter on the twenty-fifth anniversary of the San Francisco Opera House, November 1979 (photo Ron Scheri)

whom return regularly for extra coaching and advice, as Hotter did with Matthäus Roemer through all the early years of his career.

In the summer of 1960 he was invited to be one of the instructors for a course at Aspen College in the USA. This consisted of private lessons with each of a dozen students, rather than class teaching, although there was a big weekly interpretive class, and the teachers themselves sang in the weekly concerts. He returned to Aspen for the same course the following year. The students were young professionals, American, Chinese, Japanese, and it was here that Hotter first started his discussion sessions.

Later came more master classes and courses through the '60s and '70s in Japan, Australia, Canada, in the USA at the Eastman School in Rochester, New York State, and in California, and in several other countries. For three years, 1971-73, he took a class at the summer school at 's-Hertogenbosch in Holland.

During the seventies he did much teaching in Britain at the Opera Centre, held a master class series for the Park Lane Group and worked with Scottish Opera and the National Opera Studio in London.

Curiously there were few invitations for regular classes or courses in Germany — apart from one in Berlin — until quite recently. In the 1982–3 academic year, he gave masterclasses at the Munich Hochscule für Musik, returning to the place where he had given a class twenty-five years earlier. Austria came into the picture early with a lieder class at the Mozerteum in Salzburg during the festival of 1959. That was unlucky because it had to be cut short owing to a leg injury he acquired during *Schweigsame Frau* rehearsals. Then in 1976 Hans was invited to take a lieder class in the Vienna Master Courses which are arranged by the Council for Intercultural Relations, and sponsored by the City of Vienna each summer. A number of his Dutch students came to Vienna to attend the course that year and it was a great success. With the exception of 1980 he has been one of the course leaders each year since then.

I have been able to attend a few sessions of these classes in different years, and to watch Hotter's technique with a variety of students, men and women from many different countries. Each has their turn to sing selected lieder. He asks them to explain first what they themselves see as the character and style of the song. Then he will comment on their performance, correct or suggest differences in technique or approach, perhaps singing a few bars himself and often adding a story or anecdote, giving fresh insight into the particular piece of music or the composer. After that the rest of the class, some of whom attend as observers, not as singers, are drawn into the discussion. Their criticisms or comments are an integral part of the class work, helping the performer of the moment and deepening their own knowledge. The whole has a deceptively informal atmosphere. It is really like the professional performer's art which conceals art, for an immense amount is taught and learned in these friendly, relaxed sessions. When there is a short break, individual students come up to the teacher to discuss a particular problem or to ask him to elaborate on some point mentioned.

The three weeks of intensive work ends with a public concert given by a selected number of those who have taken part, but before that there are other wholly relaxed occasions, as for example when Hans and his students go off together to Grinzing and spend a typically Viennese summer evening, eating and drinking together at a *heuriger*.

The very first of these courses in 1976 led to Hans' most important teaching appointment. Rumours of the success and standard of the course filtered through to the authorities, and as a result he was officially invited to become a professor of singing at the Hochschule early in 1977, an appointment which he held for five years. Today his busy teaching life includes regular visits to

Vienna, and there are other annual lieder classes at summer schools in Austria. One of these is a class for American and other English speaking singers which is part of a major series of classes given by well known musical teachers such as Elly Ameling, Brigitte Fassbaender, Irmgard Seefried, Kim Borg and others, and held at Baden near Vienna each summer.

With the development of his work in classes and special courses came invitations to act as a judge at a number of singing competitions. He has served as a member of the jury at competitions organised by the ARD radio in Munich, at two of the Benson and Hedges Gold Award contests at the Snape Maltings, and at various specialised competitions in Austria, but he does not really agree with the competition concept.

'I have ruined my reputation as a judge, I think, because on various occasions I have made it clear that I do not believe very much in competitions, and the way they are handled. I do not think the system can work properly.

'For example one may ask for the competitors to be "mature and ready for stage and concert work" and also that they should still be developing. This seems to me to be an impossible demand. You give prizes for development, but you cannot expect people who have had no experience to be ready for the stage. That is a discrepancy in itself.

'Then there is the choice of judges. You have classes for opera and lieder and you have judges from different countries in some of which there is almost no lieder singing. You may have one judge who is excellent for opera but if they have no real experience of lieder how can they judge the subtleties between the songs of Wolf, Schubert, Mozart? It seems so silly. Certainly variety in a jury should create a happy medium. But the mixture can cause problems. Mostly the judges are famous singers, some of whom will have passed their peak as performers. You have conductors, perhaps musicologists, singing teachers who may have had no career of their own as singers. They may have had great experience as teachers, but that does not necessarily make them good judges. Then there is the difficult position of the president of the panel of judges – I have been put into that office!

'There is also the fact that most of the judges teach themselves. Sometimes they are not permitted to judge their own students; sometimes it is allowed. There are always liable to be harsh feelings in one way or another. Occasionally there are even political influences.

'Why I am not happy about competitions is that there are clever contestants who know how to hide their own flaws. Sincere ones are at a disadvantage. Adjudicators are human. You cannot always judge totally impartially. Some competitors have a personality. Others you cannot fault, but they make no impression. So the judge must have a personal, subjective opinion, but that means that a clever, superficial competitor may impress even experienced adjudicators. I speak against myself here, because sometimes when I was not on the jury I was very successful with my students, and they have proved their quality. But mostly competition prize winners do not become great names later.

'There have been a few notable exceptions of course. Jessye Norman and Ileana Cotrubas both won first prizes. But there are a great many competitions. Where are the winners? There are very few that one hears of again.

'Competitions must not be overrated. Some are known for being very hard to win, others for being easy. Some are overpaid in the prizes. And whatever the standard there is always the danger of the winner becoming self-important. If they come first among two hundred contestants some of them think themselves a king of kings, and are absolutely ruined for professional work.

'I tell my students — enter a competition more to see

who and what is on the market, than to expect that the judgment will be a criterion of real quality. Try to be prepared for the fact that you may not be judged properly, for many reasons. There would not be so many prizes if there were more quality! Sometimes the entrants are of high standard, sometimes it is difficult to find enough merit to give the prizes at all. Then so much depends on the singer's quality and vocal condition on the day when they sing. They may do well at the first session, badly at the second, but still get into the finals when they may be at their best again. Or they may make a bad start and get knocked out at the beginning when they could have done much better. Singers have to learn to try to maintain a constant professional standard, but that depends on experience. Very few young ones can achieve that, especially with the nervous tension of a competition. The result is that the whole thing is very much a matter of luck.

'The same thing is true of auditions. Singers are not accepted simply because they do badly on that day. I am very much against auditions too, but you cannot do without them. You may possibly be able to do without competitions.

'Teaching singing is something quite unlike other musical teaching. A dead instrument is different. You have to bring it to life. You put life into a violin or a piano. The organ is nearest to the human instrument because of the air in the pipes, but it is still dead.

'With a voice you project much more because it is alive. It is a way of transmitting emotion, and is much more direct and natural than when an artist conveys emotion through the playing of a dead instrument, however great an artist he may be.

'Air is the carrier in all the media of expression in ordinary life. It is used in any emotional projection: a gasp of surprise or a sigh of relief. You push it in anger or excitement, you sob in sorrow, you hold your breath in fear. When you are excited the breathing becomes

233

shorter. Air is such a vital element in expression. Voice is the most direct projection in the artistic world. It is a direct projection to the listener, and here personality is more important than with a dead instrument. But it is also harder to make the congruence between the artistic intention and the result.

'This is partly because the singer does not hear himself in the same way as the audience does. Everyone knows that most people are surprised — sometimes shocked — the first time they hear a recording of their own speaking voice. It is even more so with singing. I may think I put my emotional feeling into the voice but the result is completely different. You can record it on tape and then you will hear it acoustically, but there is much more than that.

'From a tape you may correct yourself if you are flat or sharp, if you are wrong in rhythm, even to some extent wrong in colour — not assimilated. But in some ways it can be dangerous to work from your own recordings. You will never hear your own voice live as others receive it, because of many factors: sheer sound, vibrations, the direct result not only of what you do in sound but what the hearer receives. It can be dangerous to listen too much to your own recorded voice. You have to learn what its effects are in relation to what you hear yourself from inside, and how to control and recognise its expression. It is very hard to control in this way. Most people, unless they are psychologists, have trouble in controlling and recalling emotional expression of this kind.

'That is why it is so important that when a singer starts to learn, he learns to teach. To be able to express and understand. And for the basic technical things. Just as the painter needs to know how to mix paints. That is not art, but a technical requirement of art, and it is the same with the technique of singing.

'Even the use of technical words and expressions can be confusing because not all teachers give them the same meaning. For example there is the well known term "cover". A singer has to cover the voice, or he has to darken it, or he has to widen the throat. Some teachers say, "You may cover, but you must never widen the throat". But in fact all these expressions mean exactly the same thing. It is simply a stupid, childish fight about words. I hear it so often when my students come for auditions. They have been confused by being told — this, yes; that, no — about the same thing.

'Therefore it is very important to know about technique, how it works and why, and for a young singer to be sufficiently secure, whenever he starts as one of a group under a conductor in some small company. That can be good, or it may do harm. It is very important to have enough knowledge of the craft first to control and correct your own singing.

'By teaching — or in discussion — you have to name, describe, express things which may otherwise remain unformed in your mind. That is a great help. And one of the reasons why singing is so different, so difficult to explain is that so much of the instrument is hidden. Like the iceberg, only about one-sixth of it is visible!

'Learning to listen to one's own voice is very important, and very few singers know how to do it in the right way. When I am learning to teach as well as to sing, I am listening to the good and bad things with the teacher, and that trains my ears to listen to what *I* am doing. When I am teaching the student expects that I sing it to him — that I show it to him by voice.

'What makes a good teacher? So-called good singers are certainly not as a rule good teachers; in fact it happens only occasionally. I think one must have a real feeling for teaching, a love for it, to be successful in imparting one's own knowledge and experience to others. The fact that a person is a successful singer does not mean that he can teach. Some of the lucky ones have so many natural gifts, everything is so well co-ordinated and like nature that they do not have to do very much.

235

They still have to know how the voice functions and where it comes from, but they will have little understanding of others who are not so well endowed. Those who have had great problems and overcome them are perhaps more apt for teaching.

'Many of those who study singing do so simply to become teachers, not to perform themselves. Voice teachers can often be excellent without having a very good voice. But young people are more likely to trust someone who has been successful. They think — if my teacher has been successful for thirty years then there is a good chance that his technique is sound. But they do not always realise that not all can hand it on. A fine voice or even good technique is not always proof of being a good teacher. It is tremendously important that a young singer should be able to trust his teacher, and that the trust is not misplaced.

'There are many reasons why a singer may take up teaching, and they are not always the right ones. It may be just to make money. It is much better if a teacher does not have to do it out of financial necessity. Or it may be to prolong his own career in the musical limelight. Some just try to make their pupils copy them. Then there are those who were not themselves successful. They may become critics or teachers, and that is dangerous because they do it out of frustration. They may think that because they did not succeed themselves they must teach their students to do things in a different way, and they get things mixed up. There is an unnatural approach.

'When you go to an instrumental teacher you can hear yourself whether they are good or not. A young singer is mostly not able to judge whether his teacher is good or not if the teacher is no longer singing professionally or has never done so, having been simply a teacher.

'Some teachers are good with some people. Very few are equally successful with all types because the personal understanding is so important. But I think it is a mistake to limit the range too much. There are those who only take students of their own type of voice, or of a psychological type.

'Often young singers want to imitate their teacher. There is nothing wrong with that, but there is a difference between whether you imitate because the teacher is a good singer or because it is his system, "I show you the way you must do it." As in producing, the teacher should help the student to be a thinking, creative artist, not just a copyist. It is the style, the taste which should be handed on.

'The singer must learn not to be wholly dependent on a teacher, or on a conductor for that matter. Furtwängler used to say "You are waiting too much. You are waiting for me to give cues. I am not giving cues. You are to come in, and I come with you. I want you to take over!"

'Then again there are some teachers who are best with pupils at different stages of their musical development, just as some parents are at their best with the children when they are very young, or in the school years, and some who come to the closest understanding with their sons and daughters when they are grown up. In the same way some singing teachers are wonderful for the elementary stages. Others are very good for interpretation and style, how to do things, how to express, and perhaps less for technique. Others specialise in the professional singer's periodic check-ups: like those who come from time to time as one goes to a doctor to see that all is well. Famous artists who do this are the most difficult to help because they are not accustomed to listening to themselves. If you tell them there is something wrong they may be affronted, almost angry, until they realise that there is something they lack, which may be quite small.

'After my first Munich *Siegfried* Roemer wrote to me, very pleased, but adding "I hate to be a Beckmesser, but have to tell you one or two things. . ." They were things

44. Hans Hotter, San Francisco 1979, at the twenty-fifth anniversary celebration.

I had not noticed at all, but afterwards I was grateful to him.

'No two voices are exactly alike, so no teaching can be stereotyped. For those who are lucky enough to find the right teacher, it is better to have only one. The majority of students have more, perhaps four or even five in the course of their training. Some may run from one to another, which is not good. Its a matter of temperament. Some are always mistrustful. Some have had bad experiences. They are very difficult to help because you feel right away that they do not trust you, which is quite understandable if they have been unhappy with others. One of the first things to be impressed on a beginner is the importance of finding the right teacher.

'I was very fortunate to have found Matthäus Roemer or rather that he found me. He was the ideal teacher for me, and I had no other, apart from the short spell of special coaching with Rudolf Bockelmann; though I learned a lot from colleagues and famous singers in the years when I was young: watching them, listening to them, knowing them. Roemer said "to learn you must teach, and you must listen." He guided me as to where real art lay: "listen to *her*, but not to him . . ."

'Wilhelm Rode was a great idol of mine in Wagner singing, so was Friedrich Schorr who sang in Prague while I was there, Jaro Prohaska, and of course Bockelmann. Later I heard that someone had asked Bockelmann why he had recommended me for Hamburg where I could be a rival to him, to which he replied "To be a rival he must beat me in my art, not just the voice. If he wants to beat me he must do it as a personality. But if he is a personality, he is himself, and not a rival!" I always thought that was a very wise and interesting remark. It should be the answer to professional jealousy.

'I had another valuable insight into the need always to go on learning and listening from Richard Tauber when he was singing some guest performances in *Dreimädelhaus* by Heinrich Berfe in Prague. He used to come regularly to the opera and sit in the artists' box and I asked him once why he came. He said "You always learn something. What to do and what not to do. You see things you do yourself."

'I always try to help my students to have this kind of approach to singing.

'To be a good teacher you must enjoy teaching. Apart from any gifts you must love it, more I think than with other musical teaching because of the need for so much psychological understanding. First to help the student to find the balance between self confidence and insecurity. Not to be too conceited. Many young singers are lucky enough to be fairly successful in their early years. Then there is a danger that they think they know everything. Others do not have this quick success and one has to help them to know that it is not a fault, and it may even be an advantage in the long run. It is not easy for those who have the opportunity to go ahead quickly to know how fast they should try to develop their career or how long they should wait. Especially today when many people are forced to make decisions early.

'In my own case the fact that there was no money, and that my father had died had an enormous influence on me and on my career. That was why I started so young. It could easily have gone the wrong way if I had not had a wise teacher, and good luck with the contracts and the conductors and colleagues with whom I worked.

'Today young singers have more help, more schooling, more scholarships. The internationality of the singers' life is quite helpful and competitive, but there are dangers because in all fields, not only in music, people expect to get to the top very young.

'When I started there were very few foreign singing students in Germany, today there are hundreds, especially Americans and Japanese. Many of the German singers resent them, but it is better for them to know what is on the musical market, with whom they will have to compete for places in opera companies or in the concert world. Not to take things for granted.

'Everything is on a bigger scale now. There are more opportunities but also more problems in starting a career wisely, although the singer's personal training does not change. The student has to learn this and to see both levels, and not lose faith in what they can do. A great part of the teacher's task is to help them understand themselves in this context, and the fact that average or just above average musical gifts can be just as successful, with the right approach, as the great voice. As Clemens Krauss said, given basic talent it is hard work that counts. That may sound old fashioned, but I find many students are ready to listen and to accept this.

'A good balanced sense in the approach to life is very important. Contrary to the public's idea of artistic lives it helps tremendously to be methodical, but on the other hand one must not take everything too seriously. A sense of humour is an enormous asset, especially the gift of being able to laugh at oneself. That prevents self pity in the bad times.

'Many young singers say, "if only I had this or that." I try to remind them that there are disadvantages in anything. They see other students who seem to have everything, a gift for acting, personality, poise, and so get good chances. But that may not result in real and lasting success.

'Some develop quickly but never really mature. I learned that myself. I used to see them in the companies where I began, where they were so polished and I felt so clumsy and discouraged. But in fact many had only superficial skill. They did not go any farther. Often the slow developers are the ones who go farthest and last longest.

'It is important to learn to be critical in the right way. To assess the gifts and skills of others, and to see faults and recognise the same faults in yourself. "Ah, thats how it sounds," or "that is something one should not do!"

'It is not enough just to admire a great artist; those who are going to be a professional themselves must learn to understand what and why they admire. Most of the time there is personality present, and this comes partly from the singer's whole experience and development in life, not just from within his career.

'There must be a consent between the basic approach to things in your private life and what you do professionally. I think this is easier for women than for men, because by a woman's nature her private and public life are almost always more closely integrated than is the case with men. Generalisations are dangerous, but it is very rare for a woman to live a professional life without her personal life entering into it, and vice versa. The effect can be both good and bad from the artistic point of view. When things are unhappy in private life, she may throw herself into her professional vocation with much greater intensity, bringing to it her own deeper emotional understanding. When things are very good at home she may be so content that she takes less interest in her art. Sometimes the reactions are just the opposite, but either way it proves a basic difference of nature between men and women. I always say a man's professional and private lives are like parallel lines, one or other is ahead, but they do not cross each other. They can be combined in some ways but they are treated separately. With a woman the lines are concentric circles and either the profession is in the middle and the private life round it looking inwards, or the other way round.

'Women never do anything in one of these fields without letting the other come into it. That can be good because in many ways it gives them a much more natural approach to bringing personal experience and understanding to professional work. There is less discrepancy. This means that they can bring their own natural personality into the service of their stage or concert work.

'Personality also helps in succeeding as a teacher, not only his or her public personality as an artist, but also in gaining the trust and confidence of the student, for without that trust and confidence you can do very little for them.

'There are so many things about himself that the singing teacher needs to consider before he takes it up. The decision eventually to teach should be made early, even if it cannot be put into practice until much later, but if it is delayed there is time to judge oneself for the task. Is one really made for it? It is a great responsibility, for a bad teacher or the wrong teacher can do great harm to the young singer's voice or technique, or their whole approach to a career.

'Often you have to try to erase former mistaken teaching in a student's work before you can begin to help them develop in the best way for their own gifts.

'I think I am better fitted for working with students who have already mastered the elementary stages. This means that you work with people who need improvement either by adding certain things, or trying to eradicate some faults or problems. Each one is different. Some come as if to a doctor with a specific problem, but it is much better to treat them when they are "well" rather than wait until trouble appears.

'One throat specialist said to me, "If only you singers would come to me when you are completely well I could see what your throat really looks like!"

'That is of course true for the teacher too. Some of the problems are psychological rather than physical. Some people come to you after a disaster, when the voice has failed completely or something like that, and they cannot regain confidence. When they come for an audition I ask them if they have any problems. Sometimes they say no — either they are not aware of them or they do not want to own up. Others have nothing but problems! Some just come for a clean-up. Some say, "I only want interpretation not technique," while another will ask for technical help. Its a fairly wide psychological field, and of course very often they do not recognise just what they do need. That is where the teacher has to diagnose and help them to see what — if anything — is wrong.'

'There are different kinds of framework for teaching, all of which I enjoy. Each has its own value and they are complementary to each other. Many students take part in them all.

'The first is private lessons. Here I can of course give the most individual attention, and I concentrate on the person. First I have to find out what he needs, what his interests are, where I can help and how, what needs to be corrected, what I can add or what I must subtract. That is the starting point, and if we develop a good understanding we can then work together regularly or from time to time, building up the young singer's personal musical character, technique and expression.

'Second is the regular class in a musical academy such as I had at the Vienna Hochschule. Auditions are held at the beginning of the academic year and then we work together regularly right through the student's year or years of study there. This means we all get to know each other well. There are individual lessons and at these I quite like to have listeners present — unlike private lessons in my home — because the listeners can learn and sometimes contribute. In the general classes we have discussion, so that it is not just my own comments and corrections.

'The third group consist of master classes, special lieder or oratorio classes sometimes devoted to one or two specific composers. These are specially organised courses, sometimes part of a large musical summer school, and the students are often drawn from many parts of the world. They may last for only three or four days, or as many weeks. Some of the students may be private pupils of mine or come from a musical school, but many will be strangers to me and to each other, so there is a different often constructive challenge in getting to know people and establishing a creative community in a short time.

'It is particularly important that the students learn to talk about the whole meaning of lieder singing, for example, the influence of poetry on the musical side and vice versa. The importance of the piano part which is often neglected. How to treat the language so that it fits, and the special gifts of one or another poet or composer. It is a part of such courses to get young singers to develop their own musical judgment and know how to express it, as well as to sing better. It is also good for them to comment, constructively, on each other's performances, and to accept it themselves. It is the first remark that is important and they have to learn how to be positive without offending.

'I prefer lieder to opera classes because I think lieder is more interesting and more generally helpful in the singer's development, whatever form of singing he will take up. In my view classes devoted to opera are more difficult, less cohesive, because you always find many of the participants have special interests. Some are specialists in Italian opera, some German, others Slav, some in modern works. How can one form a unity among them *in a class*? And I believe the success of a class is team work. Therefore I am more enthusiastic about lieder classes because the participants have something in common.

'In my case it is of course natural to concentrate on the German Lied, and that covers a very wide range, the largest of all. My knowledge of French is not good enough for me to work with the French repertory of songs which others can do so much better. English is easier, and as far as the actual teaching and discussion are concerned in many of my classes we work in both

German and English because a lot of the students come from English speaking countries.

'One should always build on positive things. But there is a limit to the amount you can teach students in a short time. There is a point at which they do not hear any more. I can see it in their faces and I understand it very well because I can remember feeling like that myself. I could not absorb it all. That is the time to let them relax a bit. In the classes I often tell them anecdotes or stories of composers or artists I have known which they enjoy, though I do not do this so much in private lessons or they might think I was wasting time and their money!

'Often it is the students themselves who expect too much in a short time. The teacher's help is not like a medicine or an injection to produce an instant cure or transformation. Some things are caught in a week or a month, some will only show in their work a year or more later. One is taught something without fully understanding it, but it is there in the background, and long afterwards the teacher's meaning becomes plain. I have proved that so much in my own work, and my students today can testify to how often I refer to Roemer, how much I learned from him about teaching as well as singing.

'There are many practical things, too, to learn which are not strictly musical. The singer, especially the recitalist, has to know a lot about the audience, for the audience forms a living, reciprocal part of each performance. It matters what sort of personal impression you make; how you walk, how you stand, the way you behave, the way you hold your hands. Facial expression means so much for this is the only way you can act on the concert platform apart from with the voice, but it must not be overdone. There is style in this as well as in singing.

'The singer must win his audience. Once you have won them you can carry them with you. The choice of programme is very important. It takes about ten minutes for an audience to settle down and relax, to forget all the rush and problems of the everyday life they have left. Never choose a long song which needs a lot of concentration on the listener's part as the opening piece. Then a proportion of the audience will be hearing some of the music for the first time. It is the singer and pianist's responsibility and privilege to show them the beauty or splendour of it. A first impression may last a lifetime, and it can be good or bad. But it is equally important that the singer does not take himself too seriously.

'To appear effortless in singing and performance is one of the marks of a great artist; an audience will very quickly sense strain or insecurity and it worries them and spoils their enjoyment, but the singer has to accept that the more successful he is the less will people realise how hard he has worked to achieve it. It is a very silly assumption that famous singers are so gifted that they do not have to do anything, it just happens, but I suppose that is just the impression we must try to give.

'A few years after I started opera singing I remember saying to Matthäus Roemer "What annoys me is that people say — of course its so easy for you!" And he replied "You should take that as the highest praise. It is nobody's damn' business to know how much effort it took you to sound so natural."

'It was a part of his teaching that you should never use the whole voice, and that of course means that the singing should sound easy, free. Normally use sixty or seventy per cent of the voice, was his maxim. Occasionally seventy-five per cent, once eighty! Never more. Good orchestras play better when they do not go to the extremes of their volume. If you sing very loud the orchestra will play louder, but when a singer has a good concentrated piano, the conductor and orchestra will meet him.

'Pressure of time and money are two things which do

not help artistic development in any field. In the old days there was more time, or there seemed to be; there was a more relaxed atmosphere. In opera companies one never had a rehearsal on the day of a performance and very seldom on the day before. Now it happens sometimes that you are asked to rehearse an hour or two before a performance with some great singer who has flown in from another country. That is death to real artistic work, and it is impossible to develop anything like good comradeship, everyone is edgy.

'When I was a young singer we worked hard but we also had a lot of fun among ourselves. I remember once when I was at Hamburg several of us had a contract to do an Italian opera for the Frankfurt radio. We had a morning rehearsal which was scheduled to go on till one o'clock. Then we had to take a train, and there was another rehearsal when we arrived, in the evening. We wanted to take an earlier train because there was a friend who was anxious to play cards with us, but that meant leaving before noon, so we wanted to shorten the morning rehearsal. We planned an artificial quarrel. One singer accused another of making mistakes. The other said, "How dare you speak to me like that?" First one walked out of the rehearsal, then the other. We caught the train!

'We played tricks in performance too sometimes. There was a very charming production of the *Barber of Seville* which we did at the Cuvilliés Theatre in Munich, the smaller more intimate house. The public loved it. It was always difficult for me to be allowed to sing a comic role once I had become identified with the Dutchman, Wotan, Scarpia and so on, and Don Basilio was one of my favourite parts. One performance was on April 1 and as we did it in German with spoken dialogue instead of recitative it was possible to ad-lib a bit. In the scene where everyone is trying to get rid of Basilio and to their horror he keeps coming back, I beckoned them all to gather round me — that was part of that production — but instead of singing I just said "April Fool!" I had of course arranged it with the conductor beforehand because he had to come in, but no one else knew.

'Even in teaching there is this pressure on time, like the young singer's anxiety to succeed quickly and not be lost in the competition for opportunities. And there are the more actual, economic pressures too. A student may come from a distance for a series of private lessons. He wants to do as much as possible in a few days because of the cost of accommodation and the time away from his regular studies or his professional work. Then the teacher has a full schedule too. There is always a danger of pressure, of tension, and that is not good because real teaching, real learning is a gradual development, a growing of understanding and technique.

'It is an important part of the teacher's work to remove tension; to give the student a feeling of calm, wise guidance which makes him find strength and resilience in himself. But that calls for a certain kind of understanding and outgoing personality on the part of the teacher. Some have given up because they were too shy, too much afraid of the responsibility to show and to give the right kind of confidence and trust.

'There is, I feel, a shortage of individualists, of "all-rounders" today. Everyone specialises even in everyday life. No one is expected, sometimes not even allowed, to do anything except the job for which they have been specially trained. That does not help you to be a real person or to be self reliant. We used to sing all kinds of operatic roles which were within our own voice range — Wagner, or Rossini, operetta or Handel. It was good training and if one was specially well fitted for certain roles specialisation came later. Of course this all-round experience still happens in regular companies, but there is less of it, and young singers want to specialise early in the roles they study. They tend to be more earnest. There is not so much chance for a sense of humour to develop.

'I remember a number of musical "characters" at different times whom we all loved and enjoyed. One was a bass in Breslau who always used to "tune" his voice. He would walk into his dressing room, take out the tuning fork, put it down on the A, and run his voice up and down the scale — and in between he would call for his dresser, singing the name! He did it quite seriously. I do not know of any characters like that now.

'I would be the last to say that everything was good in the past. I think there are quite a few things that are more helpful now, but the musician from an early stage becomes a specialist. Before the real development of radio, recordings, television, people of all ages played instruments themselves, even if they played badly, they sang in choirs and choral societies, or at home. When they went to a concert they knew from experience what the artist was experiencing. Now they judge the performance from the impossibly high standard of hi-fi recording, not through their own struggles. The artist and especially the student is always conscious of that. You must win your audience by being more than human! That is disheartening for beginners. It is not fair.

'The public should not know too much of what goes on behind the curtain, so to speak, certainly the artist must not pass on his own anxieties or problems if he has them. That is not fair either. But the audience is a living part in the creation of a performance and therefore if they bring a personal experience of music making there is a real bond between performer and listener, a wave which goes in circles linking them and which the artist feels almost physically.

'That is something which the individual must discover for himself, you cannot explain it, but he will discover it if he has any gift for transmitting the essence and the love of music. The living contact with an audience may happen without your knowing quite what has achieved it, but the artist has to learn what is his own way of winning and holding an audience.

'Partly, this can come with age and some experience of people. I am not very much in favour of starting to study singing too young. It is not easy for me to say that, because when I do, people turn on me and say "You did it! You started to sing big operatic roles when you were twenty-one!" But I was very lucky, lucky in my teacher, conductors, companies, colleagues. I know now that it is not at all wise to start too early, especially for men. Women's voices are formed earlier, they grow bigger and more powerful but they do not have to change and start afresh as with the break in a male voice. It has been said that bass voices, and those below tenor, are not fully developed until the mid-thirties. I think that is perhaps going a little far, but certainly the development continues until about thirty-two years of age.

'Musical judgment comes with years, experience, thinking, both in the pupil and the teacher. Of course a person cannot become a great singer without certain prerequisites which have to be there and have to work. In addition you need complete command of technique and complete command of your own voice. You have to understand economy in its use, and to exercise this without people recognising when you are saving your voice. As I have said, a good average voice with full understanding of these things can often create a finer singer than one with an exceptional voice who lacks the stability of hard, painstaking work. On the other hand a "voice owner" who is not particularly intellectual can often learn enough to enable him to equal others who have all the gifts but do not know how to co-ordinate them. Much more is expected of singers now, in the way of acting and appearance for example, but this can be learned and, at least for opera, it can produce very good results. To succeed with lieder you must be a true musician.

'There is so much to learn that from time to time it

251

becomes bewildering for any student. That is the point when one says to a student — forget all the technical tools. Throw everything overboard and sing as you did when you were twelve years old! Then you will know how much has become an instinctive part of you.

'So often in teaching one has to take away rather than to add. To uncover the really splendid natural thing. Civilisation distorts, covers up; so does some teaching. It is like one of those beautiful carved wooden madonnas of the 15th or 16th century which you cannot see because some idiot has painted it over in the 1800s. It looks terrible, and then a restorer very delicately scratches and chips away the thick, crude later paint. Gradually the beauty of the original work, the inspiration of the carver's art, the glow and harmony of the old colours reappear. Teaching singing can sometimes be like that. A natural instrument can so often be wrongly used. But of course you do not always know what is there underneath, what is lacking. A lot of teaching must be of style, or to supply musical education if it is lacking or if it is wrong.

'Most of the worthwhile things in life are learned by experience. Sometimes one can pass them on and help others or save them from making unnecessary mistakes. In music much can be learned from colleagues, but not everyone will reveal his methods, like cooks, preferring to keep the recipe secret.

'I was blessed in Matthäus Roemer. He gave me so much that he had learned and proved, and I try to hand it on to my students through the experience of my own career. A singer who has been through all the stages, the ups and downs, the disappointments and the self doubting, and can still put himself back into that mentality of years ago, is better able to help those who are starting out. Especially if you tell them about your own difficulties. At school I remember that the teachers who said, "I too found this hard," were those we loved best.

'At first, if you have been famous students are very

252

apt to think — he was always a "god", always an idol, he never had any problems like mine. . . But we have all been young, we have all been overshadowed by former stars. I remember when I began lieder singing people used to say — "You will have a hard time to follow so-and-so."

'Just as the performer needs to gain the audience, the teacher needs to win students by being human, not weak, but having trodden the same path which they may be finding so difficult. When I read the book of letters written to Richard Strauss by his father, who was a practising musician, I found in it many of the things which Richard Strauss later told me.

'In the same way, looking back, I remember how often Roemer quoted what Jean de Reszke had taught him, just as I quote Roemer to my pupils.

'A past student of mine Brian Hansford, now head of the vocal department of Melbourne's musical conservatory became very interested in this genealogy of music teaching, and did quite a lot of research into it. Jean de Reszke studied with Antonio Cotogni, a great Italian baritone who sang at Covent Garden for more than twenty years up to 1888. Gigli and Stabile were other pupils of Cotogni.

'Brian Hansford writing to me after one of my master classes in Australia in 1974 had been struck by my own way with vowel-sound in singing, compared it with Gigli's singing in this respect, and traced both back to Cotogni! He sent me a quotation from E. Herbert Caesari's *Tradition and Gigli*, in which Gigli quotes Cotogni's words about shaping vowel sounds before utterance, and to my amazement I find I use almost the same phrases in talking to my own students. That is, I suppose the living tradition in music which is handed on, in person, from one generation to another.'

Silence fell in the big comfortable sitting room of the Hotters' home just south of Munich. A companionable silence in a setting of antique Bavarian furniture, large easy chairs, books, scores. At one end stands the grand piano open, awaiting the next student. On the walls are a striking modern picture with bold command of colours by Peter Hotter and a series of delicate medieval scenes painted on glass by Helga. On the table in front of us coffee cups and papers showed the passage of a morning's work, and underneath it Tucker the cocker spaniel snored gently, conscious of his right to comfort with no work at all.

Outside in the garden the swimming pool was under its winter shield and bright sunshine touched the snow-covered branches with the beauty of perfect simplicity. A handsome black and white bird with a russet swathe of feathers under the body — *buntspecht*, a variety of woodpecker — hung from a suspended net of nuts and fat, pecking in ecstasy.

'I suppose there is no one who does not think — who will succeed me?' said Hans Hotter thoughtfully. 'No one who is not vain enough to wonder who will follow him. Now I can look at it objectively, and enjoy and admire new singers. But I do not envy them.' He looked at his watch. 'And now comes the next hopeful one!'

'You do too much,' said Helga, with wifely concern.

He stood up laughing, towering above the domestic circle and looking remarkably young and vigorous. 'I am not always doing too much. And I have done too much so often in my life — why should I not do it sometimes now, when I enjoy it?'

APPENDICES

IMPORTANT DATES IN HANS HOTTER'S LIFE

1909	January 19, born in Offenbach-am-Main.
1929	First public concert, *Messiah* in Passau.
1930	First contract, Troppau Opera.
1931	Member of Breslau Opera.
1932–1934	Member of Prague Opera.
1934–1945	Member of Hamburg Staatsoper.
1936	Kammersänger City of Hamburg.
1936	July 7, married Helga Fischer.
1937–1972	Member of Bavarian Staatsoper, Munich.
1938	Sang leading role, the Kommendant, in world première of Richard Strauss' *Friedenstag*, Munich.
1939–1970	Member of Vienna Staatsoper.
1941	First *Winterreise* recital, Hamburg.
1942	Sang Olivier in world première of Richard Strauss' *Capriccio*, Munich.
1944	Sang Jupiter in 'première' dress rehearsal of Richard Strauss' *Die Liebe der Danae*, Salzburg.
1947	First performances in London.
1948	First season in Buenos Aires.
1950	Debut at the Metropolitan, New York, as the Flying Dutchman.
1952	First Bayreuth season, singing Kurwenal and Wotan.
1955	First Australian tour.
1956	Kammersänger Bavarian Staatsoper.
1962	First concert tour of Japan.
1964	Honorary Professor of Music, City of Vienna.

1966	Bavarian Order of Merit.
1972	June 29, farewell Wotan performance, Paris.
1972	Hon. Member of the Royal Academy of Music, London.
1974	Grosse Bundesverdienst Kreuz.
1977	Appointed guest professor of singing, Vienna Hochschule für Musik.
1978	December 10, farewell performance at Vienna Staatsoper, as the Grand Inquisitor in *Don Carlos*.
1979	Goldener Ehrenmedaille, Vienna.

REPERTOIRE OF OPERATIC ROLES

Composer	Title	Role
D'Albert	*Tiefland*	Moruccio
Beethoven	*Fidelio*	Pizarro
		Second Prisoner
Berg	*Lulu*	Schigolch
Bizet	*Carmen*	Escamillo
		Morales
Borodin	*Prinz Igor*	Galitsky
Cornelius	*Der Barbier von Bagdad*	Kalif
Dvorak	*Der Jacobiner*	Monk
Egk	*Die Zaubergeige*	Kaspar
von Einem	*Der Besuch der Alten Dame*	Teacher
Flotow	*Martha*	Richter
Giannini	*Das Brandmal*	Doctor
Gluck	*Alceste*	Herald
	Iphigenie in Aulis	Agamemnon
Goldmark	*Die Königin von Sabe*	Beal Hanan
Gounod	*Faust*	Mephistopheles
Handel	*Julius Caesar*	Caesar
	Joshua	Othniel
Humperdinck	*Hänsel und Gretel*	Father
Kienzl	*Der Evangelimann*	Johannes
Leoncavallo	*Pagliacci*	Tonio
Malipiero	*Julius Caesar*	Brutus
Mascagni	*Cavalleria rusticana*	Alfio
Milhaud	*Der arme Matrose*	Friend
Moniuszko	*Halka*	Janusch
Mozart	*Die Entführung aus dem Serail*	Bassa Selim
	Le Nozze di Figaro	Almaviva
	Don Giovanni	Giovanni
		Masetto
	Die Zauberflöte	Speaker
		2nd Priest
		2nd Armed Man
Mussorgsky	*Boris Godunov*	Boris
		Rangoni
		Tchelkalov
		Tschernjakovsky

Offenbach	*Tales of Hoffmann*	Four roles.
		Schlemihl
		Spalanzani
Orff	*Der Mond*	Peter
	Trionfo de Afrodite	Leader of chorus
Pfitzner	*Der arme Heinrich*	Dietrich
	Palestrina	Borromeo
		Morone
Pizetti	*Murden in the Cathedral*	Becket
Puccini	*Bohème*	Schaunard
	Madam Butterfly	Bonze
	Il Tabarro	Marcel
	Gianni Schicchi	Schicchi
	Manon Lescaut	Captain
	Tosca	Scarpia
	Turandot	Mandarin
Rossini	*Il Barbiere di Seviglia*	Basilio
Saints-Saens	*Samson and Dalila*	Abimelech
Schillings	*Mons Lisa*	Francesco
Schönberg	*Moses und Aron*	Moses
Smetana	*Die verkaufte Braut*	Krushina
		Indian
Strauss	*Arabella*	Mandryka
	Capriccio	Olivier
		La Roche
	Der Rosekavalier	Notary
	Die ägyptische Helena	Altair
	Die Frau ohne Schatten	Geisterbote
	Die Liebe der Danae	Jupiter
	Die schweigsame Frau	Morosus
	Elektra	Orest
	Friedenstag	Kommendant
	Salome	Jochanaan
Verdi	*Aida*	Amonasro
	Don Carlos	King Philip
		Grand Inquisitor
	Falstaff	Falstaff
	Macbeth	Duncan
		Macbeth
	Forza del Destino	Marchese
	Otello	Iago
	Rigoletto	Monterone
	Simon Boccanegra	Simone
	Sicilian Vespers	Montfort

Wagner	Das Rheingold	Donner
		Wotan
	Die Walküre	Hunding
		Wotan
	Siegfried	Fafner
		Wanderer
	Götterdämmerung	Gunther
	Der fliegende Holländer	Holländer
	Lohengrin	Herald
		King Heinrich
		Noble
		Telramund
	Meistersinger von Nürnberg	Kothner
		Nachtigall
		Nightwatchman
		Pogner
		Sachs
	Parsifal	Amfortas
		Gralsritter
		Gurnemanz
		Titurel
	Tannhäuser	Biterolf
		Wolfram
	Tristan und Isolde	Kurwenal
		King Marke
		Steersman
Walter Fried	Königin Elisabeth	Don Antonio
Weber	Euryanthe	Lysiart
	Der Freischütz	Eremit
		Kasper
		Ottokar
Wolf-Ferrari	I Quattro Rusteghi	Simon
	Il Segreto di Susanna	Graf Gil
Zillig	Das Opfer	Scott

OPERETTA

Adam	Blume von Hawaii	Stone
Kalman	Die Zirkusprinzessin	Zirkusdirektor
Millöcker	Der Bettelstudent	Officer

HOTTER PRODUCTIONS

1954 Strasbourg: *Siegfried.*
1960 Amsterdam: *Die Walküre.*
1961 London, Covent Garden: *Die Walküre* (new decor).
1962 London, Covent Garden: *Siegfried* (new decor).
1963 London, Covent Garden: *Götterdämmerung* (new decor)
1964 London, Covent Garden: *Das Rheingold* (new decor)
1964 Munich: *Der Fliegende Holländer* (new decor).
1964 Vienna: *Palestrina* (new decor)
1966 Zürich: *Tannhäuser* (new decor).
1966 Dortmund: *Der Fliegende Holländer* (new decor).
1967 Dortmund: *Lohengrin* (new decor).
1968 Vienna: *Die Schweigsame Frau.*
1968 Hamburg: *Parsifal* (new decor).
1968 Bayreuth: *Der Ring des Nibelungen.*
1969 Dortmund: *Die Zaubergeige* (new decor)
1969 Vienna: *Arabella.*
1970 Dortmund: *Tristan und Isolde* (new decor).
1972 Paris: *Die Walküre.*
1981 Chicago *Fidelio.*

DISCOGRAPHY

a) *Recordings on 78 r.p.m.*

September 1938, Berlin, 'His Master's Voice' (Electrola)
Die Walküre: Zweiter Aufzug, Erste und Zweite Szene with Marta Fuchs,
Margarete Klose
Orchester der Staatsoper, Berlin, Conductor: Bruno Seidler-Winkler
In Deutschland: DB 4599/4604
In England: DB 3719/28 resp. DB 8737/46 (Automatic) zusammen mit in Wien
unter Bruno Walter aufgenommenen Szenen
LP: E 80 687/88 (WCLP 735/36) Electrola, 1962

1942, Berlin, Deutsche Grammophon Gesellschaft (Polydor Meisterklasse)
Carmen: Euren Toast kann ich wohl erwidern
Bajazzo (Pagliacci): Schaut her, ich bin's (Prolog)
67854
Die Meistersinger von Nürnberg: Was duftet doch der Flieder
1. und 2. Teil
67855
LP: DL 9514 (Decca, USA)
Orchester des Deutschen Opernhauses, Berlin, Conductor: Artur Rother
Die Walküre: Wotans Abschied
1. und 2. Teil
67972
LP: DL 9514 (Decca, USA)
Die Meistersinger von Nürnberg: Wahn! Wahn! Überall Wahn!
1. und 2. Teil
67973
LP: DL 9514 (Decca, USA)

Staatskapelle Berlin, Conductor: Robert Heger
Winterreise (Schubert) Piano: Michael Raucheisen
68160/71
LP: DX-111 (Decca, USA), 2700 704 (Heliodor)
1943, München, Deutsche Grammophon Gesellschaft (Polydor Meisterklasse)
Der fliegende Holländer: Die Frist ist um
1. und 2. Teil
68297
LP: DL 9514 (Decca, USA)
Otello: Ich glaube an einen Gott (Credo)
Otello: Zur Nachzeit war es (Il sogno)
68298
Bayerisches Staatsorchester, Conductor: Heinrich Hollreiser

November 1946, Wien, Columbia. Piano: Hermann von Nordberg
Die beiden Grenadiere (Schumann)

Wer machte dich so krank?/Alte Laute (Schumann)
LX 997
Der Wanderer (Schubert)
Der Doppelgänger (Schubert)
LX 1004
LP: HQM 1030

October 1947, Wien, Columbia
Ein deutsches Requiem (Brahms) with Elisabeth Schwarzkopf
Singverein der Gesellschaft der Musikfreunde
Wiener Philharmoniker, Conductor: Herbert von Karajan
LX 1055/64
LP: SL-157 (Columbia, USA), EAC-30103 (Angel, Japan)

November/December 1947, Wien, Columbia
Sinfonie Nr. 9 d-moll (Beethoven) with Elisabeth Schwarzkopf, Elisabeth Höngen,
Julius Patzak
Singverein der Gesellschaft der Musikfreunde
Wiener Philharmoniker, Conductor: Herbert von Karajan
LX 1097/1105
LP: EL-51 (Columbia, USA) EAC-30101 (Angel, Japan)

December 1947, Wien, Columbia
Liebeslieder Walzer op. 52 (Brahms) with Irmgard Seefried, Elisabeth Höngen,
Hugo Meyer-Welfing: at two pianos: Friedrich Wührer und Hermann von Nordbert
LX 1114/17
LP: SH 373 (World Records, EMI)

October 1949, London, Columbia. Piano: Gerald Moore
Wanderers Nachtlieder 1 & 2 (Schubert) LP: HQM 1030
Am Bach im Frühling (Schubert) LP: C 147–01 633/34
LX 1261
Im Frühling (Schubert)
An die Musik/Meeresstille (Schubert)
LX 1305
LP: C 147–01 633/34
March 1950, London, Columbia

Ich habe genug, Kantate Nr. 82 (Bach)
The Philharmonia Orchestra, Conductor: Anthony Bernard
LX 1290/92
LP: C 147–01 633/34, HQM 1030 (Aria only)

September 1950, Berlin, Columbia. Piano: Michael Raucheisen

Sonntag/Ständchen (Brahms)
Ich liebe dich (Grieg)
LW 45

Mondnacht (Schumann)
Wohin? (Schubert)
LWX 392

Am Meer (Schubert)
Der Doppelgänger (Schubert)
LWX 393

May 1951, London, Columbia. Piano Gerald Moore
Feldeinsamkeit (Brahms)
Mit vierzig Jahren (Brahms)
LX 1403
LP: VS 805, C 147–01 633/34

Der Tambour (Wolf)
Ob der Koran von Ewigkeit sei? (Wolf)
Solang man nüchtern ist (Wolf)
LB 141
LP: C 147–01 633/34

Anakreons Grab (Wolf)
Schon streck ich aus im Bett die müden Glieder (Wolf)
Ein Ständchen Euch zu bringen (Wolf)
LB 142
LP: C 147–01 633/34

November 1951, London, Columbia
Joshua: Soll ich in Mamre's Segens Au'n (Handel)
Samson: Wie willig trägt mein Vaterherz (Handel)
LX 1516
LP: C 147–01 633/34

Giulio Cesare: Dall'ondoso periglio. . .Aure, deh, per pieta (Handel)
LX 1538
LP: C 147–01 633/34
The Philharmonia Orchestra, Conductor: George Weldon

November 1951, London, Columbia. Piano: Gerald Moore
Vier ernste Gesänge (Brahms)
LX 8933/34
LP: VS 805, C 147–01 633/34

b(*Long play recordings*

May 1953, London, Columbia. Piano: Gerald Moore
Hugo Wolf Lieder Recital
Drei Gedichte von Michelangelo
Cophtisches Lied I und II
Grenzen der Menschheit
Prometheus
Harfenspieler I, II und III
Geselle, woll'n wir uns in Kutten hüllen
CX 1162

May 1954, London, Columbia. Piano: Gerald Moore
Winterreise (Schubert)
CXS 1222 & CX 1223

Schwanengesang (Schubert)
CX 1269

May 1956, London, Columbia. Piano: Gerald Moore

A Brahms Lieder Recital
Wie Melodien zieht es
Sonntag
Minnelied
Komm bald
Wir wandelten
Wie bist du, meine Königin
Sapphische Ode
Botschaft
Sommerabend
Mondenschein
Ständchen
Heimweh 2 (O wüsst' ich doch den Weg zurück)
Auf dem Kirchhofe
Heimkehr
In Waldeseinsamkeit
Wenn du nur zuweilen lächelst
Verrat
CX 1448

October/November 1957, London, Columbia
Sinfonie Nr. 9 d-moll (Beethoven) mit Aase Nordmo Lövberg, Christa Ludwig, Waldemar Kmentt
The Philharmonia Orchestra and Chorus
Conductor: Otto Klemperer
CX 1574/75, SAX 2276/77

October/November 1957, London, Columbia. Piano: Gerald Moore

Lieder Recital No. 1
An die Musik (Schubert)
Im Abendrot (Schubert)
Ständchen (Schubert)
Abschied (Schubert)
Wer machte dich so krank? (Schumann)
Alte Laute (Schumann)
Erstes Grün (Schumann)
Odin's Meeresritt (Loewe)
Die wandelnde Glocke (Loewe)
Hinkende Jamben (Loewe)
Verborgenheit (Wolf)
Der Musikant (Wolf)
Fussreise (Wolf)
CX 1626

Lieder Recital No. 2
Im Frühling (Schubert)
Der Lindenbaum (Schubert)
Sei mir gegrüsst (Schubert)
Wanderers Nachtlied No. 2
Geheimes (Schubert)
Ach, weh mir unglückhaftem Mann (Strauss)
Ich trage meine Minne (Strauss)
Die beiden Grenadiere (Schumann)

Mondnacht (Schumann)
Nimmersatte Liebe (Wolf)
Anakreons Grab (Wolf)
Der Erlkönig (Loewe)
Edward (Loewe)
CX 1661

November 1957, London, Columbia

Duets from 'Der fliegende Holländer' & 'Die Walküre'
Der fliegende Holländer: Wie aus der Ferne
Die Walküre: War es so schmählich with Birgit Nilsson
The Philharmonia Orchestra, Conductor: Leopold Ludwig
CX 1542, SAX 2296

Capriccio (Richard Strauss)
Role of La Roche with Elisabeth Schwarzkopf, Christa Ludwig, Nicolai Gedda,
Dietrich Fischer-Dieskau
The Philharmonia Orchestra, Conductor: Wolfgang Sawallisch
CX 1600/02

October 1958, London, Columbia
Der Mond (Carl Orff)
Role of Petrus
The Philharmonia Orchestra and Chorus
Conductor: Wolfgang Sawallisch
CX 1534/35

March 1961, Wien, Deutsche Grammophon Gesellschaft
Aida-Highlights (Verdi)
Role of Amonasro with Gloria Davy, Cvetka Ahlin, Sandor Konya, Paul Schöffler
Wiener Volksopernorchester, conductor: Argeo Quadri
LPEM 19 402, 136 402

December 1961, Wien, Deutsche Grammophon Gesellschaft
Winterreise (Schubert)
Piano: Erik Werba
18 778/79, 138 778/79

1962, Bayreuth, Philips
Parsifal (Wagner)
Role of Gurnemanz with Irene Dalis, Jess Thomas, George London, Gustav
Neidlinger
Chor und Orchester der Bayreuther Festspiele Conductor: Hans Knappertsbusch
A 02 342/46 L, 835 220/24 AY

1963, Wien, Decca
Siegfried (Wagner)
Role of Wanderer with Birgit Nilsson, Marga Höffgen, Wolfgang Windgassen
Wiener Philharmoniker, Conductor: Sir Georg Solti
LXT 2061/65, SXL 20 061/65-B

November 1963, München, Deutsche Grammophon Gesellschaft
Die Frau ohne Schatten (Richard Strauss)
Role of Geisterboten with Inge Borkh, Ingrid Bjoner, Martha Mödl, Jess Thomas

267

Chor und Orchester der Bayerischen Staatsoper Conductor: Joseph Keilberth
138 911/14

November 1963, München, Eurodisc
Die Meistersinger von Nürnberg (Wagner)
Role of Veit Pogner with Claire Watson, Jess Thomas, Otto Wiener Chor und
Orchester der Bayerischen Staatsoper Conductor: Joseph Keilberth
70 850, S 70 851 XR

June 1964, Berlin, Deutsche Grammophon
Die Zauberflöte (Mozart)
Role of Sprecher with Evelyn Lear, Roberta Peters, Fritz Wunderlich, Franz Crass
Berliner Philharmoniker, Conductor: Karl Böhm
138 981/83

1966, Wien, Decca
Die Walküre (Wagner)
Role of Wotan with Birgit Nilsson, Regine Crespin, Christa Ludwig, James King
Wiener Philharmoniker, Conductor: Sir Georg Solti
SET 312/16

1968/69, Wien, Preiserrecords
Hans Dokoupil accompanies Hans Hotter, Eberhard Wächter, Heinz Holecek
Der Kreuzzug (Schubert)
Greisengesang (Schubert)
Frühlingsfahrt (Schumann)
Komm, wir wandeln zusammen (Cornelius)
Es hat die Rose sich beklagt (Franz)
Aus meinen grossen Schmerzen (Franz)
Das macht das dunkelgrüne Laub (Franz\
Der Musikant (Wolf)
Der Soldat I (Wolf)
Der verzweifelte Liebhaber (Wolf)
Seemanns Abschied (Wolf)
SPR 9951

May 1969, Tokyo, CBS SONY. Piano: Hans Dokoupil
Hans Hotter in Tokyo I
Winterreise (Schubert)
Grenzen der Menschheit (Schubert)
Am Bach im Frühling (Schubert)
An eine Quelle (Schubert)
Geheimes (Schubert)
Heliopolis II (Schubert)
Auf der Donau (Schubert)
SONC-16007/08-J

Hans Hotter in Tokyo II
Deutsche Lieder Abend
Erstes Grün (Schumann)
Wer machte dich so krank? (Schumann)
Alte Laute (Schumann)
Wie bist du meine Königin (Brahms)
Wie Melodien zieht es mir (Brahms)
Ständchen (Brahms)

Minnelied (Brahms)
Komm bald (Brahms)
Die Nacht (Strauss)
Gefunden (Strauss)
All mein Gedanken (Strauss)
Nachtgang (Strauss)
Ruhe, meine Seele (Strauss)
Erlkönig (Loewe)
Die wandelnde Glocke (Loewe)
Hochzeitlied (Loewe)
Du meines Herzens Krönelein (Strauss)
SONC-16013-J

December 1971/March 1972, Wien, Decca
Parsifal (Wagner)
Role of Titurel
with Christa Ludwig, René Kollo, Dietrich Fischer-Dieskau, Gottlob Frick
Wiener Philharmoniker, Conductor: Sir Georg Solti
SET 550/04

May 1973, Wien, Decca. Piano: Geoffrey Parsons
The Art of Hans Hotter
Der Tambour (Wolf)
Nimmersatte Liebe (Wolf)
Jägerlied (Wolf)
Der Mond hat eine schwere Klage erhoben (Wolf)
Heb auf dein blondes Haupt (Wolf)
Schon streck ich aus im Bett (Wolf)
Ein Ständchen Euch zu bringen (Wolf)
Denk es, o Seele (Wolf)
Wohl denk ich oft (Wolf)
Alles endet, was entstehet (Wolf)
Fühlt meine Seele (Wolf)
Gruppe aus dem Tartarus (Schubert)
Im Frühling (Schubert)
Alinde (Schubert)
An die Entfernte (Schubert)
Liebesbotschaft (Schubert)
Die Stadt (Schubert)
Der Doppelgänger (Schubert)
Die Taubenpost (Schubert)
SXL 6625

The Art of Hans Hotter Vol. II
Odins Meeresritt (Loewe)
Die wandelnde Glocke (Loewe)
Hochzeitlied (Loewe)
Hinkende Jamben (Loewe)
Wenn du zu den Blumen gehst (Wolf)
Der Musikant (Wolf)
Wer sein holdes Lieb vorloren (Wolf)
Der Soldat I (Wolf)
Anakreons Grab (Wolf)
Der verzweifelte Liebhaber (Wolf)
All' mein' Gedanken, mein Herz und Sinn (Strauss)

269

Nachtgang (Strauss)
Du meines Herzens Krönelein (Strauss)
Gefunden (Strauss)
Himmelsboten (Strauss)
Ach weh mir unglückhaftem Mann (Strauss)
Auf dem Kirchhofe (Brahms)
Ruhe, Süssliebchen, im Schatten (Brahms)
Mit vierzig Jahren (Brahms)
SXL 6738

November 1976, Wien, Decca
Lulu (Berg)
Role of Schigolch
with Anja Silja, Brigitte Fassbaender, Horst Laubenthal, Walter Berry, Wiener
Philharmoniker, Conductor: Christoph von Dohnanyi
D48D 3

Stars of the Vienna Opera 1946–1953 (1982)
includes 3 recordings of Hans Hotter not previously issued:
Die Meistersinger von Nürnberg: Und doch, 's will halt nicht gehn
Die Meistersinger von Nürnberg: Doch eines Abends spat
Die Walküre: Leb' wohl, du kühnes, herrliches Kind
Aufgenommen im Dezember 1948 in Wien
Wiener Philharmoniker, Conductor: Meinhard von Zallinger
EMI RLS 764 (137–43 187/9M)

Radio recording
Falstaff (Verdi)
Title role
with Henny Neumann-Knapp, Hedwig Fichtmüller, Else Tegetthoff, Chor und
Orchester des Reichssenders Leipzig Conductor: Hans Weisbach
Preiserrecords 120046/47 (9. April 1939)

Capriccio (Richard Strauss) Highlights
Role of Olivier
with Viorica Ursuleac, Franz Klarwein, Georg Hann
Orchester der Bayerischen Staatsoper, Conductor: Clemens Krauss
BASF/Arcanta 10 21363-3 (1942)

Der fliegende Holländer (Wagner)
Title role
with Viorica Ursuleac, Luise Willer, Karl Ostertag, Georg Hann, Chor and
Orchester der Bayerischen Staatsoper Conductor: Clemens Krauss (1942)
Mercury MGL-2, BASF/Arcanta HA 23135/37

Aida (Verdi) Highlights
Role of Amonasro
with Hilde Scheppan, Margarete Klose, Helge Rosvaenge Chor, und Orchester der
Staatsoper Berlin   .
Conductor: Artur Rother
BASF/Arcanta 10 22025-7 (1942)

Taillefer (Richard Strauss)
with Maria Cebotari, Walther Ludwig, Rudolf Lamy, Chor
Berliner Rundfunkorchester, conductor: Artur Rother Urania URLP 7042 (1943)

Opernarien und Szenen
Hans Heiling: An Jenem Tag
Der Barbier von Sevilla: Die Verleumdung
Aida: Himmel! Er ist's, mein Vater!
Aida: Zu dir führt mich ein ernster Grund (with Hilde Scheppan)
Falstaff: He, Page!
Falstaff: Es verzehrt uns heisse Reue
Otello: Zur Nachtzeit war es
Der fliegende Holländer: Die Frist ist um
Der fliegende Holländer: Wie aus der Ferne
Der fliegende Holländer: Erfahre das Geschick (with Viorica Ursuleac)
Die Meistersinger von Nürnberg: Was duftet doch der Flieder
Die Meistersinger von Nürnberg: Wahn! Wahn! Überall Wahn!
Die Walküre: Leb wohl, du kuhnes, herrliches Kind
BASF/Arcanta DE 22017 (1939/44)

Lieder von Schubert, Brahms, Loewe und Wolf
Der Schäfer und der Reiter (Schubert)
Orest auf Tauris (Schubert)
Die Liebe hat gelogen (Schubert)
Totengräbers Heimweh (Schubert)
Greisengesang (Schubert)
Schiffers Scheidelied (Schubert)
Dein blaues Auge (Brahms)
Versunken (Brahms)
Mit vierzig Jahren (Brahms)
Kein Haus, keine Heimat (Brahms)
Odin's Meeresritt (Loewe)
Trommelständchen (Loewe)
Graf Eberstein (Loewe)
Selig, ihr Blinden (Wolf)
Fussreise (Wolf(
Piano: Michael Raucheisen
Arcanta BB 23037 (1943/44)

Lieder von Franz Schubert
Alinde
Die Liebe hat gelogen
Wie deutlich des Mondes Licht
Greisengesang
Das Zügenglöcklein
Orpheus
Des Sängers Habe
An den Tod
Tiefes Leid
Totengräbers Heimweh
Der Kreuzzug
Piano: Michael Raucheisen
Melodia (UdSSR) 33 M 10–40951/52 (1943/44)

Arabella (Richard Strauss)
Role of Mandryka
mit Maria Reining, Lisa Della Casa, Horst Taubmann, Georg Hann, Chor der

Wiener Staatsoper, Wiener Philharmoniker Conductor: Karl Böhm (12. August 1947)
Melodram MEL-S 101

Das Rheingold (Wagner)
Role of Wotan
with Margaret Harshaw, Karin Branzell, Set Svanholm, Jerome Hines, Orchester der Metropolitan Opera, Conductor: Fritz Stiedry Private edition, USA (27. January 1951)

Requiem d-moll KV 626 (Mozart)
with Elisabeth Grümmer, Gertrude Pitzinger, Helmut Krebs
RIAS-Kammerchor, Chor der St. Hedwigs-Kathedrale
RIAS-Symphonie-Orchester Berlin, Conductor: Ferenc Fricsay
Deutsche Grammophon Gesellschaft 2535 713 (5. März 1951)

Salome (Richard Strauss)
Role of Jochanaan
with Inge Borkh, Irmgard Barth, Max Lorenz, Lorenz Fehenberger
Orchester der Bayerischen Staatsoper, Conductor: Joseph Keilberth
Melodram MEL-S 106 (21. July 1951)

Salome (Richard Strauss)
Role of Jochanaan
with Ljuba Welitsch, Elisabeth Höngen, Set Svanholm, Orchester der Metropolitan Opera, Conductor: Fritz Reiner
Private edition, USA SID-724 (1952)

Die Schöpfung (Haydn)
Role of Raphael
with Irmgard Seefried, Walther Ludwig
Chor und Orchester des Bayerischen Rundfunks Conductor: Eugen Jochum
Melodram MEL 208 (1952)

Dichterliebe (Schumann)
Ausgewählte Lieder (Schubert)
An eine Quelle
Des Fischers Liebesglück
Wie deutlich des Mondes Licht
Auf der Donau
Der Wanderer an den Mond
Greisengesang
Gruppe aus dem Tartarus
Piano: Hans Altmann
Preiserrecords PR 3145 (1952/59)

Kleine Weihnachtsgeschichte op. 51 (Mark Lothar)
Piano: The Composer
Private edition 60.531

Boris Godunoff (Mussorgski) Originalfassung von 1874
Title role
with Martha Mödl, Hans Hopf, Kim Borg, Lorenz Fehenberger
Chor und Orchester des Bayerischen Rundfunks Conductor: Eugen Jochum (3. — 10. Mai 1957)

Ausgabe des Bayerischen Rundfunks 66.30 005

Der Ring des Nibelungen (Wagner)
Role of Wotan
with Astrid Varnay, Birgit Nilsson, Ludwig Suthaus, Ramon Vinay, Chor and
Orchester der Bayreuther Festspiele
Conductor: Hans Knappertsbusch (1957)
Bruno Walter Society IGI-292

Die schweigsame Frau (Richard Strauss)
Role of Sir Morosus
with Hilde Güden, Georgine von Milinkovic, Fritz Wunderlich
Wiener Staatsopernchor, Wiener Philharmoniker
Conductor: Karl Böhm
Melodram MEL-S 105 (8. August 1959)

Die Zauberflöte (Mozart)
Role of Sprecher
with Lisa Della Casa, Erika Köth, Leopold Simoneau, Kurt Böhme
Wiener Staatsopernchor, Wiener Philharmoniker
Conductor: George Szell
Melodram MEL 007 (1959)

Der Ring des Nibelungen (Wagner)
Role of Wotan
with Astrid Varney, Ira Malaniuk, Wolfgang Windgassen, Josef Greindl, Chor und
Orchester der Bayreuther Festspiele
Conductor: Clemens Krauss (1953)
Foyer FO 1008/11

All-Schubert Lieder Recital
Der Wanderer
Meeresstille
Wanderers Nachtlied I
Gesänge des Harfners I-III
Geheimes
An die Musik
Pilgerweise
Atys
Abschied
Orest auf Tauris
Liebesend
Alinde
Die Liebe hat gelogen
Der Wanderer II
Greisengesang
Das Zügenglöcklein
Orpheus
Des Sängers Habe
An den Tod
Tiefes Leid
Totengräbers Heimwehe
Der Kreuzzug
Der Schäfer und der Reiter
Schiffers Scheidelied

Piano: Michael Raucheisen
Educ Media Associates, USA IGI–386 (1943/44)

La Damnation de Faust (Berlioz)
Role of Mephistopheles
with Elisabeth Schwarzkopf, Frans Vroons
Lucerner Festspielorchester, Condoctor: Wilhelm Furtwängler
Fonit Cetra FE 21 (26. August 1950)

INDEX

Aachen 157
Adler, Kurt Herbert 151
Aldeburgh 148
Alfio, 78
Almaviva, Count 89, 109, 151
America 118
Amfortas 71, 89, 119, 126, 132, 161
Amonasro 71
Amsterdam 96, 180
Antwerp 89
Appia, Adolphe 160
ARD (radio, Munich) 231
Argentine 116, 149
Arosa, 32, 33
Aschaffenburg 34, 35
Aspen College (USA) 229
Australia 152, 206, 229

Bach, Johann Sebastian 59, 62
Bacon, Elmore 150
Baden (Vienna) 231
Barcelona 82
Bassermann, August 74
Baum, Vicki 71
Bavarian Staatsoper 159
Bayreuth 18, 22, 51, 54, 61, 62, 67, 98,
    120–135, 144, 145, 149, 152, 153,
    185–6
BBC 111
Becket, Thomas 156
Beethoven's 9th Symphony 148, 149
Belgium 89, 96, 118
Benson and Hedges Gold Awards 148,
    231
Berlin 56, 72, 73, 77, 85, 89–91, 96, 98,
    157, 203
Bernheimer, Martin 173
Bing, Rudolf 118, 119, 120, 150
Blutenburg church 84
Blyth, Alan 147
Bollen, Tom 153
Boris Godunov 88, 161
Borromeo 86, 156, 166
Brahms, Johannes 199, 207, 215
Brahms Requiem 157, 220
Brecht, Bert 69
Breslau 70–73, 76, 78, 126, 250
Bristol 148
British Council 154
Brüderlein fein (film) 109
Buenos Aires 116, 149

Caesar, Julius 108

Caesari, E. Herbert 253
Canada 206, 229
Cape Town 152
Chemnitz 81
Chéreau, Patrice 196
Chicago 74, 120, 149, 151, 187, 191
Chicago Symphony Orchestra 150
Cleveland News 150
Cologne 89
Conductors:
    Adam, Frédéric 180
    Beecham, Sir Thomas 89, 110, 137
    Böhm, Karl 96, 128, 163
    Boulez, Pierre 128, 153
    Cluytens, André 124, 128, 160
    Dohnányi, Christoph von 165
    Furtwängler, Wilhelm 71, 85, 89, 237
    Gibson, Sir Alexander 170
    Gierster, Hans 181
    Goodall, Reginald 138
    Heger, Robert 181
    Jochum, Eugen 84, 88, 124
    Karajan, Herbert von 122, 124, 126,
        256–7
    Keilberth, Joseph 122, 124, 159
    Kempe, Rudolf 138, 141, 227
    Klemperer, Otto 139, 140
    Klobucar, Berislav 172, 186
    Knappertsbusch, Hans 19, 61, 90, 91,
        97, 98, 121, 124, 128, 159, 181
    Konwitschny, Franz 138
    Krips, Josef 112
    Kraus, Clemens 13, 75, 76, 85, 89–
        92, 94–98, 108, 112, 124, 126,
        128, 131, 137, 155, 182, 191–2,
        194, 241
    Leitner, Ferdinand 110
    Ludwig, Leopold 160, 185
    Matacic, Lovro von 170
    Mehta, Zubin 172
    Rankl, Karl 136
    Sawallisch, Wolfgang 124
    Scherchen, Hermann 69
    Schmidt-Isserstedt, Hans 161
    Schüchter, Wilhelm 182
    Seidler-Winkler, Bruno 89
    Solti, Sir Georg 19, 135, 139, 141,
        144, 150, 165, 180, 190
    Stein, Horst 164
    Stiedry, Fritz 138
    Szell, George 74, 149
    Toscanini, Arturo 54
    Varviso, Silvio 184

275

Walter, Bruno 54, 74, 86, 100, 220
Zallinger, Meinhard von 166, 202–3
Cornides, Cilla von 199
Covent Garden 13, 21, 22, 89, 99, 111, 112, 115, 116, 118, 136, 140, 144, 150, 157, 180
Cuvilliés Theatre (Munich) 248

Daily Telegraph 146
Demel, Paul 74
Denmark 206
de Reszke, Jean 51, 253
Deutsch, Ernst 74
Dichterliebe 290
Dietrich (*Der arme Heinrich*) 84, 85, 89
Dokoupil, Hans 153, 204
Don Basilio 248
Dorsch, Käthe 109
Dortmund 89, 182, 191
Downes, Olin 118
Durban 152
Dutchman (*Fliegende Holländer*) 54, 67, 75, 98, 99, 118, 119, 127, 151

Eastman School (USA) 229
Edinburgh Festival 148
Eger, Dr. Paul 72, 73, 77, 78, 79
Egk, Werner 88
Elgar, Sir Edward 85
England 118, 135–149
Esch, Fr. Ludwig 45
Escamillo 89, 96
Esslingen 31
European Association of Music Festivals 153

Falstaff 89, 161
Feasey, Norman 225-6
Festival of Britain 136
Financial Times 147
Fischer, Helga (see Helga Hotter)
Fischers, parents of Helga 81–82
Fishmongers' Hall, London 148, 203
France, 118, 206
Frankfurt 34, 150, 164, 248
Friedrich, Götz 196
Fukuoka 153

Galitzy (*Prince Igor*) 156
Geneva 160
Gianni Schicchi 161
Gieseking, Walter 71, 85
Giovanni, Don 112, 116
Goebbels 97, 100
Goette, Rudolf 203
Goppel, Dr. Alfons 159
Graf, Herbert 160
Grand Inquisitor 97, 118, 119, 156, 161, 169, 172
Grieg, Edvard 62
Gunther (*Götterdämmerung*) 116, 119, 138

Gurnemanz 22, 127, 128, 160, 161, 169, 185
Gurrelieder 173

Habsburgs 31, 80
Haferung, Paul 183
Hall, Peter 150
Hamburg 72, 77–82, 84, 86, 88, 90, 91, 94, 96, 97, 109–111, 132, 134, 135, 157, 161, 183, 203, 239, 248
Handel, George 88, 220
Hansford, Brian 253
Harewood, Lord 139
Harrison, Jay S. 119
Hartmann, Georg 70, 71, 91
Hartmann, Rudolf 54, 91, 92, 95, 138, 159, 196
Hay fever 117
Heinrich, Rudolf 184, 189
Heisenberg, Werner Karl 45
Hindemith, Paul 69, 96
Hitler, Adolf 62, 97, 100, 108, 110, 121
Hitler youth movement 44
Holland 89, 96, 100, 118
Holzamer, Karl 47
Hong Kong 153
Hotter, Crescentia (mother) 32, 33, 35–37, 40–43, 52, 82, 98, 225
Hotter, Eberhard 31
Hotter, Gabriele (Strauss; daughter) 20, 84, 99, 116
Hotter, Helga (wife) 80–82, 84, 116, 146, 153–4, 156, 254
Hotter, Karl (father) 31–36, 41, 42
Hotter, Dr. Karl (brother) 20, 32, 33, 37, 39, 57, 100
Hotter, Peter (son) 20, 84, 116, 254
Hotter, Sippe 31
House and Garden 138
Hunding 120
Hurry, Leslie 138
Hussey, Dyneley 205

Iago 89, 157
Ingpen, Joan 110, 111

Japan 152–156, 206, 229
Jochanaan 71, 97–99, 119
Jugendbewegung 43–45, 47, 49
Jupiter (*Die Liebe der Danae*) 108

Kaspar (*Freischütz*) 116
Kaspar (*Zaubergeige*) 88
Kennenburg 31
Kent, Duchess of 149
Kern, Herbert 141–2
Kingsway Hall 138
Klien, Walter 152
Kurwenal 89, 122, 126

Lefort, Bernard 171
Legge, Walter 89, 110, 111, 157

276

Lehrstück 69, 201, 220
Leicester 81, 82
Lert, Richard 71
Leudesdorff, Ernst 80–82
Listener, The 205
Loewe, Karl 86, 87, 207, et seq., 218
London 21, 82, 89, 134, 135, 148, 151, 170, 177, 194
London Opera Centre 148
Los Angeles 172–3
Los Angeles Times 173
Löwenstein, Arthur 69–70

Macbeth 84
Mahler, Gustav 215
Main river 34
Mainz 34
Mandryka 99
Marke, King 119, 128, 153, 183
Maschat, Erik 85
Mathis (*Mathis der Maler*) 96
Max Gymnasium 45
Messiah 50, 202, 220
Metropolitan Opera 99, 118, 119, 120, 150
Milan 157, 160
Missa Solemnis 220
Mitchell, Donald 146
Moore, Gerald 204
Morone (*Palestrina*) 97
Morosus (*Die Schweigsame Frau*) 162
Moses (*Moses und Aron*) 150, 164, 169
Moussorgsky, Modest 88
Mozart, Wolfgang 62, 218, 220
Munich 13, 19, 20, 25, 31, 33, 34, 36, 41, 42, 45, 49, 51, 53, 54, 56, 57, 61, 69, 70, 72, 74, 78, 82, 84, 87–92, 94, 96–99, 102, 110–112, 116, 127, 129, 134, 135, 149, 156, 159, 163, 165, 170, 181, 203, 237, 253
Munich Hochschule für Musik 50, 52, 56, 227, 229
Munich University 50
Mutterliebe (film) 109

Nagoya 153
Naples 160
National Opera Studio 229
National Socialism 45
Nazis 73, 79, 90, 99, 100, 107, 108, 110, 121
Neudeutschland 45, 46, 47
New Otani Hotel 153–4, 156
New York 25, 75, 149, 150
New York Herald Tribune 75, 119
New York Times 118
Ney, Elly 85
Niigata 154, 156
Nottingham 81, 111
Nuremberg 150

Offenbach-am-Main 31–35, 41
Olivier (*Capriccio*) 107
Opera Centre 229
Opera magazine 118, 171
Operas:
  Arabella 99, 186
  Barber of Seville 248
  Besuch der Alten Dame, Der 164, 169
  Boris Godunov 88, 151
  Carmen 96, 110
  Capriccio 107, 108
  Cavalleria rusticana 78
  Cosi fan tutte 112
  Der arme Heinrich 84, 86, 89
  Don Carlos 97, 118, 172
  Don Giovanni 112
  Fidelio 84, 112, 139, 150, 151, 187, 191
  Figaro, Marriage of 109, 112
  Fliegende Holländer, Der 95, 127, 181, 182, 192
  Frau ohne Schatten, Die 159
  Freischütz, Der 116
  Friedenstag 97, 99
  Götterdämmerung 116, 119, 122, 142, 144
  Julius Caesar (Handel) 88, 97
  Julius Caesar (Malipiero) 109
  Liebe der Danae, Die 108
  Lohengrin 67, 131, 183
  Lulu 163, 169
  Macbeth 71
  Mathis der Maler 96
  Meistersinger von Nürnberg, Die 69, 112, 119, 126, 136, 137, 159
  Mona Lisa 98
  Moses und Aron 150, 164
  Murder in the Cathedral 156
  Pagliacci 69, 78
  Palestrina 84, 85, 86, 88, 166, 181–2, 192
  Parsifal 22, 67, 89, 119, 126, 127, 128, 136, 152, 160, 184, 190
  Prince Igor 156
  Rheingold, Das 76, 89, 97, 119, 122, 124, 144, 146
  Ring des Nibelungen, Der 13, 14, 17, 18, 117, 122, 124, 125, 127, 128, 129, 134–139, 141, 142, 144, 146, 147, 156, 157, 160, 169, 170, 177, 180, 185
  Salome 91, 95–99, 112
  Schweigsame Frau, Die 162, 183
  Siegfried 69, 88, 90, 97, 122, 126, 134, 138, 142, 144, 146, 148, 180, 237
  Tales of Hoffmann 71
  Tannhäuser 69, 76, 182
  Tristan und Isolde 96, 112, 119, 122, 126, 128, 136, 153, 183
  Walküre, Die 13, 14, 21, 89, 97, 112,

114, 115, 116, 119, 120, 122, 126, 134, 138, 141, 142, 144, 146, 148, 150, 151, 153, 160, 170, 180, 182, 186
Zauberflöte, Die 69, 74, 140, 150
Zaubergeige, Die 88, 183, 191
Orestes 119
Osaka Festival 153
Otto, Teo 162

Paris 51, 89, 118, 170
Park Lane Group 229
Parsons, Geoffrey 203
Passau 49, 50, 202
Pfitzner, Hans 84–89, 94, 95, 97, 165, 215, 216–7
Philip, King (*Don Carlos*) 161
Pitz, Wilhelm 144
Pizarro 84, 89, 139, 151, 156, 161
Pogner 119, 127, 159, 169
Pomeroy, Jan 111
Ponnelle, Jean-Pierre 196
Porter, Andrew 147
Potter, Peter 138, 147
Prague 73–79
Prague German Theatre 72
Prague Opera 56, 100, 202, 240
Princess Margaret 116
Prinzregenten Theater 96
Puccini, Giacomo 62

Queen Elizabeth, the Queen Mother 116
Quickborn 47

Rangoni (*Boris Godunov*) 151
Raucheisen, Michael 203–4
Rennert, Günther 163, 196
Rhine 34
Rimsky-Korsakov, Nikolas 88
Roemer, Matthäus 51, 52, 53, 55, 56, 57, 60, 61–63, 67, 70, 73, 201, 220, 225, 229, 237, 239, 246, 247, 252–3
Roman Catholic Church 36, 44, 45
Rome 25
Rosenthal, Harold 138, 171
Röthlisberger, Max 160
Royal Academy of Music 149
Royal Festival Hall 138, 148
Rudkin, David 150
Russian prisoners 39
Rüttenauer, Frau (maternal grandmother) 41, 43

Saam, Dr. Josef 49, 50, 51
Sachs, Hans 26, 46, 69, 71, 116, 126, 127, 137, 215
St. Matthew Passion 220
Salzburg 74, 108, 109, 110, 129, 131, 202, 229

San Francisco 151
Sapporo 153
Scala, Milan 89, 160
Scarpia 156, 161
Schigolch (*Lulu*) 163
Schenk, Otto 163, 164, 196
Schlemihl 71
Schneider-Siemssen, Günther 142, 144, 145, 163, 164, 180, 181, 190
Schöne Müllerin, Die 210
Schubert, Franz 62, 206 et seq., 215
Schumann, Robert 206 et seq., 215
Schuh, Oscar Fritz 196
Scottish Opera 229
Sehnsucht des Herzens (film) 109
Seine beste Rolle (film) 109
's-Hertogenbosch 229
Sievert, Ludwig 96
Sinden, Donald, 151
Singers:
    Ådam, Theo 153, 185
    Aldenhoff, Bernd 122, 124, 180
    Aragall, Giacomo 172
    Barbieri, Fedora 118
    Bender, Paul 61
    Berry, Walter 150, 182
    Bjoner, Ingrid 159
    Bockelmann, Rudolf 56, 57, 77, 78, 79, 239
    Borkh, Inge 159
    Braun, Helena 114–5
    Carlyle, Joan 140
    Cassilly, Richard 185
    Cebotari, Maria 112
    Chaliapin, Feodor 74, 75, 77, 130
    Coates, Edith 226
    Coertse, Mimi 182
    Collier, Marie 141, 142
    Conley, Eugene 149
    Cotogni, Antonio 253
    Cotrubas, Ileana 232
    Cox, Jean 170
    Crespin, Régine 128, 170
    Czerwenka, Oskar 184
    Dalis, Irene 185
    Dermota, Anton 182
    Dobson, John 139
    Dongen, Maria van 183
    Dvorakova, Ludmilla 181
    Estes, Simon 172
    Evans, Geraint 140
    Feuge, Elisabeth 61
    Fischer-Dieskau, Dietrich 124, 159
    Fisher, Sylvia 136
    Flagstad, Kirsten 112, 114, 115, 136
    Franz, Ferdinand 120
    Frick, Gottlob 136, 139, 142, 166, 181, 182
    Fuchs, Martha 89
    Geister, Martha 84

278

Gigli, Beniamino 253
Gorr, Rita 141
Greindl, Josef 47, 124, 129, 131
Günter Nöcker, Hans 181
Gutstein, Ernst 163
Harshaw, Margaret 138
Herrmann, Theo, 84
Hofman, Hubert 170
Holl, Robert 204, 227
Hopf, Hans 182
Huni-Mihacsek, Felicie 61
Hunter, Rita 144
Ivogün, Maria 159
Janowitz, Gundula 182
Jones, Gwyneth 144, 147, 172
Jurinac, Sena 112, 139, 181
Kalter, Sabine 84
Kaslik, Václav 165
Kingsley, Margaret 170
Klein, Peter 136, 182
Kmentt, Waldemar 163
Konetzni, Anny 136
Konetzni, Hilde 112, 163
Kötter, Paul 84
Kozub, Ernst 170
Kraus, Otakar 136, 142
Kreppel, Walter 182
Kronenberg, Karl 78–9
Kuhn, Paul 159
Kunz, Erich 112
Kusche, Benno 136
Langdon, Michael 141, 161, 170
Lear, Evelyn 163
Lewis, Richard 140, 151
Lindermeier, Elisabeth 226–7
Lindholm, Berit 170
Lipton, Martha 149
London, George 128
Lorenz, Max 114
Ludwig, Christa 164, 181
M arshall, Margaret 227
Mazura, Franz 170, 171
Meier, Johanna 187
Metternich, Anton 160
Meyer, Kerstin 164
Milinkovic, Georgine von 92
Mödl, Martha 124, 134, 159, 163
Morbach, Günther 183
Morrison, Elsie 139
Neidlinger, Gustav 124, 132, 180
Nilsson, Birgit 124, 128, 142–150, 151, 153, 157, 160, 190
Nissen, Hans Hermann 61, 97
Norman, Jessye 232
Patzak, Julius 91, 112
Pölzer, Julius 91
Popp, Lucia 182
Prohaska, Jaro 239
Ranczak, Hildegarde 61, 91
Reinhardt, Delia 159
Ridderbusch, Karl 183

Rode, Wilhelm 61, 74, 239
Robinson, Forbes 139
Schlüter, Erna 114
Schoeffler, Paul 112
Schorr, Friedrich 138, 239
Schreier, Peter 204
Schwarzkopf, Elisabeth 112, 157
Seefried, Irmgard 112, 150
Shuard, Amy 147
Siepi, Cesare 118
Silja, Anja 160, 163
Sladen, Victoria 110
Stabile, Mariano 253
Stewart, Thomas 128, 142, 160, 190
Stolze, Gerhard 131, 142, 182
Strauss, Isabelle 160
Svanholm, Set 136, 137
Sutherland, Joan 140
Tauber, Richard 239
Thomas, Jess 128, 159
Uhde, Hermann 122
Unger, Gerhard 182
Ursuleac, Viorica 76, 97, 159
Välkki, Anita 141
Vandenburg, Howard 183
Van Rooy, Anton 54, 139
Varnay, Astrid 122, 124, 128, 131, 134, 136
Veasey, Josephine 141, 142
Vickers, Jon 128, 139, 141, 150, 187
Vinay, Ramon 124
Waechter, Eberhard 164, 186
Ward, David 142, 146
Watson, Claire 141, 186
Weber, Ludwig 112, 114, 124, 129, 136
Welitsch, Ljuba 112
Wiener, Otto 181
Wildermann, William 150
Willer, Luise 61
Windgassen, Wolfgang 124, 128, 131, 142, 144, 153, 160, 181, 183, 190
Wunderlich, Fritz 181
Yeend, Frances 149
Smith, Cecil 118, 119
Sondai 153
South Africa 152
South America 206
Speaker (Die Zauberflöte) 69, 109, 140, 150, 156
Spessart hills 20, 32–35, 37, 41
Steiger 34, 35, 37, 39
Strasbourg 180
Strauss, Franz Josef 45
Strauss, Gabriele (see Gabriele Hotter)
Strauss, Pauline 92, 199
Strauss, Richard 20, 91, 92, 94, 95, 97, 107, 108, 193, 199, 207 et seq., 215, 216–7, 253
Strohm, H. K. 78, 90

Switzerland 100

Thalia Theatre 80, 82
Theresien Gymnasium 42, 45
Thomson, Virgil 75, 118
Tietjen, Heinz 98, 160
Times, The 139, 144, 182
Tokyo 153, 154
Tonio 69, 78, 89
Troppau 56, 62, 67, 69, 70, 71, 73, 76, 78, 202

United States 100, 206, 229

Valk, Frederick 74
Verdi 62, 220
Vienna 25, 31, 72, 75, 76, 79, 89, 91, 97, 98, 108, 111, 116, 127, 134, 135, 149, 156, 157, 163, 164, 169, 172, 181, 183, 194, 204
Vienna Hochschule für Musik 230, 244
Vienna Master Courses 229

Wagner, Cosima 61, 67, 120
Wagner, Richard 17, 21, 26, 62, 67, 121, 136, 144, 160, 193, 218,
Wagner, Siegfried 51, 61, 67, 121
Wagner, Wieland 121, 122, 124, 126, 128, 129, 130, 131, 137, 138, 153, 160, 170, 185–6, 189, 193, 218
Wagner, Winifred 67, 98, 121, 129
Wagner, Wolfgang 121, 127, 129, 131, 185
Wanderer (*Siegfried*) 69, 88, 89, 90, 96, 122, 124, 126, 128
Wandervogel 44, 45
Webster, Sir David 111, 112, 115, 116, 136, 140
Werba, Erik 204
Wessaly, Paula 74
Wiesbaden 82
Wigmore Hall 138
Winterreise, Die 111, 148, 152, 153, 154, 199, 203–6, 209, 216
Wirk, Willi 53, 54, 55, 56, 62, 92
Wittelsbachs 31, 35, 51, 159
Wolf, Hugo 207, 210–212
Wolfram 69, 76, 161
Wotan 13, 17, 18, 19, 21, 26, 54, 89, 97, 114, 115, 119, 120, 122, 124, 125, 126, 128, 132, 136, 141, 146–7, 157, 160, 161, 169
Würzburg 34, 43

Yokohama 153

Zilcher, Hermann 43
Zürich 13, 160, 182